D1038240

IN SEARCH OF
SHAREHOLDER
VALUE

Managing the drivers of performance

ANDREW BLACK

PHILIP WRIGHT

JOHN E BACHMAN

with

JOHN DAVIES

London · Hong Kong · Johannesburg
Melbourne · Singapore · Washington DC

PITMAN PUBLISHING
128 Long Acre, London WC2E 9AN
Tel: +44 (0)171 447 2000
Fax: +44 (0)171 240 5771

A Division of Pearson Professional Limited

First published in Great Britain 1998

ISBN 0 273 63027 X

British Library Cataloguing in Publication Data
A CIP catalogue record for this book can be obtained from
the British Library.

1 3 5 7 9 10 8 6 4 2

Typeset by Northern Phototypesetting Co. Ltd., Bolton
Printed and bound in Great Britain by
Biddles Ltd, Guildford and King's Lynn

*The Publishers' policy is to use paper manufactured
from sustainable forests.*

ABOUT THE AUTHORS

Dr Andrew Black is the director of the Price Waterhouse Business Analysis Team, which is part of the firm's business development effort. He has worked extensively on shareholder value models and their application to corporate clients. He has extensive experience of financial markets and their impact on corporate behaviour as an analyst and strategist for various banks and fund managers. He has written articles and papers on many themes including corporate governance and government industrial policy.

Philip Wright, is global leader of Price Waterhouse shareholder value services and is recognized as one of Europe's leading shareholder value consultants and privatization advisers. Between 1994 and 1997 he led Price Waterhouse's Value Builder team, which now has over 300 consultants working in this field worldwide. In more than 20 years with the firm, he has been involved with major international assignments in audit, consulting, and corporate finance and recovery, including four years based in Germany and two years in the first phase of PW's work in Eastern Europe.

John E Bachman is the leader of the Price Waterhouse LLP US ValueBuilder team. Based in Boston, Mr Bachman assists senior management of top-tier companies in a variety of industries in analyzing and enhancing their shareholder value. He has considerable experience helping multinational companies implement significant acquisition strategies and address acquisition-related integration issues. Mr Bachman received his MBA degree from Harvard Business School and his BS degree from Bucknell University.

John Davies is a freelance journalist.

CONTENTS

Part 2
PUTTING IT INTO PRACTICE: THE VALUE MINDSET

FOREWORD

Change is in the air. Within the last decade or so, most companies have seen the rapid transformation of their business and the climate in which they operate. Globalization, technological change and the increasing sophistication of the markets mean that as we approach the new millennium, successful companies are under pressure as never before: if they do not adapt to the new climate, they perish. They are finding that product excellence is no longer sufficient, nor is it enough to focus on profit alone. The key to success today is the simultaneous delivery of superior returns on capital, sustainable growth rates and the proactive management of risk.

We at Price Waterhouse are not standing apart from this process. We have a long and successful history of financial analysis and assurance work that has adapted itself to, and transcended, a multitude of market and technology changes. The way we perform our services may have changed over the years – manual processes have become automated, for example – but the core business of giving credibility and clarity to the information and systems that we examine or implement has not changed. The provision of credible financial and management information is, and always has been, a necessary precondition for sound business decisions and access to financial markets.

But that's not all. We are fond of stating that Price Waterhouse is more than just a financial services firm; rather it is in the business of 'solving complex problems for top companies'. This means, among other things, that we aim to focus on our clients' priorities and make the most of our capabilities to maximize value for them. In other words, we exist so that our clients can reach their full potential.

This is where shareholder value comes in. Our well-managed clients are on a relentless quest for value; in their businesses they want to create, preserve and realize value for owners, investors and employees. To progress in this quest, they need the latest and most effective techniques of business strategy and analysis – techniques that enable them to ensure that capital is not squandered but is used wisely. Shareholder value analysis provides just such an approach. That is why we have developed our ValueBuilder™ process which is proving its worth in helping top companies in a variety of fields to improve their performance. It is doing this by offering companies analysis and strategies that facilitate value creation and enhance communication and reporting – and by establishing appropriate ways of rewarding their employees when their targets are met.

Our research and client work in the area of shareholder value, then, is the basis for this book. In fields as diverse as banking and high technology, entertainment and energy, we are encountering enthusiastic responses when we explain shareholder value ideas and systems. We hope we can arouse similar enthusiasm among you, the readers of this book.

JERMYN BROOKS
Chairman, Price Waterhouse

ACKNOWLEDGEMENTS

A book such as this is the product of more than its authors' efforts. The collective knowledge and experience, over several years, of the Price Waterhouse Business Development Group and its clients has inspired, and fed into, the writing of *In Search of Shareholder Value*.

We would particularly like to thank Mike Maskall, Ian Coleman, Jeff Bowman, Hermann Aichele, Guy Madewell, Michael Melvill, Anthony Van der Byl, Chris Neenan, Francois Langlade-Demoyen, Jane Docherty, Cedric Read, Michael Donnellan, Likhit Wagle, Gabi Black and Sigrid Wright for assistance and advice during the writing of this book.

Help with individual chapters has come from John Devereaux and Jonathan Peacock (for Chapter 7); Tom Wilson, Frank Brown and Robert Neilson (for Chapter 8); Alan Jamieson and Carter Pate (for Chapter 9); Loic Kubitza, Axel Jagle, Mohamed Bharadia, Julian Alcantara, Elisabeth Edwards, Christopher Baer and Andrew Wardle (for Chapter 10); Jens Hartwig Arnold, Tibor Almassy, Marcus Bracklo, Ian Falconer, Patrick Frotiee, Jesus Diaz de la Hoz, Jacob S Geyer, Thomas Goldman, Jean-Louis Goni, Anders Landelius, Jusbi Majamaa, Anders C Madsen, Greg Morris, Michael Octoman, Karin Pauly, Berndt Samsinger, Carol Brumer Scarlatti, Staale Schmidt, Andre Szczesniak and Joachim Wolbert (for Chapter 11); Andrew Horne and Kumiko Murata (for Chapter 12).

Some of the material in Chapters 11 and 13 has already appeared in a different form in *Converging Cultures: Trends in European Corporate Governance* (Price Waterhouse, 1997) and *Pursuing Value: The Emerging Art of Reporting on the Future* by Philip D Wright and Daniel P Keegan (PW Papers, 1997).

We are also grateful for additional help from Ella Lui, Chris Paxton, Dominic Watt, David Waller, Roger Mills, Tsurumi Hamasu, Glen Peters, Jon Bentley, Cheryl Martin, Jenny Francis, Ambreen Khokhar, Rebecca Carter, Anne Lima, Jacqueline Mitchell, Sam Roberts and Ann Stevenson. And a final thank you to Patrick Figgis for throwing down the challenge.

INTRODUCTION

You've probably heard about shareholder value. Perhaps your company has declared a commitment to shareholder value, or SHV as we will call it throughout this book, and you want an explanation. Perhaps you are an executive who wants to introduce an SHV approach in your company. You may have even thought of using some value-based management system to implement an SHV policy in your company. Or perhaps you are just curious about why *Fortune* magazine called SHV 'the real key to creating wealth'.

Certainly there is a veritable storm of acronyms out there for the interested lay person to weather. For a start, there's EVA™ (economic value added), SVA (shareholder value added) and CFROI (cash flow return on investment), to say nothing of value-based management (VBM). We hope in this book to guide you around these and other sets of potentially important initials – for call them what you will, the ideas that cluster around these labels are ideas whose time has come. Corporations in Britain, the USA and other parts of the world are increasingly putting SHV theories into practice – and benefiting from doing so.

This book aims to explain what SHV means, and how it can help companies and their managers make better, more informed and more proactive decisions. As we shall see in subsequent chapters, SHV takes the insights that market analysts, looking at a company from the outside, have developed, transfers them inside and transforms them into management tools – tools that can be used not just at the boardroom level, but throughout a company, to notch up genuine improvements in performance.

We at Price Waterhouse see ourselves as one of the leaders in the SHV trend. This book is not, however, a handbook for our particular system. Rather, it takes one step back to look at the philosophy of value creation and at the global financial environment in which value-based management can thrive. We don't promise easy solutions – and we hope we will succeed in dealing with some of the tricky questions raised by critics of the value-based approach.

It is unquestionable that in the last decade or so there has been a global momentum in the economy. Capital markets – indeed, almost all financial institutions – are increasingly global in outlook. Investors are more sophisticated than ever and want to know more about a company; more than simply what dividends it has been paying in the past. Profit and loss statements drawn up in traditional ways are no longer enough; cash flow has become a more important measure.

As one of the oldest established and largest accountancy practices in the world, Price Waterhouse is particularly well placed to observe such global trends. We are moving forward from the traditional audit that has been our bread and butter for so many years in order to keep pace with – and get ahead of – these trends. Indeed the core purpose of the firm can be described as to help clients build value: value for their shareholders, for their employees, and for their communities.

This book then, is not only a result of our experience and thinking about financial value, but also an example of what Price Waterhouse does for its clients. For what we do is help them build value through financial and business analysis, implementation of systems and procedures that facilitate value creation, and enhanced communication and reporting to their shareholders and other stakeholders.

The content of this book

The first part of *In Search of Shareholder Value* aims to introduce the basic concepts of SHV analysis, not only by describing the current economic and global conditions that make SHV so compelling, but also by arguing against a 'stakeholder' view of business. We then look at the theory behind shareholder value, and the history behind that, before asking the all-important question: what does your capital cost?

It is not until you have established the true cost of your capital that you will be able to calculate whether or not you are adding value in your day-to-day business. Working this out can, however, be a tricky business. We try to make it easier by dealing with matters such as risk-free rates of return, betas and market premiums.

These calculations have to be made because, as we show in Chapter 4, the apparently straightforward figures of profit and loss do not tell the whole story. Rather than look to profit and loss and earnings per share, the market prefers increasingly to judge a company's performance on its cash return on investment capital. This is where SHV analysis come in, with its seven 'value drivers' outlined in Chapter 5. Finally in this part, Chapter 6 outlines the various metric systems used for calculating shareholder value. Whatever refinements of calculation are used, the basic message is the same: cash is what counts.

Part 2 moves from theory to practice, and outlines the principles of value-based management. First comes corporate analysis of a standard company – the application of the value drivers to its activities, and the tools by which value creation can be measured. We then turn to the 'wartime' situation of mergers and acquisitions, and how SHV can help both acquirer and target company assess what their true worth is, and what their best course of action might be. The other problem can be the 'sickbed' situation – when a company is facing failure and it needs help to recover. Here again shareholder value analysis can be a precious resource.

Part 3 stays in the practical sphere by reporting on our experience in a range of industrial sectors, noting that while the 'value drivers' may vary, basic shareholder value analysis can apply to all of them. We also report on how shareholder value ideas are being received and applied in a selection of countries around the world. A particularly interesting case is that of Japan, whose generally accepted post-war economic success, in apparent defiance of 'Anglo-Saxon' SHV precepts, has been followed by a collapse and some rethinking of economic performance criteria.

Finally, in Part 4, we bring everything together to look at the future of value reporting, and imagine a hypothetical company report of the future, where value creation is truly taken seriously – to the benefit of all concerned.

Come with us on our journey to the future with SHV.

PART

1

WHAT IS
SHAREHOLDER
VALUE?

SHAREHOLDER VALUE: FAD VERSUS FACT

Value. It's a five-letter word with a wealth of meanings – from 'desirability' and 'utility' as a noun to 'appraise' or 'have a high opinion of' when it is a verb. But more and more, when business people and investors talk about value, it's to do with SHV or similar 'value-based' measurements of performance. In other words, techniques by which companies and corporations can be analyzed, re-oriented and then managed to conform with a value creation imperative.

Value for whom? What kind of value? In the business world it's certainly financial value that's the issue, and more specifically cash. By this we mean the cash that takes the form of the returns a company gives to its shareholders, and also cash flow – because that is the sign of a corporation's health in the eyes of the market. (More about that later.)

But, you may ask, why should it matter what the market thinks? Isn't all this just another fad that management will have to adopt and then discard a few years later? Our answers to these two questions are: yes, the market does matter; and no, it is not a fad. Because SHV is founded on the facts of economic life as they confront us today. If you are to be part of a successful company, you cannot ignore these facts. The creation of value for its shareholders is fundamental to the success of any public company.

In this book, particularly in this opening chapter, we hope to convince you of the case for SHV. We will open our case by developing the argument under three headings: why it is not a fad; what it is; and why it is so controversial. Under the last heading we will be exploring some of the arguments against SHV that use 'stakeholder' theories.

WHY SHV IS NOT A FAD

To put SHV into context, we must consider the changes that have taken place and are still taking place all over the world. In the past decade or so, companies have seen the rapid transformation of their businesses by a multitude of forces. Three forces in particular have contributed to a growing awareness of the importance of SHV and value-based management. They are: the spread of private capital; the globalization of markets; and the information revolution. Let us look at them one by one.

Increasing amount and spread of private capital

The accumulation and spread of wealth has accelerated dramatically across the globe in the last 50 years, driven by technological advance, a long period of peace in the West and increased world trade. Inherited from the first half of the century, however, was a loss of faith in capital markets and an experience of war that led people to accept the expansion of the state into areas of commercial and financial life on a massive scale. In particular, many states entered into long-term obligations in the areas of pensions, health and social security. But demographic developments – increased life expectancy, for example – have meant that in the last 20 years these states have hit the limits of their taxing and borrowing powers and have begun to withdraw from at least some of their commitments and to shift provision back to the individual.

States and politicians have a multitude of differing and often complex claims and priorities to consider. But the individual is driven by a simpler and clearer set of objectives. At the practical level this means that more and more people are investing privately to secure their pensions, as well as taking out health and other insurances to protect themselves against a variety of risks. Each individual may be thinking of different combinations of growth, risk and return, and therefore different mixes of property, bonds and equity. For longer-term commitments many take the higher-risk, higher-return option and invest in equities, often through mutual funds.

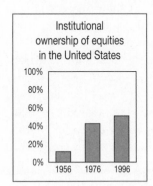  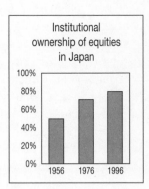

Source: International Federation of Stock Markets, London Stock Exchange and Price Waterhouse calculations

Fig. 1.1 Growth in institutional ownership

This in turn has led to the enormous expansion of equity markets – in the first instance in the UK, Japan and the USA, but increasingly as a worldwide phenomenon – and the rising proportion of equities held by institutions such as pension funds (see Fig. 1.1 but see Chapter 12 for the special circumstances of Japan). The individual investor expects funds to maximize their performance; in their turn the funds increasingly demand value from the companies they invest in.

Globalization of markets

Since 1970, true global markets have developed in an increasing range of goods and services, accompanied by various GATT (General Agreement on Tariffs and Trade) agreements which have successfully lowered trade barriers. These lowered barriers, unsurprisingly, led to an increase in international trade, and before long companies were faced with decisions about where to sell, and how to support those sales. (A strategy based on protecting or holding on to a domestic market has become untenable in an increasing number of areas.) To invest in foreign markets, capital transfers from one country to another, and arrangements for remitting profits back to the investor, are needed.

The currency markets have grown in size and sophistication since the collapse, in the 1970s, of the Bretton Woods system of fixed exchange rates. This has enabled the management of currency and interest risks to keep pace, more or less, with the demands of global traders.

By the 1980s, along with widespread domestic financial deregulation, most restrictions on capital flows had been removed by the OECD (Organization for Economic Co-operation and Development) countries. Following the establishment of global markets for financial assets, it has become possible to invest internationally in a much more proactive way than before. Companies are now competing internationally not only for customers, products and employees, but also for capital. Attracting capital depends on being best in class and the major criterion for this is the creation of SHV.

In 'capital rich' countries, local companies can no longer expect to gain access to funds as cheaply as before. Many of the larger companies in countries such as Germany and Japan are realizing that previous supplies of cheap long-term lending are drying up and are being forced to concentrate on creating SHV in ways previously undreamed of.

Nevertheless, there are paradoxes. Portfolio investors now have the technical means to invest almost anywhere in the world, yet this freedom is limited. Restrictions are imposed on the liquidity and reputation of the markets where they can place their funds, and on the type of assets they can acquire. Like huge oil tankers unable to enter smaller ports, the large institutional funds are forced to stay in the deep water channels of the financial markets. Asset and liability considerations also mean that such investors have to keep a weather eye on their base currency; at the end of the day, liabilities in one currency have to be paid in that currency. Finally, valuable local tax concessions for entities such as pension schemes may prevent funds from investing outside their home markets.

So although there has been a large increase in international investment, it still forms a relatively small part of the total. Typically only 5 per cent of US equity investors go outside the US market; in most of the world's leading financial countries, the vast majority of investments are in domestic stocks and bonds. Even if they have the capacity to be global, most funds are still very local in their investment strategies, being tied to their home markets either because of risk aversion or because local content rules require them to invest domestically.

Does this mean that globalization is not such a big thing after all? On the contrary, we believe it is a process that is still in its infancy. Non-US companies such as Daimler-Benz are increasingly being listed in New York, and non-UK ones on the London Stock Exchange. We will see more and more of such phenomena as NASDAQ – the US-based National Association of Securities Dealers Automated Quotation System – advertising its services in countries outside North America.

Information

The increased sophistication of telecommunications and computers means, as we know, that money can now travel across the world in a matter of seconds. Two further developments in the information revolution have facilitated the application of SHV and at the same time increased the demand for information to create an efficient market.

First, the advent of PC-based modelling software has relieved investors of the need to spend time on the complex calculations underlying SHV methodology. This has enabled them to focus on the quality of a company's strategic thinking, its product and market knowledge.

Second, the quantity and quality of information now available to investors are far superior to even ten years ago. Companies such as Reuters and Bloomberg provide on-line news and market information; the Edgar database provides immediate access to US financial filings; and product and market data proliferate. Many companies also now spend a considerable amount on investor relations and communications.

The value of disclosing fuller and more comprehensive information is perhaps best illustrated in Switzerland. There, companies that have chosen the disclosure route regularly attract capital at a lower cost than those that remain secretive.

All these trends, taken together, have one message: you can't hide from the markets. Any company that wants to do well – and that means attract investment funds, and continue to attract them – will (unless it can sustain its investment need from its own resources) have to submit itself happily to the scrutiny of the people whose money it is using.

WHAT IS SHV?

What then does the investment community understand by SHV? One definition of it is simply 'corporate value minus debt' – or, put another way, a company's SHV is calculated as the present value of future cash flows of the business discounted at its weighted average cost of capital, less the value of debt. But the more fundamental principle is that *a company only adds value for its shareholders when equity returns exceed equity cost*. If an investor is considering buying your company's equity, he or she ought to take account of the *opportunity cost* of having capital tied up there rather than elsewhere. We shall return to this crucial question of the cost of capital in Chapter 3.

You may already be feeling uneasy, however. 'Sure, the markets want to know the value of my company – there's nothing wrong with that,' you will say. 'But why introduce new methods? What's wrong with looking at the balance sheet and the profit and loss statement? Aren't measures such as EPS (earnings per share – a company's total profits after tax and interest is deducted, divided by the number of shares at issue) sufficient for analysts?'

Unfortunately they aren't. Economists have looked back over the past and have been able to show that there is little correlation between historical accounting earnings and stock market performance. With GAAP (generally accepted accounting practices) varying markedly from country to country, it is possible for the same company, using the same figures, to declare a profit in one country and a loss in another. Profit, in other words, is an opinion rather than an established fact.

The gaps in GAAP

For this reason, among others, there has been a growing disenchantment with company results as reported. In particular there is a feeling that too much attention is given to EPS measurements. (The overuse of EPS and anomalous accounting measures is discussed in Chapter 4.)

But of even more concern to investors is the question of whether accounting measures in Europe – and indeed around the world – are consistent. As one would expect, they are not. The treatment of goodwill, deferred taxation and the valuing of inventory varies from country to country.

There is now a healthy industry in recasting reported accounts for use by investors. But it is questionable whether managements are arriving at their internally compiled figures – upon which they base operating and strategic decisions – in the same way. Without a focus on SHV principles, pan-European businesses or businesses that cross different trading blocs could be in danger of relying on internal accounts that have the same fault lines as external accounts. The result is bad decision making.

It is no surprise, then, that investment analysts are looking behind the headline figures to find other numbers that can measure more informatively the long-term prospects for a company. Shareholder value analysis based on free cash flow and the cost of capital can produce such numbers. Later on, we will examine the different ways of making the necessary calculations. Look out for acronyms such as CAPM, CFROI, EVA™ and TSR, all of which manipulate the source data on cash flow, capital or its cost to show different aspects of value. The important thing to take on board now is that these are the measures increasingly being used by the market to take investment decisions, and they concentrate on economic or cash flow measures rather than earnings or traditional accounting measures.

WHY IS SHV SO CONTROVERSIAL?

Understandably, boardrooms and middle managers are suspicious of the stock market. A superficial glance at the behaviour of share prices in the market might lead you to think that short-termism has priority over long-term evaluation. Companies are convinced that investors are driven by short-term targets and do not therefore understand management strategies. This view has its counterpart in the investment community: many shareholders feel managements take too little account of their needs, in particular for information about companies' future plans and strategies.

Paradoxically, this misunderstanding between management and investor concerning the short and the long term arises because of the enormous immediate effects on value of announcements made by companies, even concerning short-term results, if these change the market's perception of their long-term cash flows.

So perhaps there is less conflict than is at first apparent. An essential component of value-based management is an emphasis on communication, both internally and externally. As our own research at Price Waterhouse has shown, investors are not simply looking for short-term rewards in the form of dividends and an increasing share price; they want long-term prospects for growth. There is a great deal of evidence that the market evaluates management decisions according to their impact on long-term discounted cash flow.

All the same, it cannot be denied that tensions exist between investor and management. This tension can all too easily be repeated elsewhere. Within many companies the culture of the strategist and creative visionary clashes with that of the manager and controller. Shareholder value demands a consistent link between both. Similarly, tension can arise between corporate and divisional management.

In a company structured to maximize SHV, the divisional manager will have to be more aware of what the shareholders want – which is nothing but better returns. He or she will have to think much more as an entrepreneur, rather than just as an employee. Accustomed perhaps to carrying out head office's requirements without too much thought, divisional managers may face some difficult adjustments. The quiet life they long for will not be an option as they become both more empowered and also acquire more responsibility and accountability. For many, this will be uncomfortable – as will the scrutiny that comes with the new focus on value creation. With that bad news, however, should come the promise of better things in the shape of rewards for value creation. The measurements that SHV brings in its train are ideal tools for the incentivization of management. (We will deal with such incentivization in Chapter 7.)

Shareholders and stakeholders

So far we have argued that significant trends at work in the economy and society are pushing for an increased role for SHV. However persuasive such evidence is, it has to be compared critically with a number of alternative approaches. For many people, it is not self-evident that the equity-based approach is the best. Emphasizing the interests of shareholders over those of other groups, they argue, is misplaced. In this 'stakeholder' view of companies, the interests of suppliers, customers, creditors, employees and the state are at least as important as those of shareholders.

If a company is focused simply on SHV, the argument goes, the only stakeholder to get any benefit will be the investor; employees in particular will suffer. There is a close correlation in people's minds between companies performing poorly, redundancy programmes and share price increases. Taking a stakeholder view, on the other hand, means taking a less 'callous' view and considering the sometimes competing interests of worker, shareholder, customer and supplier – and indeed the wider community.

This 'stakeholder corporation' does, on the face of it, make sense: wouldn't it be fairer if everybody's interests could be weighed against each other and reconciled by management? The trouble is, ultimately, they can't be. The management of a business must have one prime focus: maximizing the value of its equity. If it is accountable to more than one interest, it will sooner or later be faced with the problem of deciding between them, and it can only give preference to one or the other by using some further criterion. This is all the more true in today's decentralized corporation where middle managers are continually taking decisions with value implications; for instance, should an investment that adds value and keeps customers satisfied – but reduces the workforce – go ahead? Corporate paralysis would ensue without a clear, common criterion. When interests conflict, such as those of employees and shareholders, a choice has to be made, and stakeholder theory offers no help in making that choice.

Putting SHV first, however, does. While it concentrates on its one objective, a company managed for value cannot afford to ignore the other stakeholders. Staff will leave if under-rewarded or otherwise mistreated; customers will leave if not satisfied; suppliers have to be kept happy, too. By adopting the measures necessary to maximize corporate value, a company can advance the interests of other stakeholders as well its shareholders. It also adds value to the society in which it operates. And it is of no use to its employees or to the community at large if it fails to make money, whatever else it does.

Indeed, SHV principles will not always necessarily support the 'downsizing' with which it has sometimes been linked. A company can be performing badly but still justify its investment in cash and retention of valuable human resources through a temporary downturn, to save the investment and training costs that would be involved in re-acquiring a skilled workforce when things get better. However, if the downturn is structural, spending cash on retaining employees will not only reduce SHV but also destroy further a company's competitiveness, and reduce job security for all.

Roberto C Goizueta, former CEO of The Coca-Cola Company, argued the case for putting shareholders (or as he described them, 'share owners') trenchantly:

> Saying that we work for our share owners may sound simplistic – but we frequently see companies that have forgotten the reason they exist. They may even try in vain to be all things to all people and serve many masters in many different ways. In any event, they miss their primary calling, which is to stick to the business of creating value for their owners. ... [W]hile a healthy company can have a positive and seemingly infinite impact on others, a sick company is a drag on the social order of things. It cannot sustain jobs, much less widen the opportunities available to its employees. It cannot serve customers. It cannot give to philanthropic causes. ...
>
> The real and lasting benefits we create don't come because we do good deeds, but because we do good work – work focused on our mission of creating value over time for the people who own the company.[1]

It is this focus on one overriding aim that simplifies everything, even as it incidentally brings other benefits in its train, for example motivation of a company's managers. As Samuel Brittan has remarked, 'People function best if they have specific responsibilities for which they are held accountable by means which are transparent, verifiable and respect the realities of human nature.'[2] The objective of maximizing SHV affords just such a responsibility, and the means by which it is measured, as we shall see in later chapters, are indeed transparent and verifiable.

---

[1] Remarks delivered to Executives' Club of Chicago, quoted in 1996 annual report of The Coca-Cola Company.
[2] 'The snares of stakeholding,' *Financial Times*, 1 February 1996.

Corporate governance

It has to be said, however, that SHV theories raise some important questions about corporate governance. These in turn feed back into deeper questions on the ownership and control of financial and economic assets. Yet so far there has been little effort to link discussion about how companies should be governed with the equally interesting question of what impact any particular form of governance might have on the creation of SHV. This omission is all the more extraordinary given that when SHV is discussed in connection with organizational and management structures, emotions often run high.

Broadly speaking there are two models for capitalism. The first, loosely called the 'Anglo-Saxon' model, is characterized by large and liquid capital markets, a growing concentration of power into the hands of institutional investors, and a market for corporate control via takeover bids, many of them hostile.

Some figures make this clearer. In the UK the total market capitalization of the 2000-plus companies quoted on the Stock Exchange comes to around 124 per cent of GDP, compared to an EU average of 44 per cent of GDP. (In the USA the figure is some 94 per cent.)[3] Institutional investors account for well over 70 per cent of total equity investments, while over half of all European takeover bids occur in the UK.

By contrast, in Germany, much of the rest of Europe and possibly Japan (countries where the 'stakeholder' model applies), equity markets are less liquid and often smaller. Shareholder power is concentrated among banks, governments and families. For example in Italy single majority shareholdings account for about 60 per cent of the total market capitalization compared to just 5 per cent in the UK and the USA. The largest five shareholders of Italian listed companies typically hold nearly 90 per cent of the shares between them, compared to only 21 per cent in the UK.

More significantly, mainland Europe has a much less well-developed market for corporate control. Hostile takeovers are virtually unknown in most European markets, and changes in control are normally negotiated by banks and governments; typically, the market is informed after it is all over.

We discuss these contrasting models for corporate governance in more detail in Part 3, where we will also consider the possible convergence of the two variants of capitalism as SHV becomes a more unifying global framework.

[3] Figures, from OECD and FIBV (Fédération Internationale des Bourses de Valeur), are for June 1996.

SUMMARY

In this chapter we have introduced the global context in which companies have to operate as competitors for (among other things) capital. Cash flow, however it is measured, is a better indicator of a company's value than more traditional measures. Consequently, investors increasingly look at cash flow figures when estimating SHV, and hence the potential value of an investment. We also looked at the question of 'stakeholding' and rejected it as a viable way of managing a company.

THE
HISTORY OF
VALUE

Value has existed as a concept as long as humanity has conducted trade and accumulated 'capital' and 'wealth'. As economies and societies have developed from subsistence, through agriculture and industry to service, value has been the consistent measurement used by those with freedom of choice to trade or to invest and preserve their capital.

Of course this historical development has taken place against occasional catastrophe (war, disease, environmental difficulties) and a background provided by government, which is involved in value in four ways: war and peace, the administration of justice (particularly property rights), the redistribution of wealth and income, and the provision of infrastructure. On the last, Professor George Stigler[1] argues that:

> The propensity to use the state is like the propensity to use coal: we use coal when it is the most efficient resource with which to heat our houses and power our factories. Similarly, we use the state to build our roads or tax our customers when the state is the most efficient way to reach those goals.

With the global economic development of the last 50 years has come an increasing study of the value creation process. From a political and social standpoint this has concentrated largely on the shareholder/stakeholder debate referred to in the previous chapter, where the superior effectiveness of the capital market approach to creating value is now widely recognized. The argument now revolves basically around how to provide infrastructure in the case of the market's perceived failure to do so (for example, in health and education), how much to redistribute wealth and income, and what legal framework is needed for the operation of the market – what laws are necessary, for example, to deal with monopolies, health and safety, environmental protection and minimum wage levels.

---

[1] George Stigler, 'The Regularity of Regulation', David Hume Institute, 1986, pp. 3–4, quoted in Cento Veljanovski, *Selling the State* (Weidenfeld, 1987).

CUSTOMER VALUE

From a business perspective, two main themes are rapidly converging: customer value and SHV. On customers and markets, much work on strategy and operations has been done by business schools and strategic consultants who have examined the competitive forces that drive them. Leading thinkers in this area include Michael Porter, who developed the 'five forces' model to analyze competition for custom in an industry and identified the generic strategies for achieving competitive advantage (overall cost leadership, differentiation and focus)[2]; and Gary Hamel and C K Prahalad, who coined the term 'core competencies' to describe those attributes that give an enterprise a competitive advantage.[3]

Clearly we are living in a market economy where winning maximum share and keeping customers satisfied is key. And customers are satisfied if a product meets or exceeds their expectations at a price no higher than its perceived value. This drive to customer value has been accompanied by other processes designed to lower costs and improve quality and performance, such as Total Quality Management (TQM), process and systems re-engineering and change integration.

Customer satisfaction is, of course, only ultimately of value when it produces over time an economic cash return on the investment – a return in excess of a company's cost of capital. Thus the strategic thinking aimed at customers needs to be reconciled with the financial thinking behind SHV, which brings us to the development of SHV theories.

SHAREHOLDER VALUE

Theories about SHV have a long and illustrious history stretching back to the 1950s and 1960s, with their intellectual roots in the path-breaking work of Markovitz, Modigliani and Miller, and Sharpe, Fama, and Treynor (to name but a few). Many of these economists have subsequently been honoured with the Nobel Prize for economics, thus putting what had started out as a 'fringe' activity in economics firmly at the centre of that discipline's development.

SHV started to take on a life of its own as a result of work done on what has become known as the Capital Asset Pricing Model (CAPM). In essence this model argues that the returns both received and expected by investors are related to the risk incurred by owning particular financial assets. Broadly speak-

---

[2] Michael E Porter, *Competitive Strategy* (New York: Free Press, 1990).
[3] C K Prahalad and Gary Hamel, 'The Core Competence of the Corporation', *Harvard Business Review*, May–June 1990.

ing the higher the risk, the greater the return should be. (It is useful to recall that what today seems to be a commonplace, and is now widely accepted as part of our thinking, was initially greeted with suspicion and scepticism. Some of what became path-breaking articles were at first rejected for publication.)

The key insight of the CAPM model – one that is central to the SHV view of the world – is that there is a risk-weighted discount factor which allows you to assess the value today of tomorrow's developments, profits and cash flows. This discount rate is derived from observations of capital markets, and defines what the *opportunity cost* of equity to an investor in the market is. It states what the company has to earn in order to justify the use of the capital resources tied up in the business.

THE DEVELOPMENT OF A THEORY

It was sometime during the late 1970s and early 1980s that work in applying some of the insights of CAPM to the corporate sector got under way. These efforts first gained prominence with the publication in 1986 of *Creating Shareholder Value* by Professor Alfred Rappaport of Northwestern University. He subsequently went on to found the Alcar group, a company dedicated to the production of software to help executives achieve some of the goals laid out in his book.

Brought down to its simplest, the SHV approach is well summarized by the late Coca-Cola CEO Roberto Giozueta: 'We raise capital to make concentrate, and sell it at an operating profit. Then we pay the cost of that capital. Shareholders pocket the difference.' This surprisingly simple statement raises a number of questions. Traditionally, for example, managements have been encouraged by being set growth objectives. They have also been encouraged to reduce borrowing costs and diversify their enterprises (possibly in pursuit of the growth goal already mentioned). Looked at from the point of view of SHV theory, all three policies can be seriously flawed, not to say destructive.

A growth policy can tie up considerable capital resources, which are then applied inefficiently and yield inadequate returns. Seen in SHV terms, this policy has destroyed SHV, even though the company may have grown larger as a result. Debt repayment schemes may also help to reduce SHV when they have the effect of increasing the cost of capital, and thus raising the threshold rate which the company has to meet before it begins to add to SHV.

Finally, efforts to diversify the company's portfolio by getting involved in extensive mergers and acquisitions activity has been described by a leading proponent of the SHV approach as being 'equivalent to charitable contributions made to random passers-by', as the acquirer regularly overpays for the privilege of managing a decidedly mediocre business. (But see Chapter 8.)

FURTHER WORK ON SHV

Interest in the SHV approach received a further boost with the 1990 publication of *Valuation* by Tom Copeland and others from the McKinsey Group. This book contained a detailed exposition of the issues and how to deal with them, showing that the application of SHV principles to companies is both feasible and highly desirable. Furthermore, it can yield substantial benefits not only to shareholders, the book argued, but also to other 'stakeholders' in a company.

Subsequent developments have been materially assisted by the emergence of a number of software products. These, combined with the skills of consultants and managements, have brought the analysis of SHV within the reach of companies who had previously never considered it, or had not felt competent or comfortable with the idea of applying it to themselves.

AFTER THE HISTORY, WHAT?

If business and capital markets are going to be increasingly value oriented, what are the implications? What will success look like for companies in the new millennium? If SHV is the new game, how will corporate players win?

Certainly the rules are changing. Product excellence and customer satisfaction is still necessary but is no longer sufficient, nor is it enough to focus on profit alone. This is now a game in which success requires both sustainable superior returns on capital and peer-leading growth rates. Combine these with a proactive management of the risks associated with optimizing returns and growth, and you have a whole new set of trade-offs and strategic permutations to challenge the corporate sector.

These challenges may be new, but in a sense they are the same old challenges in a different guise. The three aspects of market activity just referred to – risk, growth and return – continue to be central. The economic reality, that cash is king and investors require compensating returns for the risks they bear, is not new. It has always been the case that investors buy securities based on their expectations of future performance, not merely as a belated recognition of past performance. Growth, too, has always been a good thing, other variables remaining constant. It is these basics on which SHV theory is founded.

Paradoxically, then, we are going forward to the past. Although the capitalist system has always appeared to be structured to serve the interests of the owners of equity – the shareholders – it is only now, with the increased global pressures described in Chapter 1 now applying, and with the increased sophistication of software tools, that shareholders' interests are really being considered. Value for shareholders has finally reached the top of the agenda.

SHV IN PRACTICE

The basic SHV approach is a simple one, then – although some aspects of the theory and calculations are complicated, and will be dealt with later. It addresses the relationship between what a company is using in terms of capital resources, how they are allocated throughout the firm, and what the likelihood is of their earning their 'keep' over the planning horizon. Although it all sounds very straightforward, it is surprising how often it has to be explained.

Meanwhile, it is worth noting that 65 per cent of all large companies in the USA claim that they have adopted SHV as a primary goal. Indeed, they might be slightly offended at any suggestion they had not taken this issue seriously. But it is also clear that only a relatively small number of companies has seriously embarked on detailed SHV programmes, let alone had the patience and forbearance to hold on until they are finished.

Companies that are on record as having embarked on, or having signed up to, SHV programmes include such names as Coca-Cola, Pepsi Cola, Quaker Oats, Reuters, Lloyds Bank, Hoechst, Veba, General Electric, Briggs and Stratton, ICI, Boots, Novo Nordisk and many more. Many of the companies on this list have indeed experienced above average share price performance – which is one good indication that the companies have really taken SHV seriously.

What then are the reasons why companies adopt a SHV approach? There are the external stimuli:

- when they are faced with strong external pressure from investors. This can be because of an actual or threatened takeover situation;
- when incumbent senior management is faced with a new CEO who understands SHV concepts;
- when a new CEO wants to implement a SHV project as part of finding out what is going on in the company;

But there are other reasons, too:

- to 'empower' the work of lower management, and encourage it to take steps that will explicitly consider SHV, and match empowerment with accountability and incentivization;
- to give additional focus to other consultancy projects, to ensure that the new systems are aligned with SHV goals;
- when there are serious mismatches between corporate expectations and subsidiary performance;
- when there is confidence that the programmes can be implemented properly, reliably and within budget.

Companies are less likely actually to implement SHV programmes if these conditions are not met. They may also stall if there is serious disagreement at a senior level about the wisdom of the exercise – which may reach unpleasant conclusions, thereby upsetting a fragile consensus at board level.

These are general issues that affect many consultants and programmes offering change to a corporation. Companies may give up on SHV programmes if it is felt that they are not getting anywhere, and if there is too little support from the top to ensure that everyone is co-operating. SHV programmes work better if the wider circle of managers and employees can be convinced that they are necessary and that they will yield some benefits over and above the laying off of staff. Indeed, to be successful, such programmes will often have started a lively discourse about where the company is going, and how it can set itself feasible goals that will raise SHV.

SUMMARY

In this chapter we took a brief view of the historical context of value. Alongside the development of customer value approaches in business, SHV theories have arisen from academic work on the cost of capital. Underlying all these theories is a belief that companies have to earn a certain amount of returns to justify the use of the capital they have tied up in their enterprise. In effect, this belief is a reassertion of one of the basic facts of capitalism – that shareholders have to be rewarded for investing in you.

Finally, we identified the circumstances in which companies in practice have sought to adopt SHV-based programmes.

WHAT DOES YOUR CAPITAL COST?

It sounds so simple, and yet it is probably one of the most commonly overlooked aspects of business. All enterprises require some capital, and it does not come free.

Although capital comes in more than one form – as equity or debt – we are primarily concerned here with a company's shareholder capital, since this is the most common form of corporate finance. When we say capital is not a 'free' good, we mean that if it is not adequately rewarded it will migrate into areas where it can earn a reasonable rate of return – equivalent to what is sometimes called the *opportunity cost* (the term we introduced in Chapter 1).

This chapter, then, is all about ways of identifying what a company's share and debt capital actually costs. These calculations have two sides. The suppliers of capital look to a maximum risk-weighted return to compensate them for putting up the money in the first place; while the consumers of capital have to ensure that the suppliers obtain a minimum return at least as high as any that could be earned elsewhere. (Obviously, if a company can achieve a higher return, so much the better.) Afterwards, we will link the cost of capital to a general SHV model and introduce the concept of the drivers of SHV.

HURDLE RATES

The cost of capital is a very important concept – indeed, it is a concept that is central to this book. In simple terms, it is not unlike the situation described by Mr Micawber in Dickens' *David Copperfield*: 'Annual income twenty pounds, annual expenditure nineteen nineteen six, result happiness. Annual income twenty pounds, annual expenditure twenty pounds ought and six, result misery.' Cost of capital calculations are similar: there exists a figure which marks the boundary between misery and happiness. This is the *hurdle rate*, or the rate of return that a company should realistically be able to earn on a risk-adjusted basis.

Suppose the hurdle rate is set at 10 per cent a year. If this represents the cost of capital – a concept to which we will return in more detail below – then a company is creating SHV if the return on capital is greater than this (say 12 per cent a year). It is destroying SHV if its return on capital is lower that this, at say 8 per cent a year.

In our experience, corporate hurdle rates can vary considerably. One rate might be very low because the investment is regarded as strategic, and hence will not be obliged to earn a realistic rate of return. This approach is often adopted by governments, and to a degree by nationalized companies. It reflects what might be termed the social rate of time preference, or the willingness of society to postpone consumption today in order to receive higher consumption tomorrow. A low hurdle rate might also be used if the investment is regarded as intermediate to the production process, with the money to be recouped elsewhere.

On the other hand, a company might use a more 'realistic' approach, perhaps using an apparently arbitrary number established during the days of high inflation, and never subsequently adjusted downwards in the light of new circumstances. You might find a 25 per cent hurdle rate being used, irrespective of the actual risks incurred.

The use of global hurdle or discount rates across an entire group of activities in a company gives rise to some odd results. Not only does the firm's internal planning process become clogged up with various draft proposals all managing to pass the conditions set by senior management, it can also seriously bias the direction of investment policy. Discount rates that are uniformly too high will generally push the company into taking bigger risks than are justified – even though the actual probability of reaching the rate set may be quite low. By the same token, the use of the high discount rate will rule out many apparently unprofitable projects that might have earned the company a respectable addition to its SHV.

The key weakness of the 'conventional' hurdle rate is that it fails adequately to include any *market risk* component in making a calculation. The SHV approach, on the other hand, will include a risk factor in assessing what the appropriate rate of return for investors (and hence management) should be. It thus provides a more satisfactory way of measuring the return a company should be achieving on the capital resources it uses.

CAPM: THE KEY RISK EQUATION

We used the phrase 'risk-weighted discount factor' in Chapter 2, when we introduced the Capital Asset Pricing Model (CAPM). As we said then, this discount factor states what a company has to earn in order to justify the use of the capital resources tied up in the business. We call this the *cost of equity*. Let us now look at this model in more detail.

There is a key relationship in the CAPM. Expressed as a formula, it looks like this:

$$r_i = r_f + \beta r_m$$

Here, r_i refers to the return on an individual security, r_f is the risk-free rate of return, and r_m represents the market risk premium. β (beta) describes the systematic risk attached to investing in that security – a concept we will return to later in this chapter. This is saying that the return on an individual security r is a function of β, a risk-free rate of return r_f and the market risk premium r_m. Let us look in more detail at these components starting with r_f – the risk-free rate of return.

ELEMENTS OF THE CAPM EQUATION

Risk-free rates of return

The notion that there is something called a 'risk-free' rate of return may bring a smile to a bond trader's or fixed income investment manager's face. For our purposes, though, we treat interest rates available in the government bond market at a given point in time as if they were risk free. What we are saying is that these are the current ruling rates, and an investment decision made today will be able to achieve those rates.

Since we are looking ahead, however, we want to know what the 'risk-free' rate is over the length of time used for the forecasted cash flows. In many cases it may be convenient to use the benchmark yields on ten-year government bonds; for shorter cash flow forecasts of say five years we would use bond yields over this maturity. This yield is preferable to whatever interest rates short-term deposits are currently able to attract; short-term deposits have to be rolled over, and it is not easy to say whether these roll-over rates will stay constant over the life of a project. Generally they will not, so we prefer using the longer-term bond rates.

Incidentally, when we talk of 'interest rates available on the market', we may sometimes have a problem deciding *which* market. In our view, SHV analysis should try and keep everything as local as possible, at least to start with. We look at where a company is paying its dividends – its home country. The returns on investment will have to be made in that currency and bear some relationship to current interest rates available on that market.

The situation can become much more complicated when a large corporation has multiple borrowings in multiple currencies, or is registered in several countries. For a more detailed discussion, see later in this book.

Betas (βs)

Why are betas important? Why have economists discussed them so much? The beta measures the association between changes in an individual share price and the changes in an underlying share index. It measures the systematic risk taken on when an investor buys that share, and gives an idea of how much the share will move in line with the market. This is important because while investors can offset specific risks associated with individual shares by holding diversified portfolios, they remain exposed to systematic risks associated with the market as a whole which cannot be diversified away. The higher its beta, the riskier the share: thus a share having a beta greater than one will move more than the market, and is sometimes described as being a volatile share. A share having a beta of less than one moves less than the market, and is sometimes thought of as a defensive investment (see Fig. 3.1).

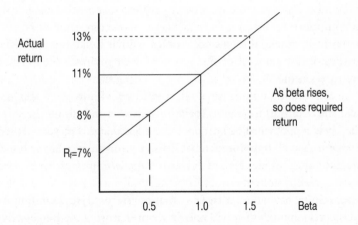

Fig 3.1 Investors' required rate of return

This has a number of implications about the returns expected from a share. Work by Friend and Blume[1] looked at the link between the betas on shares (here aggregated into portfolios), and subsequent share performance. It produced the results summarized in Table 3.1, where the most risky portfolios are at the bottom of the table.

---

[1] 'A New Look at the Capital Asset Pricing Model', *Journal of Finance* (1973) pp 19–33.

Table 3.1 More risk means higher returns – but less than the CAPM predicts

| Portfolio No | 1939–69 | | 1948–69 | | 1956–69 | |
	β	Mean return	β	Mean return	β	Mean return
		%		%		%
1	0.19	0.79	0.45	0.99	0.28	0.95
2	0.92	1.26	0.94	1.35	0.91	1.17
3	1.29	1.53	1.23	1.33	1.3	1.18
4	2.02	1.59	1.67	1.36	1.92	1.10

Source: Friend and Blume (1973)

Table 3.1 shows that the average returns of a number of portfolios increased with their riskiness. Interestingly, however, after a certain point mean return did not rise commensurately with risk, so that not much is gained from taking on riskier portfolios. Another interesting feature is that the gap in performance between the most risky and the least risky portfolios appears to have narrowed over time – supporting the idea that markets have become more efficient.

Other work by Black, Jensen and Scholes[2] which looked at the risk/return characteristics of different US stocks over a 35-year period, concluded that the average returns on the stocks increased by 1.08 per cent a month (13 per cent annually) for a one-unit increase in ß. While providing good evidence for CAPM, the strength of the observed relationship was only about three-quarters of what had been expected. The authors concluded that their tests: 'provide substantial support for the hypothesis that realised returns are a linear function of systematic risk value. *Moreover, it shows that the relationship is significantly positive over long periods of time.*'

This research suggests, then, that less volatile, low beta stocks will on balance perform less well than their more volatile competitors. In other words, as an investor you can only achieve a higher performance by exposing yourself to higher risk.

Measuring betas

Measuring betas is relatively straightforward: basically, it is a matter of using data from the past – but doing it in order to estimate what the future beta will be. We start with the assumption that the relevant beta for investors will measure a share's volatility relative to the main market index where the share is quoted. In most cases this is clear cut, and follows the principle adopted for

---

[2] Black, F, Jensen, M and Scholes, M, 'The Capital Asset Pricing Model: some empirical tests', in *Studies in the Theory of Capital Markets* (Praeger, 1972).

identifying the risk-free rate of return. Using a historic measure, we can take a five-year (60-month) moving average. We think this provides the best estimator of the future beta, which is what we are actually looking for. It may not always be a particularly good estimator, though: the variance (or degree of dispersion) of the estimates can sometimes be quite large, meaning that we cannot always attach a high degree of confidence to them. But tests we have done suggest that on balance a five-year period is better than most others at providing a long-run and relatively stable estimate of betas over a business cycle.

A few additional factors need to be considered, though. The first is that a share may not be traded very frequently, thus giving rise to deceptively low beta values. This can be adjusted for by using more detailed benchmarking and peer group analysis (benchmarking is covered in more detail in Part 2). Second, in some circumstances differences in the debt-to-equity ratio can also impact on the beta. On occasion, it is more suitable to adjust for leverage levels to find a 'truer' estimate of what the underlying volatility of the share is.

Finally, there may have been substantial changes in what a company actually does. It may have been through an extensive restructuring process, making it no longer the same company it was a few years ago. Here judgement is necessary, and it may be useful to take a shorter time period. Remember, the main object is to find the best estimator of what the beta is likely to be over a forecast period taking into account likely business cycle changes.

All this serves to underline the point that while the basic mechanics of a CAPM-related SHV approach are not particularly complicated, its actual implementation can be, and is full of pitfalls. There has been a long and spirited academic discussion about the validity of CAPM and the role of beta; the general conclusion has been that 'theoretical' betas in CAPM are probably larger than those observed in real life.[3] But the important thing to be aware of is that a forecast is being reached on the basis of past performance.

Market risk premiums

The SHV approach is all about comparing future outcomes with each other. One of the most important ways of doing this is to establish the opportunity cost of capital in general, and the opportunity cost of equity in particular. This is done by estimating what are called market risk premiums. In other words, the additional return an average investor can obtain from investing in equities (which are risky investments) as compared with 'risk-free' alternatives such as government bonds. As with betas, we have to rely primarily on history to help find the best estimator of a future risk premium.

---

[3] There are alternative methodologies for estimating betas such as the Arbitrage Pricing Model: readers interested in this approach should look at Ross, S 'The Arbitrage Theory of Capital Asset Pricing', *Journal of Economic Theory*, December 1976.

There are two basic ways to calculate market risk premiums: *ex post* (back-ward looking) – based on the actual performance of equities as compared to bonds – and *ex ante* (forward looking), based on the expected future perform-ance of equities, or what is realistically needed to get an institutional investor to give up the relative security of the bond market for the more uncertain pastures of the equity market.

Ex post: looking at history

The ex post method relies on identifying a historical period likely to give a good estimator of future market risk premiums. Within this, two calculation methods can be used: an arithmetic average of the excess equity returns, which assumes a re-balancing of the portfolios after every year, or a geometric average which assumes a long-term buy-and-hold investment strategy (often used as a bench-mark for investment performance comparisons in asset management). Many of the numbers quoted for market risk premiums use arithmetic rather than geo-metric calculations, and tend to be larger.[4] (Note that the arithmetic return is always higher than the geometric return: the spread increases as a function of the variance of the return and the interval chosen.)

How can we be sure of identifying the right time period for an ex post esti-mate? How relevant will it be? There are several answers, frequently coloured by the amount of information available. In the USA, where equity market per-formance has been long and reliably documented, the approach has often been simply to put as much information as is available into an analysis and calculate an average number. Doing this provides a figure of around 7 per cent a year 'extra' equity performance.

Simple though it seems, this approach has a number of difficulties. The first is that, as Table 3.2 shows, there are some striking differences in the market risk premium on a decade-by-decade basis. Indeed, the performance achieved by equities in one decade has very little correlation with that of the next. A cursory examination of US economic history can provide plenty of reasons why this should be; indeed, the apparently high overall number is buoyed up by two very exceptional periods – the 1920s and the 1980s. Generally we do not expect to see such good bull markets as we saw then, despite very good recent perform-ance, particularly in US equities.

Table 3.2 throws some light on other issues too. It is often asserted that equity markets are the best hedges in times of high inflation; but the figures show that this is not generally the case. During the 1960s, when inflation was beginning to accelerate, and more noticeably in the 1970s, when even the USA suffered from relatively high rates of inflation, equity performance was modest. The market risk premium virtually disappeared in the 1970s.

---

[4] Ian Cooper, *Arithmetic versus Geometric Mean Risk Framed: Setting Discount Rates for Capital Budgeting*, IFA working paper 174–95, Sept 1995.

Table 3.2 Market risk premiums, USA

Period	Percentage
1920s	7.0
1930s	2.3
1940s	7.8
1950s	12.9
1960s	4.0
1970s	0.2
1980s	3.7
1990–94	3.5
Overall average, 1920s–1990s	7

Source: Ibbotson Associates, 1993[5][6]

Let us look at the history another way, then. Table 3.3 adopts a moving average approach to the issue of the market risk premium. Here you can see how the numbers look year by year when the geometric mean of the excess returns is taken over a constant 30-year period.

Table 3.3 Longer-term average MRP (30-year) S&P compared to return on US Treasuries

Period	Percentage
1986	4.3
1987	4.7
1988	3.6
1989	4.1
1990	3.9
1991	3.8
1992	4.3
1993	3.7
1994	3.2

Source: Ibbotson Associates, 1996[6]

---

[5] *Stocks, Bonds, Bills and Inflation Yearbook, 1996* (Ibbotson Associates, Chicago).
[6] *Ibid.*

So when we try and use a constant length of historical time to estimate the market risk premium, the values look substantially more conservative than the longer run average figures shown in the first table.

We must remember, of course, that so far we have been talking exclusively about the USA. As soon as we look at other countries, it becomes increasingly clear that the USA is more an exception than a rule. On the basis of our research, countries like the UK, France, Switzerland and the Netherlands show a positive market risk premium more often than not, with the UK taking the premier position. The ability of equities to consistently deliver superior investment performance in other countries is more questionable. In Germany, equities underperform bonds for substantial periods of time, thus giving lie to the idea that the riskier investment is always the better one in the longer run. In countries like Canada, Australia, Italy and Spain the outcome is also more uncertain.

Why is this? Part of the reason is that all these countries have experienced lengthy periods of high inflation and high government deficits. Government investment needs tend to 'crowd out' those of the private sector, simply because the government is generally able to offer investors a positive real rate of return, which equities sometimes find difficult to emulate. In all the countries mentioned, equities underperformed bonds for substantial periods of time, and although a positive equity risk premium has returned recently, it is probably too early to say whether this will become a truly permanent feature of equities.

As for Japan, it offers an extraordinary spectacle of sustained equity outperformance until the late 1980s, after which it has been virtually downhill all the way for the stock market. If a reminder is needed of how risky equities can be, then you need look no further than the land of the rising sun. (There is more information on Japan in Part 3.)

Ex ante: looking to the future

Establishing a market risk premium by selecting the 'right' historical period can seem too complicated – or maybe too arbitrary – a task. In any case, the MRP measures observed actual returns, not required or expected returns which is of interest to us in looking forward . Perhaps then we should look at current market opinion about the extent by which equities are expected to outperform bonds in the future. That is what we have done – and have found no hard and fast opinion. A recent Price Waterhouse survey came up with market risk premium estimates ranging from a low of 2.7 per cent to a high of 4.5 per cent. Answers varied not only according to the time period under consideration, but also in relation to who we were talking to. People more closely associated with equity trading tend to be more optimistic about equities' chances in the future, while people actually involved in managing funds – the asset managers and strategists – tend to be more cautious about future equity performance.

As with the ex post analysis, SHV practitioners need to realize that judgement is needed. The aim should always be to provide the best 'estimator' for the market risk premium over the period being considered; which will typically involve combining estimates about the future with evidence from the past. But, once a judgement has been made, it should be open and transparent, and should come close to most analysts' and other observers' opinions of the underlying market. We would argue that this ultimately is less arbitrary than other approaches.

We have dwelt on the subject of the market risk premium at some length because it is crucially important. All discounted cash flow (DCF) approaches are very sensitive to the choice of discount rate, and so great care has to be exercised to 'get it right'. Inevitably, estimates will contain errors. As we have seen, market risk premiums shift substantially from one decade to the next, and observers in one period may not be all that good at accurate predictions of the next period's risk premium. From a practical point of view, we favour an approach that provides a judicious mixture of historical and *ex ante* views on the market.

THE COST OF EQUITY

After identifying the components of the CAPM formula, it is relatively easy to calculate the cost of equity. It cannot be stressed too much that this is an *expectational* cost, and differs from what some would argue is the actual cost of equity.

For traditionalists, the cost of equity is something that is limited to dividend payments made to shareholders, with an eye being kept on dividend yields that are currently available in the market. It is this type of view that underpins the dividend discount model (DDM) frequently used by actuaries. But in the SHV view of the world, the message of the cost of equity concept is different. It is telling both investors and managers that while dividends are important they are only part of the picture. The investor is concerned with the overall rate of return, which in addition to the stream of dividend payments also includes capital appreciation – any increases in the share price. We think of this as total shareholder return (TSR)[7]; over a period of time investments in the equity of a company have to minimally attain the cost of equity target. How it is done is of secondary consideration for the time being – it could be all capital appreciation, as in the case of start-up, venture capital types of enterprises, or it could be entirely dividends as in the case of more established companies. The investor is concerned with the overall rate of return, not just with the stream of dividend payments.

---

[7] Total Shareholder Return represents the change in capital value of a company over a one-year period, plus dividends, expressed as a plus or minus percentage of the opening value.

THE COST OF DEBT

We also need to calculate the cost of debt for SHV analysis. Companies use both equity and debt in their operations, and just as equity has a 'cost' to management – and a return to investors – so does debt. However, debt differs from equity in one important respect. Interest charges on debt are normally tax deductible, so that the effective cost of debt to management is lowered by the extent of a 'tax shield'. From the corporate perspective, this tends to make debt costs lower than the cost of equity. The tax shield argument does not apply to investors them-selves, however, or at least not in the same way. Investors may be interested in their post-tax rate of return, where their individual tax positions will have to be taken into account. This is one aspect dealt with by the Cash Flow Return On Investment (CFROI), which we will look at in more detail in Chapter 6.

Where a company has some publicly quoted debt – corporate bond issues, for instance – an idea of the current cost of debt can be obtained directly by look-ing at market price and yield quotes. Where this information is not directly available, then an estimate of the cost of debt has to be made. Here we are once again looking at debt from the outside, from a market-based point of view, and asking what value the market place would put on this debt at a particular point in time. Rating agencies such as Moody's and Standard & Poor's are useful in this context, since their ratings allow us to estimate a credit risk premium based on the current market yield structure.

Following the previous logic of the risk-free rate of return, we can use the rat-ing agencies' figures for competitors and the relevant sector, and add a risk pre-mium for the specific company. This may sound simple, but in practice it can involve some judgement, especially where the company has extensive borrow-ings in different currencies over different maturity periods. Various forms of hybrid financing such as warrants and convertibles introduce further complexi-ties. This means that a view has to be taken about how the debt structure could evolve, especially if we know that certain debt instruments will be retired at some point during the period for which we are forecasting.

THE WEIGHTED AVERAGE COST OF CAPITAL (WACC)

The point of calculating the cost of equity and the cost of debt is to bring them together to create the weighted average cost of capital (WACC), as in Fig. 3.2. Having, in this hypothetical example, established the 'risk-free' cost of debt cur-rently ruling in the market as 7.9 per cent, we use that figure to determine both the cost of equity and the cost of debt for this particular company. For the cost of equity, we add to that 7.9 per cent a market risk premium of 3.5 per cent based on a consolidation of historical expectations and information, which is then discounted at the beta of the company's share price – in this case it is 0.86, indicating a fairly 'safe' investment. The cost of equity, then, is 10.91 per cent. For the cost of debt, we simply take the same figure of 7.9 per cent and add a company risk premium of 1.5 per cent to reach 9.4 per cent. However, the cost of debt for the company is offset by the tax shield, which in this case is assumed to give relief at a rate of 35 per cent. The total capital of the company is made up of 38 per cent debt and 62 per cent equity, so we reduce the costs of the debt and equity by the relevant percentages and then add them together to arrive at a figure of 9.08 per cent.

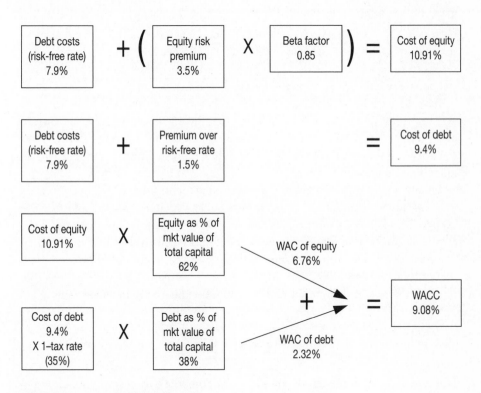

Fig. 3.2 Cost of capital calculation

One of the important points to note is that the WACC is sensitive to changes in gearing (leverage), so that as debt levels rise the WACC will fall (over a certain range of ratios). As with other components of the SHV approach what looks simple at first glance turns out to be quite complex in implementation. (See Appendix 3.) But before looking at these issues, let us consider just what the WACC is telling us.

A measure of success

The WACC is an expression of what return a company must earn if it is to justify the financial assets it uses – in other words, the opportunity cost of the assets in use. It is entirely market driven: if the assets cannot earn that return, then investors will eventually withdraw their funds from the business. Share prices will fall relative to the market, and the company could then become a takeover target. Pushed to its extreme, the failure of the company to earn its cost of capital could result in the management being replaced by another.

From the manager's point of view, the WACC establishes *the market relevant hurdle rate against which success has to be measured.* It is a risk-weighted measure, since it specifically includes a measure of the riskiness of the investment. Since we are saying that the costs of both equity and debt have to be exceeded if the business is to survive in the longer term, it is important to realize that these differ from other ways of measuring financial success. The cost of equity is different from the cost of dividend payments, and the cost of debt is different from the apparent interest rate actually charged on outstanding debt.

Indeed, the SHV approach is saying something even more serious to managers. It is not just a question of ensuring that the business earns returns that are equivalent to its WACC. If the business is to prosper in the longer term, it has to earn *more* than that WACC. It is only when this condition is met that we can talk about the creation of SHV.

Finally, we need to remember that everything mentioned so far has concerned publicly quoted companies, and our analysis has been assumed to be of entire quoted companies or entities. As we shall see in the following chapters, the approach can be fine tuned to accommodate both subsidiaries and divisions of companies. Private companies can be dealt with too. Although more complex, these ultimately come down to finding the best estimators for the risk-free rate of return, beta and the market risk premium for the unit being analyzed.

SUMMARY

Having emphasized the importance of calculating the true cost of your capital – not the same as the conventional hurdle rate – we then looked at the elements that contribute to such a calculation: risk-free rates of return, market risk premiums, and betas, which measure the volatility of a share. These are all part of the CAPM formula which is used to determine a company's WACC, the market relevant hurdle rate against which you measure success.

PROFIT IS AN OPINION; CASH IS A FACT

Having a good estimate of the cost of capital is a fundamental first step for conducting SHV analysis. However, against what cash flow should it be used to measure value creation? Earlier we drew attention to weaknesses in conventional accounting measures: here we want to consider them in more detail. We also want to examine how the large institutional investors in the equity markets are assessing the market value of corporates.

ACCOUNTING PROFIT

The EPS calculation has long been recognized by investment management firms as a convenient shorthand for valuing stock. But it is based on accounting profit, which is arrived at using different accounting methods in different countries – making earnings comparisons difficult.

Consider Table 4.1, compiled as part of a management training exercise in the early 1990s. For this, managers were given a basic set of data about a company, and were then asked to disclose a profits figure using their own local accounting conventions. There are several striking things about the results shown. The UK is particularly generous in its view on profits. The most likely number struck is close to the feasible maximum. This is due in part to the different basis on which UK and US accounts are constructed, independently of the tax calculations and more oriented towards investors. Nevertheless, seen from a Continental European point of view, UK accounts may be too ready to declare as profit items which are more prudently held in reserve elsewhere – even if the main motivation for the reserves is one of tax efficiency.

Another striking feature is that the range of profits in other countries is very wide, and hence the most likely number struck is an arbitrary one. At the extreme, for German managers and analysts anything between 27 and 133 is a feasible profits number – undoubtedly calling into question the usefulness, and hence undermining the credibility, of much profit-based and earnings-based analysis and information.

Considerable effort is going into improving the comparability of earnings through the development of international accounting standards (IAS). The largest equity market in the world, in the USA, requires the consistent reporting of earnings in accordance with the country's Securities and Exchange Commission (SEC) reporting requirements. Despite this, accounting profit has other well-known deficiencies: the need for investment is fixed, and working capital is only dealt with partly through depreciation, while risk, future expectations and the true cost of money are not taken sufficiently into consideration.

Table 4.1 Accounting profit can vary from country to country

	Most likely net profit	Maximum net profit	Minimum net profit
	Ecu millions		
Belgium	135	193	90
Germany	133	140	27
Spain	131	192	121
France	149	160	121
Italy	174	193	167
Netherlands	140	156	76
United Kingdom	192	194	171

Source: Henley Management College

CORRELATING SHARE PRICE MOVEMENTS AND CASH FLOW

Even if an underlying earnings figure could be defined reasonably accurately, it would still be of little help in establishing a share price or in calculating SHV, surprising though this sounds. Figure 4.1 dramatically shows the wide disparity between EPS data and share price movements in Germany.

The dots in the chart represent combinations of changes in company share prices and changes in EPS. The EPS changes are prospective forecasts for 1994 made in January, while the change in share price is what actually happened over the year. The diagonal line gives an idea of the preferred relationship. Ideally, a positive expected move in earnings should (all things being equal) be associated with a positive change in share prices along the 45 degree line. The cloud of measle-like spots shows that there was a very poor relationship between EPS changes and share price changes that year in Germany.

This result is confirmed in many other studies. Work by Rawley Thomas and Marvin Lipson[1] looked at correlations between the share prices (proxied by the

---

[1] Rawley, Thomas and Marin, Lipston, *Linking Corporate Return Measures to Stock Prices,* Molt Planning Associates (St. Charles, Illinois, 1985).

market-to-book ratios) and several explanatory and often used accountancy-based performance ratios. The results, set out in Table 4.2, show that cash-flow-based figures (specifically, CFROI, or cash flow return on investment) provide a superior explanation for the market to book ratios on the US stock market. (For ROE and ROI see Chapter 6.)

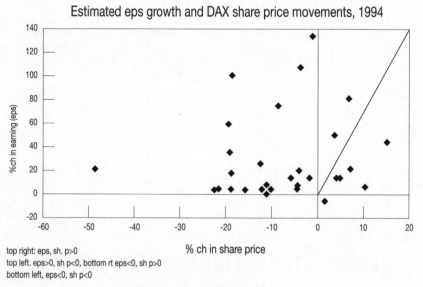

Fig. 4.1 **EPS is a poor predictor of share prices**

Table 4.2 **What best explains the variance in market/book ratios of the S&P Index? (1982/84)**

Variable	R^2
eps	<0.1
ROE	0.19
ROI	0.34
Real CFROI	0.65

The robustness of measurement systems that relate to cash flow has also been emphasized by Roger Mills of Henley Management College, who quotes 'a considerable amount of empirical research' in support of the contention that 'there is a significant relationship between cash flow and share prices'.[2] By comparison, specific accounting-based indicators of performance are poor measures, in UK studies, of what shareholders expect to receive by way of dividends and capital appreciation

Taking all this together, we are persuaded that cash flow-based measures are more closely aligned with share price movements, and indeed can more satis-factorily explain them than alternative measures.

THE INVESTOR'S NEW FOCUS

How then are large institutional investors assessing companies' economic value? They are clearly moving from earnings-based return calculations to a more sophisticated assessment based on risk, growth expectations and cash flow returns on invested capital. Here at Price Waterhouse we commissioned inde-pendent market research on 50 of the largest global investment managers and their approach to stock valuation, and the research has confirmed this trend. For these firms, cash flow-based economic models have become vital valuation tech-niques.

As one US investment manager put it, 'We feel that when push comes to shove, it all comes down to cash.' Another commented: 'We think that the mar-ket is influenced by things that we don't tend to look at in the short run, but in the long run [it] is influenced by precisely what we look at – real cash-on-cash returns on investment.' The focus on cash was emphasized by a third, who said: 'Cash is what you actually *have*. You can take your cash and you can reinvest it. You can reinvest earnings, but if your cash is in excess of your earnings then you have the ability to make more investments or pay down more debt.'[3]

In response to the changing focus among institutional investors, equity ana-lysts at securities firms have also been revising their approaches to value analy-sis. For example, the equity research group at Credit Suisse First Boston (CSFB) commented: 'P/Es may have value as a rough proxy for expectations, but do a poor job of explaining the fundamental determinants of value. How much, how well and how long capital can be successfully redeployed in the business are con-siderations explicitly addressed in a free cash flow model.'

In other words, free cash flow (FCF) is the key. Clearly it is now time to intro-duce our basic cash flow-based SHV model – and this is what we will do in the next chapter.

[2] Roger Mills, *Shareholder Value Analysis – Principles and Issues*, Technical Bulletin of the Institute of Chartered Accountants in England and Wales (forthcoming).
[3] From 'Value Transformation: Driving Shareholder Value Throughout the Organization' in *PW Review*, June 1997.

SUMMARY

Using data from the recent past, we have shown how accounting measures such as earnings per share are no guide to share values. Instead, investors are increasingly using cash flow as a measuring tool to predict future company performance.

SHAREHOLDER VALUE: A DEFINITION

In the last two chapters we have established two basic things: the importance of understanding your cost of capital, and the trend among investors towards using cash flow analysis in evaluating companies. It is important, then, to focus on the key components that contribute to your company's success in achieving a positive cash flow and thus a return on invested capital.

For this, we return to Alfred Rappaport's 1986 book *Creating Shareholder Value*. Our Free Cash Flow (FCF) model of SHV uses the seven value drivers originally put forward in that book – drivers that provide the framework for analysing the economic value of a business. Six of them feature in Fig. 5.1.

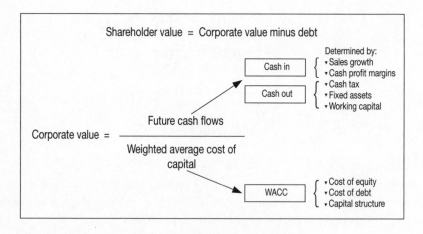

Fig. 5.1 Free cash flow model of shareholder value

RISK, GROWTH AND RETURNS AND THE SEVEN VALUE DRIVERS

Shareholder value is therefore defined as the difference between the corporate value and debt, where corporate value is the sum of the future (or free) cash flows discounted at the WACC. The free cash flows themselves are made up of the individual cash flows for each year of the growth duration or competitive advantage period and the residual value. (Residual value is covered in Chapter 6.) The cash flow is 'free' in the sense that it could be distributed to shareholders.

Let us look at this from a different angle. The FCF model can be thought of as looking at three things: growth, returns, and risk. These aspects can be explained by seven 'value drivers', six of which feature in Fig. 5.1. The seven, to which we will return in Chapter 7 and later chapters, are:

- sales growth (or turnover growth);
- cash profit margin (EBITDA – earnings before interest, tax, depreciation and amortization);
- cash tax rate;
- working capital (to grow the business);
- capital expenditure (or fixed capital);
- WACC – the risk-adjusted and inflation-adjusted weighted average cost of capital;
- competitive advantage period.

Growth

Growth is analyzed by three drivers: *sales growth* and investments in *working capital and fixed capital*. Revenue growth is all about growing the top line of the business, and the FCF model focuses attention on this. As we will see in later chapters, we can break the revenue growth driver out into a large number of industry-specific micro-drivers, as well as allowing for the impact of changes in price, volume and product mix.

As the business grows, so additional working capital is required, which is a deduction from the free cash flow. Similarly, any shrinkage of the business will release resources. *Fixed capital investment*, on the other hand, has a more ambiguous status. In the short run, it ties up resources, and is a deduction from free cash flow. In the longer run, though, it is highly important for growing the business. Knowing just how much to invest and what to spend the money on is one of the most crucial decisions managers have to take. Similarly, shareholders are sensitive to decisions on investment, since this will have a material impact on future cash flows.

All the same, it has to be realized that we are moving into a 'knowledge economy'. In other words, increasingly capital expenditure in the traditional sense of money spent on plant, machinery and so on is irrelevant to companies in areas such as biotechnology or software development. For them, it is the 'intangibles' of R&D and intellectual property that are the important value creators. We shall return to this topic in Part 3.

Returns

For returns, there are two drivers. The *cash profit margin* driver is of great importance, and will often make the largest contribution to SHV creation. It is defined as earnings before interest, tax and depreciation, or EBITDA. As this definition implies, it is a driver that is focused on the pre-tax cash margin earned in the business before any financing or depreciation charges, thus eliminating any accounting distortions.

Also associated with revenue is the *cash tax* driver. Although it may not always appear important, it is a direct deduction from the free cash flow and so impacts on the return. Since we are interested only in the amount of cash flowing into and out of a corporation, the tax driver specifically concerns cash taxes paid. It is at this point that deviations between value-based reporting/accounting methods and more traditional accrual-based accounting occur; sometimes traditional tax figures have to be substantially adjusted.

Risk

Finally, there is risk – often described as 'appropriate risk' to distinguish it from other kinds of hazard or chance. Here we have the WACC (cost of capital) driver, crucial for bringing financial market perceptions into SHV assessment, and the *growth duration or competitive advantage period* driver. We have already explained the crucial importance of understanding the cost of capital, and we will return to this subject in Part 2. There we will see the importance in the corporate planning process not only of understanding the overall corporate cost of capital but also of analyzing differing costs of capital within a company in relation to its different businesses and geographical locations.

As for the *growth duration period*, this is normally defined as the period of time over which the company has a competitive advantage – the period during which a company has a positive net present value when discounted at the WACC. Industry studies have shown that these competitive advantage periods are often much shorter than managers think. As we shall see later, in Part 3, sectoral and industry differences in the growth duration period can make a material difference to how SHV models are applied.

A common framework

Taken together, these value drivers provide a common planning platform from which to review the variety of business units to be found within a typical corporation. The linkage of financial planning to business operations and decision making requires that these drivers be mapped on to the business-specific measures which drive success with markets, customers and production. For example, a customer services business will focus on highly valued customer segments through market penetration, customer acquisition, product extension and business retention measures, whereas an innovation-driven business will focus on research and development, intellectual property and time-to-market measurement.

In both cases the business-specific measures are mapped or translated into their anticipated effect on the financial value drivers, providing a clear linkage between the operational and the financial value drivers, and enabling a reconciliation from these through the SHV framework to the market price.

THE MARKET MIRROR

Using historical and forecast estimates of the value drivers based on consensus market estimates – or industry forecasts where available – it is possible at least to understand the derivation of the existing market capitalization and current share price. It is essential to compare this market-derived estimate with the company's own estimate of its intrinsic worth, using the same SHV framework. This comparison between intrinsic and market value will clearly indicate where the market is more bullish or bearish than the company's own management. The results can sometimes be both surprising and alarming to managements who have not used the SHV framework before, and often speak volumes about communication between company and market, or about confidence of the market in the company's management

SENSITIVITY ANALYSIS

Finally in this chapter, we should mention that the SHV approach has the advantage of showing how sensitive the share price can be to changes in the underlying value drivers over the duration of the forecast period – see Fig. 5.2 – which shows the likely effect on a hypothetical company's share price performance of a 1 per cent change in each value driver. Understanding these sensitivities can help management develop more useful forecasts while building better insights into where they should concentrate their efforts to increase value.

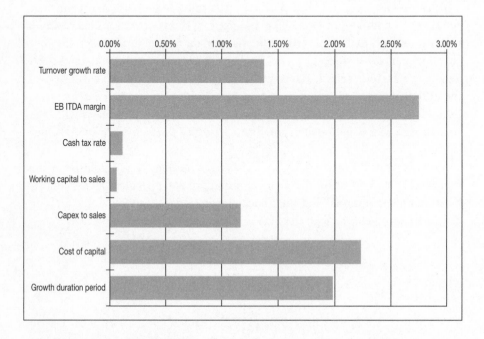

Fig. 5.2 Effect on share price of 1% favourable change in value drivers

This technique, known as sensitivity analysis, offers a bridge between the world of finance and the world of management, in that the SHV model can provide an agenda for change within the company and an idea of the effect of such a change. Even at relatively general levels of analysis, the combination of sensitivity analysis and the market mirror can provide considerable insights into what is going on inside a company, thus acting as a very useful lever for subsequent strategies. We shall return to this kind of analysis in Part 2.

In essence, any substantive idea put forward to improve a company's performance can, and should, be measured by the value yardstick – measured, in other words, against the cost and availability of capital employed to make it happen.

SUMMARY

In this chapter we have looked at the FCF model of SHV with its seven main drivers of value, and have discussed their relationship to the measurement of risk, growth and returns. The seven drivers – sales growth, cash profit margin, cash tax rate, working capital, fixed capital, WACC and competitive advantage period – provide a framework for analyzing company performance and, through sensitivity analysis, judging the effect of future strategies.

SHAREHOLDER VALUE: A SINGLE METRIC OR A COMMON FRAMEWORK?

So far we have concentrated on explaining the rise of SHV and its basic economic elements: cash flow and cost of capital. Many corporations and some advisers have sought to reduce this whole theme to a specific single metric in order to simplify the process of introducing SHV across a whole organization. They have tried to align all operating and investment decisions, performance measures and compensation using one measurement.

What measurement have they favoured? In addition to the FCF model already discussed, the two other main metrics used are economic profit, branded as economic value added or EVA™ by the US consulting firm of Stern Stewart, and Cash Flow Return on Investment (CFROI). We will examine each of these in turn in this chapter.

In our experience, however, senior executives who have been exposed to these various SHV metrics understand that each is built on a common economic foundation and each plays a useful part in the value creation process. Economic profit, for example, can be employed to track overall corporate and business unit performance; CFROI is used in evaluating a company's longer-term strategy and resource allocation; and FCF provides the bridge linking the core strategic and operational objectives to the overall goal of maximizing value via the financial value drivers.

In the FCF model we look at how a company is going to develop, based on forecasts and opinions, over the next few years – a 'multi-period' model. This has the advantage of enabling us to link the company's likely growth path with other observable macro-economic and sector trends. It also makes it easier to subject these forecasts to some consistency checks. If we start by asking what the market's perception of a company's growth duration period – the seventh value driver – is, we will establish what period of time should be considered for the cash flow forecast in the first place. The FCF and other SHV models represent important generalizations of earlier, more limited discounted cash flow models designed for investment appraisal work (see Fig. 6.1). As noted in Chapter 3, the standard DCF approach suffered from a lack of clarity with respect to the determinants of the discount rate.

SHV = Corporate value – Debt

DCF: $$\frac{\text{Cash flows – Investment}}{\text{Disc rate}} = \text{NPV (net present value)}$$

FCF: $$\frac{\text{EBITDA – Debt}}{\text{WACC}} = \text{SHV}$$

Fig. 6.1 From DCF to Free Cash Flow

SVA: CAPITAL AND CALCULATIONS

Economic profit, economic value added or SHV added (SVA) is based on the concept developed and used by Stern Stewart (see p. 56). The FCF model is entirely future oriented, assumes no opening capital or balance sheet and discounts the future free cash flow at the WACC. On the other hand, the key concept behind the SVA models is the idea of a spread between the economic return a company earns in a single period compared to the cost of the capital resources used in the business. In essence it is very similar to a multi-period FCF model. Rather than looking at the situation over several years, however, SVA models are built on a close analysis of a company's position year by year. The sum of the spreads between the return and the cost of capital for all future periods will of course be equivalent to the positive net present values achieved in the earlier 'top down' multi-period model.

The SVA or economic profit model requires a starting balance sheet based on an estimate of the capital resources needed in the company, and this is not the same as the historical financial balance sheet.[1]

The definition of SVA is expressed in the formula:

$$\text{SVA} = \text{total capital x (return on total capital – WACC)}$$

where total capital is defined as equity plus net debt and other capital.

SVAs are calculated on an annual basis. So in order to arrive at an estimate of market value added or MVA we take a discounted stream of SVAs and add a residual value to it. We do this so as to take account of a firm's continuing value after the end of the forecast period; it is a shorthand for assuming that the company would have a resale value. We will return to this point later. In other words:

$$\text{MVA} = \text{SVA} + \text{Residual value}$$

and

$$\text{Shareholder value} = \text{MVA} + \text{Opening capital}$$

[1] For further discussion of the adjustments needed see Chapter 10, pp. 146–150.

Let us look at this more carefully. The important thing in the SVA approach is to establish the 'spread' between what a company earns and what it has to pay for the capital it needs to run its business. For this we use what is known as an Economic Return on Capital Employed, or Economic ROCE, which is:

$$NOPAT - (Capital\ employed \times WACC)$$

NOPAT, or the net operating profit after tax, is a function of the value drivers introduced in Chapter 5 – revenue growth; EBITDA; cash taxes; and changes in both working and fixed capital. A company should direct all its strategies towards increasing such a spread. An idea how effectively a company is doing, thus can be obtained by using an economic index, which is:

$$\frac{Economic\ ROCE}{WACC}$$

This ratio is closely correlated with the market-to-book ratio.

The SVA approach is relatively data hungry – in other words, it requires a lot of information about the company that is being analyzed. As we noted earlier, the model needs opening balance sheets and profit and loss statements, but not simply in their customary form; they have to be adjusted to allow for various distortions found in normal statutory accounts, and to a lesser extent in management accounts. Let us consider a few of these adjustments.

Inflation and asset adjustments

One of the first things to look at is the impact of inflation, and the age mix of assets. To establish whether a company is producing any shareholder value added, it is crucially important to get a good 'fix' on the current replacement value of assets. The SVA approach depends very much on the opening balance sheet of a company, which will typically include a variety of assets with different useful lives and with different ages. These assets will for the most part, be included at their 'book' values, with their age profile playing a significant role. Even with relatively modest inflation, old assets will have book values that are significantly below their replacement value.

Since it is this asset base that is going to have to earn a return, the lower it is, the more likely it is that a firm will earn a high rate of economic return. One of the first steps in any analysis, therefore, will be to adjust the asset base and put it on an equivalent replacement cost basis. This can be quite difficult. Making an *ad hoc* adjustment to an asset to calculate its new replacement value can raise an important issue – namely, that you might not want to replace this particular asset in the same form at all. Technical progress might mean that, were you to start again, you would choose a different process or technology.

Bear in mind that, under current performance measurement systems, businesses with old assets may be earning highly respectable rates of return – which will change dramatically if these assets are revalued. What was formerly a good money earner can now turn out to be a business that has to work much harder to justify its existence.

A further consequence is that the SVA approach requires a more detailed analysis of a company's balance sheet. Again, this can be difficult. SVA analysis works very well when a corporate balance sheet can be allocated across different divisions or business units. The analysis also benefits from sensible forecasts concerning changes in balance sheet requirements both for the business as a whole and for its various subsidiaries and divisions.

Other adjustments

Other distortions from the SVA point of view are caused by accrual accounting methodology, which for prudential reasons sometimes brings forward expected losses and makes other timing adjustments. As we have noted earlier, our cash flow-based approach is primarily interested in seeing what flows across the corporate 'border' and really in little else. This means that timing adjustments have to be either eliminated or added back in.

One such adjustment would be in the calculation of the 'economic' equity involved in a business, which is defined as the sum of ordinary equity adjusted for tax effects. So we would have to add back deferred tax provisions into the equity pool, while deducting future tax benefits. Similarly, changes might be required in the calculation of NOPAT. This would typically involve adding back the tax shield effects to operating profits estimated as part of the firm's borrowing costs. Other adjustments would be needed for research and development (capitalized rather than expensed), for goodwill (likewise), and for inventory valuation methods among other items.

As if this is not enough, the careful SVA practitioner must beware of expected changes in the capital structure following the issue of warrants and convertible bonds, as well as having to incorporate a lot of off-balance sheet items that companies do not normally report. If nothing else, a company can find that simply running through such a list can help define – possibly for the first time – just what the common value-based accounting framework is going to be before it starts using SHV models.

The resulting figures are bound to be different from those generated by a typical accounts department. We would view this as being a matter of 'horses for courses'; for an interim period SHV calculations and statutory accounting calculations will continue down parallel tracks. Looking further ahead, however, we believe that the changes needed for what we will term Value-Based Accounting or Value Reporting ought anyway to become part of the mainstream of accountancy practices – a topic that we shall return to at the end of the book.

ASSESSING STRATEGY DECISIONS

Value return on investment

How, using any kind of SHV analysis, can the impact of different strategies be looked at before you take any action? In our experience, applying the SHV approach can be beneficial simply by virtue of the fact that companies have to sort out what kinds of information their internal control systems are currently producing, and what is actually needed to answer the question as to who and what is creating or destroying SHV. At the same time, though, you can easily get lost in the detail.

One way of keeping a focus on the bigger picture is to use a top-down model such as Price Waterhouse's ValueBuilder 1™ in order to compare the outcome of prospective strategies with the current market value of the company. Indeed we can also compare various future strategies with each other by this method. Alternatively, we can look at the Value Return on Investment (VROI), which is a useful way of exploring whether a prospective strategy is in the right ball-park or not. The 'pre-strategy' view is simply to capitalize the existing free cash flow – probably for the latest available year, but to correct for short-term distortions, we might generate an average based on the last five years of cash flow performance. This is then compared with the 'post-strategy' view of the world, which will include the value of cash flows generated over the forecast period. The VROI ratio can therefore be expressed as:

$$\text{VROI} = \frac{\text{post-strategy value} - \text{pre-strategy value}}{\text{present value of projected investments}}$$

where the denominator (the bottom half of the fraction) is designed to throw light on the incremental use of resources involved. The decision rule is relatively straightforward: where VROI is greater than one, SHV is being created, while a VROI of less than one implies the opposite – the destruction of SHV – since the incremental value added is smaller than the incremental value of the resources being used. In the example used in Table 6.1, the VROI ratio is 1.2 – indicating that the net investment is contributing to SHV. (We will go on to the Q ratio, the final calculation in Table 6.1, later in this Chapter.)

Like all systems of measurement, however, VROI has to be used with care. The numerator (the top half of the equation) can be quite unstable, particularly if a company's pre-strategy value is very small – if for instance it was making losses in the previous year. The ratio also requires there to be meaningful capital spending. If this is likely to be rather low, then the ratio will become unreasonably and misleadingly high.

Table 6.1 Example of VROI and Q ratios

At a WACC of 15%	Year 0	Year 1	Year 2	Year 3	Year 4	Year 5	Year 6
Profit after tax (PAT)	16						
Assets employed (nominal)	80						
Cash flow		12	14	12	14	16	12
Discount factor		0.9	0.8	0.7	0.6	0.5	0.4
Present value		10.4	10.6	7.9	8.0	8.0	5.1
Residual value (perpetuity method)							200.0
Present value of residual							84.6
Present value of cash flows							50.0
Total present value (post-strategy)							134.6
Assets employed inflation adjusted							
(3% inflation pa assumed)							95.5
VROI calculation							
Net investment		5.0	8.0	6.0	7.0	8.0	4.0
Discount factor		0.9	0.8	0.7	0.6	0.5	0.4
Present value		4.4	6.0	3.9	4.0	4.0	1.7
Total present value							24.0
Total present value (post-strategy)							134.6
Pre-strategy value = year 0							
(PAT/WACC)							106.7
Value increase post-pre-strategy							27.9
VROI = Value increase/PV investment							1.2
Q Ratio = Total PV post-strategy/assets							
(inflation adj)							1.409

Q ratios

Another approach to the question of which strategies generate value, and which do not, is based on the Nobel Prize-winning work of the economist James Tobin. The now famous Tobin's Q ratio is the ratio between the market value of the physical assets in an economy and the replacement cost of those assets measured in current currency units. From the macro-economic point of view a Q ratio of greater than one means that the stock market is valuing a company's (or an economy's) assets at more than their actual cost, while a ratio of less than one implies the opposite. A high value of Q means that corporations have a good incentive to invest in new plant and equipment since the market values each unit of investment at more than it is worth. A low value of Q reduces the incentive to invest but encourages acquisitions via the stock market, since investors are paying less for an asset on the financial markets than it would cost them to replace it on the goods market.

In the Table 6.1 example, we calculated not only the post-strategy return to the company but also the replacement cost of the assets used in the company, which we assumed to be inflating at 3 per cent a year. We arrived then at a Q value of 1.4 – which suggests that the stock market should be willing to pay a handsome premium on the price of assets used in the business. This Q ratio also suggests that the strategy is adding to SHV.

Q RATIOS AND CFROI

The insights that come from the Q ratio have been developed further using a concept called the Cash Flow Return on Investment (CFROI). This is designed to answer a number of different questions about value creation, and goes beyond just looking at share values. Its principal aim is to examine a company's aggregate performance by applying a number of techniques borrowed from approaches used for project finance – the main one here being the idea of an Internal Rate of Return (IRR).

CFROI measures can assess the rate of return on all investments made in a company, including those made by debt holders. They can therefore be utilized in any investigation into the financial viability of a company overall rather than just its viability as seen from the shareholder perspective. (Although, as we say throughout this book, the two are closely related.) CFROI aims to allow for the effects of inflation, and to subject any possible strategies to a stringent comparison with what companies on average in a particular industry or sector can achieve by way of returns to investors. It takes a top-down view of total corporate performance, treating the company almost as if it were one large 'project'.

There are some notable differences from other SHV approaches. Let us start by introducing and defining the Operating Cash Flow After Taxes (OCFAT). If:

$$\text{Revenues} - \text{costs} - \text{cash taxes} = \text{NOPAT}$$

then:

$$\text{NOPAT} + \text{depreciation} + \text{other adjustments} = \text{OCFAT}$$

We will have to make a distinction between depreciating and non-depreciating assets, since the non-depreciating assets must be adjusted by the rate of inflation in order to keep everything, initially at least, measured in nominal, but inflation-adjusted, terms. This means we have to take:

$$\text{Non-depreciating assets} - \text{current liabilities} = \text{Non-depreciating assets (adjusted)}$$

If we add in an estimate of depreciating assets – which includes plant, property and equipment, intangibles and accumulated depreciation, all adjusted for inflation – we will create a term called gross assets. We can then reach the following simple definition:

$$CFROI = \frac{OCFAT}{gross\ assets}$$

Since we know what the gross asset value is for each period, we can calculate the CFROI to be the internal rate of return on that investment – which is the discount rate needed (or calculated) to ensure that the net present value of future cash flows, minus the initial investment, comes to zero. These rates are then compared to the WACC and calculated to produce a spread, which is similar to that used in the SVA analysis.

But there are further complications. First, this analysis looks at the return to all capital holders, so there are no tax shelter effects on debt, and it is not assumed to be cheaper than equity. Tax has relevance to the capital side only through the tax position of the investor, rather than the tax position of the enterprise borrowing the money. The second complication is that we want to look at the spread referred to above in real terms, making it relevant to the perceived period of time over which a company can be expected to achieve an IRR higher than its WACC. Again, this is similar to the idea of the competitive duration period used in the SVA and FCF models.

CFROI also offers a different treatment of an enterprise's continuing or residual value. To explain that, a small digression is needed.

RESIDUAL VALUE: A DIGRESSION

Residual value is a shorthand term for any estimate of the continuing value of a company at the end of a forecast period. Residual value calculations are needed for the assumptions that have to be made about a business's value at the end of a planning period. They are an important feature of the entire SHV approach – indeed, there may be occasions when one of the main conclusions of an SHV analysis will be that almost all of a firm's value rests on its residual worth.

Another way of looking at it is to assume that the business could be sold at the end of the planning horizon; in which case we need an estimate of what its value should be. Some SHV practitioners argue that one should try to value the different parts of the business, then add them together to achieve a sale value – an approach that could be misleading as well as time consuming. It is often based on today's earnings multiples, begging the question as to what these multiples might be in ten years' time, or whenever the envisaged 'sale' takes place. More seriously, there will have been several years of inflation between current values and those in the future. Inflation does not proceed smoothly through the economy; some assets appreciate or depreciate noticeably faster than others, making a significant difference to the sort of resale values calculated.

More problematically, it is not clear whether a sale of assets would achieve a premium or a discount over the estimated 'book' value. Premiums are some-times paid for control of an asset or a group of assets, on the grounds that the value of the whole is greater than the sum of its parts. (This is the matter of syn-ergies, to which we will return in Chapter 8.)

The residual value calculation, then, is a way of trying to avoid these difficul-ties. It implies that the business is still a going concern, and that it has settled down into an equilibrium after the end of the forecast period. It is traditionally calculated as an 'equilibrium' cash flow divided by the weighted average cost of capital (WACC), with the WACC now based on some 'ideal' long-term capital structure. This is also known as a perpetuity calculation.

Other interpretations of residuals

If the residual value offers a shorthand way of understanding the continuing going-concern value of the enterprise, it also offers a number of new opportu-nities. One is that we can look more closely at the determinants of this residual, and include features specific to a particular industry or sector. In the financial area, residual value might be related to the years to maturity of various loans and other obligations, for instance insurance policies. With resources, it might be an adjustment based on depletion rates and the estimated years of life of provable reserves. In both cases, we can adapt the residual calculation to take into account the extent an organization's resources are more or less committed after the end of the planning forecast period.

In the high technology area, the treatment of residual value differs again. At Price Waterhouse we are looking at ways of linking the perception of a value gap – where market valuations are far higher than either the enterprise or the resid-ual value would justify – to the value placed by the investor on a firm's flexibil-ity in the face of rapid technical change. Work is continuing on including real options valuations as an additional factor in establishing how high technology firms create SHV.

CFROI AND RESIDUAL VALUES

The CFROI approach to residual value is different from that outlined above. Instead of the perpetuity calculation, it offers a methodology based on 'hold' and 'fade'. The 'hold' assumption deals with the number of years that a com-pany can maintain a rate of return in excess of the WACC. This is based on close observation of the US equity market, and the perception that on average com-panies are not able to 'beat' the market for more than seven or eight years at the most. The estimated real return on investment is around 7 per cent a year (this figure is just for the USA – see Chapter 3's discussion of market risk premiums), with a real asset growth of around 3 per cent a year.

After this seven or eight-year period, performance will gradually decay until eventually the return on investment will equal the WACC. This decay rate is known as the 'fade' period, and can be quite long – over 20 years in many cases. This links the analysis of cash flows to observable behaviour in the equity market, and has the benefit of pointing out just how transitory periods of competitive advantage can be. Note that the 'hold' period is similar to the growth duration period used in the FCF model.

Now the value of a company can be thought of in two ways. The first is similar to the way bond yields are calculated. An investor has a bond price and a pattern of coupon payments: if the bond coupon rate exceeds prevailing interest rates, then the bond will sell at a premium to the market. Conversely, where the coupon rate is lower than prevailing interest rates, the bond will sell at a discount to the market. A similar situation applies to the Cash Flow Return on Investment model. If the future CFROI exceeds an investor's required return (his or her cost of capital), then the company will be priced above its book value; if CFROI is lower than the investor's required rate of return, then the company will sell below its book value. In other words companies with a positive CFROI 'spread' will have a Q ratio greater than one, and companies with a negative CFROI 'spread' will have a Q ratio of less than one. Market price and the CFROI price (current inflation-adjusted book value) will only be the same – in essence, Q=1 – when the anticipated future CFROI is the same as the investor's discount rate. These relationships are summarized in Fig. 6.2.

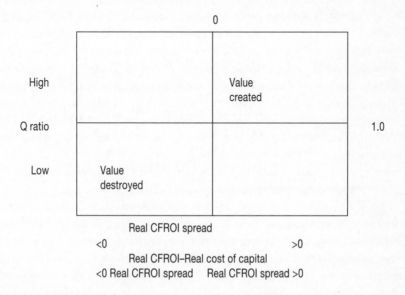

Fig. 6.2 Q ratios and CFROI spreads

The second way that the CFROI approach can put a value on a company is by looking in nominal, rather than real, terms at the discount rate that will discount the cash flows back to the company's current market price. This spot valuation therefore will relate all the various assumptions about inflation rates and assets' life expectancies and use them to generate a figure for the return on the invested resources that would justify today's observed market value (debt plus equity).

Back to Q

The one great attraction of the CFROI/Q approach is that it can 'explain' a lot of the movements in real market-to-book ratios, which themselves are derived from share price movements. The combination of real growth and the real ROI spread (i.e. real ROI less real WACC) explains over 80 per cent of the variance in the Q ratio of the S&P 400 in the USA.[1] The link between the Q ratio, real ROI spreads and SHV creation is shown in the diagram above, and this can be used to assess the usefulness of different strategies, in a similar manner to the value map (see Chapter 7). The CFROI approach also avoids some of the problems of accrual-based accounting methodologies, as well as specifically allowing for inflation.

If it is not a perfect measure, then neither are the others. What are the drawbacks of the Q ratio approach – and how far are they true for the other approaches as well?

The drawbacks ...

All the methods we have looked at so far are good at identifying strategies that could increase SHV – which of course is the point of the whole exercise. We have to consider, though, whether in some circumstances they might be too rigorous – whether they might be too harsh to some projects that fall just outside of charmed circle of their value-creation criteria. The CFROI approach, for instance, risks penalizing mature and basically profitable businesses simply because their assets are old and have been given a relatively high 'real' cost. The same problem exists for the SVA models, where one-off adjustments have to be made to those businesses with old assets. Although these businesses still have a positive cash flow, with assets that may still have many years of useful life, it is possible they do not measure up in either CFROI or SVA terms.

Another issue is that strategic choices about investing and divesting are not always as clear cut as we could wish for. For instance, when the alternatives are either to divest or to add investment in a mature business, the Q ratio approach may not always lead to the best choice. The excessively high investment needed in the denominator of the fraction on page 60 requires an unreasonably high

---

[1] Bernard C Reimann, *Managing for Value* (Planning Forum/Blackwells, 1989, p 29).

cash flow to produce either a Q ratio greater than one, or a positive SHV. Management could then decide to sell the business only to find that the cash received will not generate as a high a value for the shareholders as the old business would have done.

So, oddly enough, when we pull all these insights together, the best benchmark against which to value different alternatives is the market value of the business, which is what we do in the FCF approach. In many cases there is no reason to conclude that an inflation-adjusted figure (or indeed a value-adjusted figure) is better than the market for assessing the value of assets.

... And the advantages

The main advantages of all the approaches we have dealt with so far is that they simulate actual investor behaviour, particularly with their emphasis on expected future performance. They offer a decisive break with more backward-looking, accrual accountancy-based methods of estimating SHV. They also offer sound ways of linking companies' cash-generating capacities, the expectations of their shareholders and the creation of SHV.

The SHV approach can be thought of as a large filter through which a lot of statistical and financial material has to pass. What gets through that filter is the information that can throw light on, and be aligned with, the creation of SHV. Shareholder value is all about ensuring that external metrics – those of the financial markets – are extended internally within a company, and recognizing that the strategies it adopts internally will have an impact on the way it is viewed by the external market.

At this stage we do not want to say categorically that one SHV approach is superior to any other. In our experience we have found uses for most, if not all, of the approaches described earlier; we are not particularly interested in representing one view or another in some kind of 'metric war'. But as you may learn, in certain circumstances different models may be seen as 'horses for courses' – definite situations where some can be more successfully applied than others. Economic profit, for example, can be used to track overall corporate and business unit performance; CFROI is increasingly used in evaluating a corporation's longer-term strategies and resource allocation; and discounted cash flow methods can help implement core strategic objectives by using the financial value drivers to specify each business unit's operational objectives. In Part 2 we will look much more closely at how you can go about applying the approaches outlined here.

Complex they may be, but in expert hands some SHV approaches can provide highly relevant insights into what management needs to do to satisfy investors, as well as helping investors see what they should be asking management to do. All of which should keep their clients, the pension funds and other institutional investors, which means ultimately you and me, happy.

SUMMARY

In this chapter we have examined several variations on the SHV theme. In particular we have looked at the SVA and the CFROI approaches. We have seen how with the help of concepts like the VROI and Q ratios, we can relate the different strategies a firm might follow to the incremental use of resources this involves, and establish whether such strategies are likely to add to or detract from SHV.

From here we will now move on to Part 2, where we hope to show how these theories can be applied to 'real world' companies and linked to effective value-creating strategies. Thus the insights gained here from SHV can actually be implemented by management, to the mutual benefit of themselves and their investors.

PART

2

PUTTING IT INTO PRACTICE: THE VALUE MINDSET

THE TRANSFORMING POWER OF SHV

In Part 1 we explained why SHV has moved centre stage around the world – you will have recognized increasing market liberalization, the simultaneous rise in influence of global institutional investors, and the enabling power of computers as factors in this process. We looked at how the concept of value has developed; introduced the key elements in measuring value, cash flow and the cost of capital; and examined in some detail the three main but differing techniques that are used to derive measurements of economic value from these basic elements: FCF, EVA™ and CFROI.

But what does this all have to do with the corporate executive? Why, you will ask, should your company make SHV the focus of its strategy? One answer is simply to point to the organizations that have taken the initiative to manage for SHV – companies such as Lloyds Bank, Sony, Veba, Hoechst, Coca-Cola, General Electric, BP and Novo Nordisk. All companies that have outperformed their competitors in terms of share price – see Figs 7.1–7.6.

Part 2 will look at what it means in practice for an organization to adopt an SHV focus. We aim to explain how SHV techniques are used in corporations for analysis and planning, for action and implementation and for communication, investor relations and value reporting. This will demonstrate how the SHV framework integrates the core processes underlying the creation, preservation and realization of value.

We will also in this part be looking at how these SHV techniques should be applied not only in the ongoing business of a company, commonly called value-based management, but also in the circumstances of mergers and acquisitions and value re-creation in business turnarounds. Finally, we will reflect on the lessons we have learned as practitioners in this field and explain the issues that will need to be confronted as well as the pitfalls to be avoided.

Our approach in these chapters will not be a matter of examining case histories: rather, it will be to provide a route map for a company's journey into the world of SHV. In drawing up this map, we will of course be utilizing Price Waterhouse's experience of advising companies on the introduction of SHV systems. You can be assured, therefore, that the following chapters are grounded in the practicalities of management, not in theory – except insofar as we have found the theories of professors and consultants to have useful applications in the real world.

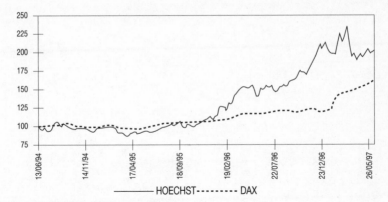

Fig. 7.1 Creating SHV at Hoechst

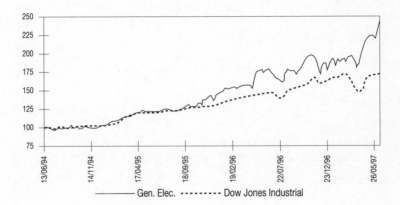

Fig. 7.2 Creating SHV at General Electric Co.

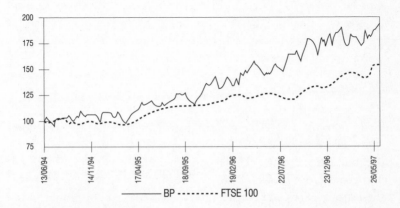

Fig. 7.3 Creating SHV at BP

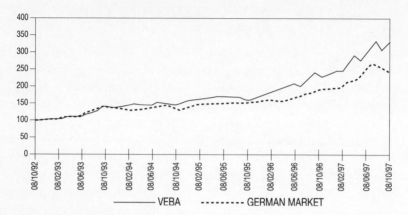

Fig. 7.4 Creating SHV at Veba*

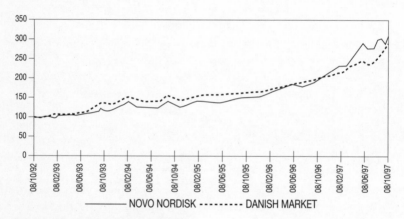

Fig. 7.5 Creating SHV at Novo Nordisk*

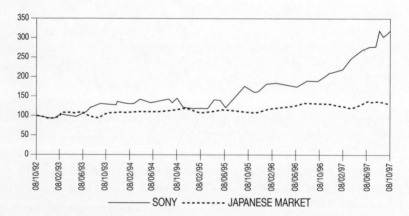

Fig. 7.6 Creating SHV at Sony*

* Country indices for Figures 7.4, 7.5 and 7.6 are Data-stream Total Performance Indices for the relevant countries.

VALUE AND ITS TRANSFORMATION

Let us return to the five-letter word that we began this book with: value. Put behind you, if you can, the apparent complications of calculating your SHV outlined in Chapter 4. Deciding between methods to use – SVA, CFROI or whatever – should not obscure the basic fact underlying the theories of SHV: that the markets require invested capital to provide returns that are equivalent to, or exceed, its opportunity cost.

Warren Buffett, chairman of the successful US investment company Berkshire Hathaway, thrives on finding investments in which value is not yet reflected in the share price. 'What counts is intrinsic value, a number that is impossible to pinpoint but essential to estimate' is how he explained his priorities in a letter to shareholders in Berkshire Hathaway's 1994 annual report. He went on to emphasize that:

> Understanding intrinsic value is as important for managers as it is for investors. When managers are making capital allocation decisions … it's vital that they act in ways that increase per-share intrinsic value and avoid moves that decrease it. This principle may seem obvious but we constantly see it violated. And when misallocations occur, shareholders are hurt.

If 'understanding intrinsic value' is paramount, SHV analysis, as long as it is applied properly, should ensure that 'misallocations' do not occur. But it's more than a matter of avoiding the negative; when you adopt SHV you are taking positive action. Applying the insights from SHV theory to a company is a powerful way of improving performance at all levels within it; turning the theory into practice can make it easier to meet apparently demanding shareholder performance targets. In our view a careful application of the methodology will result in a dramatic transformation in the way your company is run.

What it all amounts to, in fact, is the triple process expressed graphically in Fig. 7.7: *analysis* (Warren Buffett's 'understanding intrinsic value') should be followed by *action* – the transformation of your company to align it with SHV goals – and then *communication* to the market.

This trio of abstract nouns reflects the fact that if your overriding aim is to maximize SHV, every aspect of your business has to adopt an approach consistent with that imperative. What's more, by really committing yourself as a management to the SHV concept, you can make it an energizing force for change throughout your company. Value-based management – which is what this chapter is about – can be all embracing. It aligns strategies, policies, performance measures, rewards, organization, processes, people and systems to deliver increased SHV.

To succeed with a value transformation initiative, management must understand the linkage of strategy to operations and the importance for that linkage of focusing on the value drivers introduced in Chapter 4. That is *analysis*. But creating and sustaining value is not merely an analytical or planning exercise. To build long-term sustainable value in your organization you must transform its people, culture, and processes to drive for shareholder wealth. In other words, *action*. Finally, you will require excellent *communication* at all levels internally and with the outside investors and other stakeholders.

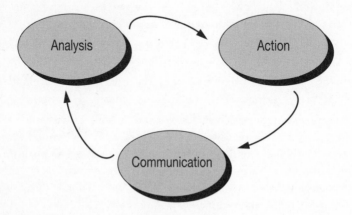

Fig. 7.7 The triple transformation process

How then does a CEO with a team committed to SHV start the process of institutionalizing it in his business's strategic and operational decision making? There is another threefold process that we believe is essential for any company that is serious about introducing value-based management. Its components, shown in Fig. 7.8, are *value creation*, *value preservation*, and *value realisation*; the triple requirement of this process – which begins by developing value with your customers and ends by delivering that value to your investors – should be borne in mind throughout this chapter. Dealing effectively with these three steps will enable you to complete the SHV mission and ensure that your promises to your investors can be delivered.

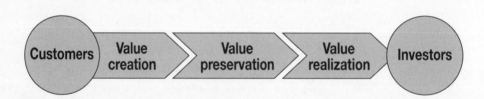

Fig. 7.8 SHV links customers to investors

The question of measurement

While we believe the SHV approach is consistent with the way that managements want to run their businesses, there is more to these three steps than might at first be apparent. Take the question of metrics – in other words, how corporate performance can connect with things that can be measured. To quote Robert Kaplan and David Norton, 'What you measure is what you get'.[1]

Oddly, although total shareholder returns can be measured to the third decimal point, attempts to link these figures to behavioural changes within a company have been very limited. Indeed, the quest for a more balanced approach to measuring performance has in most cases left managers wondering just how to decide, among all the various 'factors', 'indicators' and so on that can be measured, what they should concentrate on. The purpose of this chapter is to simplify things by arguing for the primacy of an external, shareholder-based view – to suggest that if earlier financial measures emphasized a more backward-looking, accountancy-based approach, it is now more appropriate to adopt a way of looking forward at the financial parameters within which a company is going to have operate and survive.

Shareholder value analysis, like Warren Buffet's 'intrinsic value' approach, judges a company on the basis of what it can produce in the future, rather than concentrating on what it has done in the past. This way, we believe, it is possible to pinpoint the elements that will contribute to the development of the fundamentals of your business – elements on which you can base a valuation that can be compared to the current market value.

Well-run companies, among them General Electric Co. (GE) and others referred to above, have done just such analysis. All of them, at various times, have embarked on specific SHV projects whose aim has been to shift management's attention to the raising of share price. In order to do this they have taken steps, some of them radical, not only to raise performance, but to go on doing so over a period of time. They have looked at SHV from both a corporate and from a divisional point of view, and have adopted strategies whose outcome has been an improved share price.

THE THREE STAGES OF VALUE

What then is the formula for SHV success? Let us return to the three steps of *value creation*, *value preservation* and *value realization*. The first, *value creation*, is the process whereby a company can maintain a return on capital greater than

---

[1] Robert S Kaplan and David P Norton, 'The Balanced Scorecard – Measures that Drive Performance', *Harvard Business Review*, Jan–Feb 1992.

its cost of capital. This positive 'spread', which can be retained in the business or distributed to shareholders, represents the value shareholders are looking for when they make their decision to invest in a company.

Value creation involves being able to offer something, either a product or a service, to your clients and customers at a price that satisfies the condition of earning this positive return. (This is the customer value discussed briefly in Chapter 2.) Your enterprise will need to be able to earn this positive return for a period of time – the growth duration period – and the longer this is, the greater the shareholder returns will be. Companies that do this will very often develop *competitive advantages* using proprietary technologies and favourable cost structures, or by exploiting efficiencies in manufacturing or in selling. (Competitive advantage is covered in more detail later in the chapter.)

Value creation alone does not ensure success, however. It is just as important to work towards *value preservation*, to make sure that what is created is not simply wasted or lost through inefficiency and poor management. You may therefore need to take steps to secure the appropriate management, resource allocation, cash and tax management systems. Companies need to be able to manage risk, knowledge and human capital effectively across their strategic business units. Risk, in particular, is an important area. Many companies operate from a narrow concept of risk management and as a result miss opportunities. They need to be able to consider risk in three categories – hazard, opportunity and uncertainty which can be planned for[2] – and actively manage their businesses around each of these areas.

Regrettably, there are several recent examples of firms – particularly financial services companies – that have lost money through poor management controls or inadequate risk management. As corporations become increasingly global, many are discovering additional pitfalls in tax and currency controls that trap value in certain countries and actually destroy value through poor management of the country or currency in which cash flows are generated.

The final step, *value realization*, is often neglected by corporations. Investors realize value through capital appreciation of their stock and dividend payouts. In most cases the bulk of shareholder returns comes through capital appreciation. Since markets are only as efficient as the information available, investors will not benefit unless the market understands the value created by your company and the strategies in place to build and preserve that value. Companies that deliver credible and relevant information to the market in a timely fashion, and are recognized for effectively managing value expectations, are much more likely to maintain a market value that reflects their true value than businesses with poor communications programmes.

---

[2] For more detail see Lee Puschaver and Robert G Eccles, 'In Pursuit of the Upside: The New Opportunity in Risk Management,' *PW Review*, December 1996, p7.

In recent years, there have been several companies which, in response to the market's failure to perceive their value, have fundamentally restructured themselves. To increase transparency, they have taken steps such as issuing special purpose stock on individual business units within their organization, or spinning off those businesses through stock flotations or IPOs (initial public offerings). The main effect of such initiatives has been to make the communication path from business unit to the market cleaner, crisper and less cluttered. These initiatives are examples of how written communications (what the company says) can be combined with actual restructuring of ownerships (what the company does) in a value realization programme.

It is doubtless this kind of restructuring that Jean-Pierre Tirouflet, CFO of Rhône-Poulenc, was referring to when he told a Conference Board survey of European CFOs that 'we must change our organization in order to use [SHV] measures effectively. This means we may need to redraw the company into profit centres, which make sense with their own working capital, equipment, and an economic meaning.'[3]

Challenges in achieving value transformation

Three phases

Success in applying and implementing a SHV programme is not at all easy. Businesses that set out to enhance their SHV vary widely in their levels of understanding, involvement and, ultimately, effectiveness. Normally, in our experience, large organizations pass through three distinct phases as they move towards implementation of value-based management.

First, there are the *talkers*. These are firms whose managements are aware of such things as valuation methodologies and performance metrics. They will probably refer to SHV as a desirable goal, but without having any clear idea of how they can move closer to it. Frequently, companies in this phase talk about SHV in the boardroom, but have found it very difficult to take the discussion any further. Indeed, some of them will argue strenuously that it cannot be done. And so with virtually no real transformation, a first phase company cannot expect any true value growth.

Second, we have the *partial adopters*. They are the managements that are persuaded to move cautiously down the SHV road, and have perhaps identified one area for improvement without considering the broader implications – taking an *ad hoc* approach to value transformation that frequently ends without much success.

In the final phase, a company becomes a *true value transformer*. Here, a company's management will recognize the need to integrate value across all aspects

---

[3] Quoted in *CFO 2000: The Global CFO As Strategic Business Partner* (Conference Board Europe, 1997), p14.

of the business and drive this philosophy down to the lowest levels; it will accept that value transformation is a broad undertaking that will require extensive education and several business cycles to implement completely.

The task, then, is to move your organization through these three phases of value transformation – to take the company from value awareness, through adopting a few value elements to the final goal of transforming all its major processes.

Essential requirements

There are great challenges in moving from the 'talking' phase through to value transformation. Success will mean planning and implementing a series of closely related and linked initiatives. For this process, we would like to outline what we think are the essential requirements.

First, since this is a multi-year process that affects all of the organization's central processes, your corporation needs *CEO sponsorship* of the change effort, with the support of senior management and the board of directors. Given the importance of value communications programmes, the internal communication of a value philosophy should be a major item on the agenda of your CEO and CFO. Without such endorsement from the top, the effort will fail.

A value transformation programme also requires a *value transformation team* that includes representatives from all of your major businesses. The existence of such a team encourages the building of 'ownership' and consensus to support the SHV approach among people at all levels and locations of the organization. This team can also serve to educate management and business units about measuring and managing economic value throughout the organization.

An additional challenge in the value transformation process is *motivation* – inspiring people to make decisions and take actions that support the value philosophy. Mostly this will be done by systems of compensation (see below), but it almost goes without saying that a corporate culture where the focus is on highlighting success rather than 'scapegoating' failure is one where motivation levels are likely to be higher. We shall return to this subject towards the end of the chapter, where we will suggest ways of dealing with obstacles that may lie in the path of a value transformation initiative.

FIVE CORE VALUE PROCESSES

In order to achieve the three goals of value creation, preservation and realization, there are five key processes, laid out in Fig. 7.9, that we have identified as being helpful. They are: the establishment of corporate value strategies and goals; resource allocation and planning; performance management; compensation; and value communication and reporting – in five words, *goals*, *plans*, *measures*, *rewards* and *communications*. These five processes are critical. They ensure that the value link from customer to shareholder is created and solidified.

Fig. 7.9 Five core value processes

You can achieve substantial improvement in your company's ability to create value by integrating SHV into any of your five processes. However, if these core processes are to be aligned to produce long-term sustainable value, you should focus on integrating SHV into each of them. It is these five processes that the rest of this chapter will be mostly concerned with. We will take them one by one.

Corporate value strategies and goals

This is where your SHV analysis begins. Corporate strategies define the businesses in which you are competing; they map the course for creating value across a portfolio of companies. Strategy answers four questions – all of which, you will observe, are relevant to the processes of value creation, value preservation and value realization:

- What goals do you have as a corporation?
- What businesses are you in?

- How will you win – i.e. achieve your goals?
- How will you ensure that you obtain the positive returns with which to reward your shareholders ?

There has to be a very close link between the strategy the firm intends to follow and the creation of SHV. Unless SHV is integrated into the strategy development process, a company is unlikely to meet the long-term challenge of creating value with customers and delivering it to investors.

Often, strategy is taken to be exclusively a matter of markets, customers, products, technologies, and competitive dynamics. While these are essential inputs, they are not enough; the question of value creation has to be addressed for each of these areas. In other words, for a strategy to be effective, your company will have to integrate SHV into the formulation and development of that strategy. At this level, value is driven by three basic imperatives:

- investing to achieve a return in excess of the cost of capital (Return)
- growing the business and the investment base (Growth)
- managing and accepting appropriate business risks (Risk).

As you contemplate major strategy choices, assessments of return, growth and risk can be used effectively to weigh up the implications for SHV of these choices.

A company must set specific long-term value goals; for instance, 'delivering total investor returns in the top quintile of our peers over the next five years'. Externally, these goals must satisfy the expectations of the competitive markets for capital – in effect, your investors' expectations. Internally, these same goals should be used to challenge, refine and prioritize the potential strategies of your individual businesses. When used in the strategy development process, they can help identify real constraints and priorities, and ensure that resource allocation among businesses and initiatives will be consistent with creating and delivering value.

This is where economic modelling and cash/capital/returns analyses must begin. The development of strategy will have to focus on markets, technologies, competitive dynamics and customers. Here you will need to establish what your company's *critical success factors* are and clearly define them. You will also need to go back to two terms we mentioned briefly in Chapter 2: core competencies and competitive advantage.

Core competencies and SHV

It is important to establish what your firm's core competencies are, and more important still to relate them to the creation of SHV. Sometimes described as 'integrated bundles of skills that enable a company to deliver a particular benefit to customers,'[4] core competencies harness the total learning in an organization, and in particular involve commitment to 'boundaryless' working that may involve many levels of management across all the organization's functions. A core competency should be one that competitors find difficult to copy, and should make a perceptible contribution to customer benefits. In this way, it should also materially contribute to the formation of SHV.

Core competencies need not simply be a matter of technology; they can also be defined as market understanding and know-how, strength of business process or speed of delivery. Translating these elements into products will allow you to build brands, customer loyalty, distribution channels and corporate image. Most world class corporations will have three to six core competencies. Canon, for example, has 'precision mechanics' (e.g. cameras and colour printers), 'fine optics' (e.g. videos and laser imagers) and 'micro electronics' (e.g. still video cameras and calculators).

At the same time you need to ensure that your interpretation of what your company is good at is neither defined too narrowly (is too product specific) or too broadly. As we point out in Chapter 8, synergies may be claimed in merged businesses that are not really there. As the originators of the core competency concept, C K Prahalad and Gary Hamel, put it: 'In the long run, competitiveness derives from an ability to build, at lower cost and more speedily than competitors, the core competencies that spawn unanticipated products.'[5]

As we have said, your core competencies must be related to the creation of SHV. To put it plainly, it is no use your company being good at making something for which there is little or no market demand. Your core competencies must therefore be capable of creating and sustaining a competitive advantage.

In order to compete, all organizations must demonstrate some form of real or perceived competitive advantage or unique selling point. This goal is often achieved through product and/or service differentiation linked to customer benefits. Of course, over time these advantages may well be eroded by competitors – a likelihood that is usually taken into consideration in any calculations relating to the growth duration or competitive advantage period value driver. As a conscientious manager you will have to tackle this risk head on with a stream of new products developed out of your organization's core competencies to meet customers' wants as they evolve.

While establishing core competencies is an essential element in determining strategy, it is not enough. At this point, a company needs to take its articulated strategy and link it to the other four value processes to serve ultimately both owners and customers in the effort to maximize SHV.

---

[4] Price Waterhouse Change Integration Team, *The Paradox Principles: How High-Performance Companies Manage Chaos, Complexity and Contradiction to Achieve Superior Results* (Chicago: Irwin, 1996), p 46.

[5] C K Prahalad and Gary Hamel, 'The Core Competence of the Corporation', *Harvard Business Review*, May–June 1990.

The risk factor

Before we leave this section on corporate goal setting, it is worth going back to the risk/growth/returns imperatives on page 82 to take another look at risk. This can be a neglected area. In developing and evaluating their strategies to improve total shareholder return, many corporations have concentrated on manipulating just two strategic value 'levers' – economic returns and growth. With sufficient information about a specific initiative's potential growth and economic return (net cash flow return on investment less the cost of capital), companies have been able to forecast future SHV.

But we feel that these two levels seldom reflect the full range of risks among the businesses and initiatives being considered. More importantly, however, the two-lever approach fails to consider adequately the relationship between growth and risk – the probability of actually being able to achieve the expected growth rate.

Many companies are now struggling to fulfil aggressive growth and value agendas, but fewer recognize that taking risks is essential to both growth and return. Enterprises must integrate explicit measurements of risk into their strategic planning in order to identify the possible organizational, cultural, and financial changes that will be needed to achieve their SHV and growth goals.

Resource allocation and planning

Once strategy has been established, resources – human, intellectual and financial – must be allocated to implement the strategy. As a manager, you must make decisions about where to allocate resources to support strategies and maximize returns overall, not simply because individual projects are expected to deliver higher returns.

By adopting SHV as the standard for implementing plans and allocating resources, both the corporate parent and its business units will be operating under a common framework and thus, we believe, will make better decisions. Nevertheless, management should assess performance regularly and objectively: if investments are not performing against value-based objectives, the capital should be freed for a high return strategic investment elsewhere. In this way, capital can be invested efficiently in the most productive initiatives.

Using the value drivers

Issues of resource allocation can be analyzed using a number of techniques. These include sensitivity analysis, benchmarking, and value mapping. At this point we need to go back to the seven drivers of SHV introduced in Chapter 5. Any SHV calculation will incorporate these seven value drivers – often described as macro drivers, to distinguish them from operating or micro drivers, which we shall deal with later.

In effect, these drivers can provide a common planning tool for a variety of departments, product lines and business units. By using the historical perform-ance of the value drivers to compute your company's return on invested capital for each business or product, and comparing this computation against the com-pany's cost of capital, you can determine where SHV has been created or destroyed in the past. To reach a true understanding of value, however, both management and investors must focus on likely future performance.

Sensitivity analysis

There are definite relationships between business decisions, value drivers and cash flow. By analyzing them, you can gain insights into how it might be possible to enhance SHV. Likely changes to any of the drivers can be analyzed to deter-mine their impact on value; for example, different assumptions of risk, reflected in higher or lower cost of capital requirements, can be tested. Similarly, you could study the likely impact on your enterprise's current value of a strategy to generate increases in revenues, decreased selling or marketing costs, or different required levels of working capital investment. In essence, any substantive idea put forward to improve a company's performance must be measured by the value yardstick, against the cost and availability of capital employed to make it happen.

This, then, is sensitivity analysis: as we saw in Chapter 5, the seven value drivers can be 'flexed' in a computer model to see what the effect on a com-pany's share price might be – in the case of the example in Figure 5.2, it was a variation of 1 per cent in each of the drivers. Such analysis can establish priori-ties in your management decision processes.

Once you have discovered the power of each value driver to affect the share price, you must then take a long hard look to see how possible it might be to move the relevant value drivers in the appropriate direction. If it is possible, the next question to be asked is: could this strategy be communicated to, and be believed by, the market? Whatever the answer, sensitivity analysis will illustrate how much SHV it may be possible to add if best practice can be achieved.

Benchmarking: the external scorecard

By 'benchmarking' we mean systematically comparing your own organization, its structures, activities and functions, to others. The others will often be your competitors – but here we are using a wider than usual definition of who is a competitor. Most managers see themselves competing against a clearly defined group of companies, probably offering a similar series of products or services. Investors, however, take a rather different view: their main interest is in the

return yielded by their investments. Stock markets are places where by definition all the companies participating compete with each other for capital; such
competition, as investors see it, takes place on a field much wider than most
managements envisage. Were managers occasionally to look at the way investors
group companies, they might find themselves compared with some surprisingly
unlikely companies – perhaps even companies they do not for a moment take
seriously as competitors.

Trivial though it may seem, we dwell on this point because it throws some
light on what investors are looking for in the way of corporate performance. We
know that often their main concerns are what other companies in the top 'quintile' are achieving, rather than what a particular company's immediate competitors are doing.

Benchmarking can obviously be extended along other lines too. For instance,
it may be of interest to know what the performance characteristics of your customers, suppliers, or business partners are. But to benchmark your company
against the competition, particularly the 'best in class', is a helpful starting point
in any analysis.

We recommend you start such an exercise with an 'external scorecard'
approach. By employing the same techniques as those used by market analysts,
the external scorecard – see Fig. 7.10 for an example – can offer a management
useful insights. Competitors are identified and all available information on their
strategy carefully analyzed; each of their value drivers is compared to your company's value drivers percentages. Such analysis will reveal performance gaps –
some in favour of the company and some showing stronger competitor per-

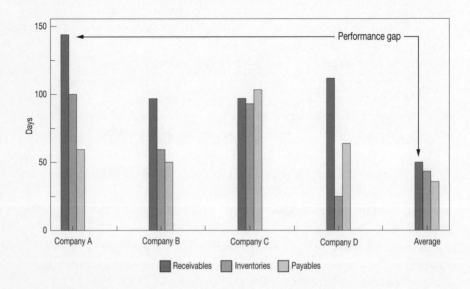

Fig. 7.10 External scorecard

formance and possible best practice. It may also be possible to join an international benchmarking alliance (for instance the Price Waterhouse Global Benchmarking Alliance) to gain further insights as to what is the best practice among competitors.

However it is done, the point of benchmarking is that you will gain an understanding of best practice, be able to set out with confidence to improve the performance of your own corporate value drivers, and thus to enhance SHV.

The value map

Another useful tool in the resource allocation stage of value-based management is the 'value map', examples of which are shown in Fig. 7.11. This is a way of showing graphically which parts of your business are contributing to the creation of value and which are not. To do this, you need to be able to divide your organization into its constituent value centres, each representing a division or business unit with responsibility for the management of revenues, costs and capital.

Assuming this is possible, you can then plot each unit's position on the first 'map' according to the value it has created (measured on the vertical axis) against the capital it has employed (the horizontal axis). Often, different business units will be positioned in different markets – in which case for each unit a cost of capital will be applied which reflects the systematic risks to which it is exposed.

At this point we have to be careful to define our terms, since there can be different value maps designed to answer different questions. One map can be concerned with the value creation possibilities of a division to all asset holders, and so you might plot the present value of a free cash flow and look at the total capital employed (drawn on the horizontal axis). Alternatively we could look at it more narrowly from a strict equity point of view. Then we would look at the present value of future cash flows and deduct the debt and compare this to the net investment involved (essentially equity).

As with other aspects of SHV metrics, it's a matter of 'horses for courses' – the right methodology for the right circumstances.

In both figures, we have a company with four divisions. Division A is creating value equivalent to the resources it uses. Division B is creating proportionately more value than it is using in resources. C is a user of capital and produces a relatively low spread. Division D on the other hand is destroying SHV while consuming resources. The total value created by the business is the size of rectangles A+B+C–D.

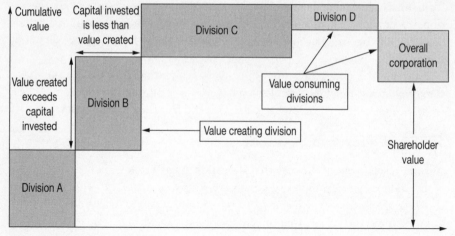

Illustrative – not based on a real company

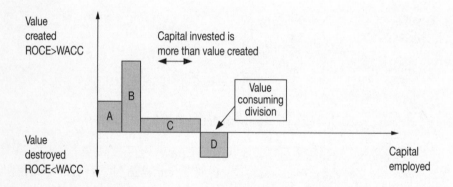

Fig. 7.11 Two kinds of value map

Whatever measurement gets used in the value map, and whatever map is used, it easy to see that your high risers will be the most valuable parts of your business; anything that turns out to be a square is 'breaking even', while there will have to be a question mark over the future of the 'bungalows', the flat value destroyers that are wider than they are tall. The important point is that in drawing the map you and your advisers will have had to undertake a thorough assessment of the cash, however defined, that is flowing into and out of each business unit. Without that knowledge, any SHV analysis can be flawed.

Of course, this kind of analysis is bound to lead to questions about what action to take and where to target investment. While some divisions that are operating less than efficiently will need additional capital in order to create value, other value destroyers will remain value destroyers whatever you do – so you will be better off without them. Equally, it may be worth investing in a high-value division, or it may not; if it is operating in a mature, saturated market, further investment may result in excess capacity and thus value destruction.

What's more, your value map can be further enhanced by benchmarking the divisional or business unit figures you have calculated – in other words, going outside the company to identify performance gaps and best practices in a group of companies. Here again global benchmarking alliances can be called upon.

Performance management

Setting the targets

As we have said, corporate analysis must be followed by the setting of targets based on share price goals. Having established what is possible at the corporate level, and having identified which business divisions are creating or destroying SHV, the next step is to convert your global targets into something much more localized and achievable at an operating level within your company. You must assess the impact of these goals on the seven value drivers as they apply to your company, its action plans and budgets. Performance measurements and incentive systems – two of the main themes of this chapter – must then be agreed and introduced. Many of the high profile global companies that have introduced SHV programmes have started with a share price goal – an objective that is easy to understand and communicate.

For example, a management may set a goal 'to increase its company's current share price from £20 a share to £30 a share over the next five years'. In order to achieve this, a 50 per cent increase in price, it will use the cash flow approach outlined in Part 1 to calculate that the following movements must be achieved in relation to the seven macro value drivers:

Revenue growth rate	increase from 12 to 15 per cent
Operating margin growth (EBITDA)	from 8 to 9 per cent
Cash tax rate	reduce from 33 to31 per cent
Working capital to sales	reduce by 10 per cent
Fixed assets to sales	from 12 to 8 per cent
WACC	from 13 to 11 per cent
Competitive advantage period	increase from 8 to 10 years

In this way companies can translate capital market investment metrics into future performance targets for their managers.

Linkages and metrics

Following on from this, you will need to link these goals to a series of other more localized value drivers. The connections between strategy, operations and compensation systems need to be identified to ensure a single consistent focus internally. These linkages are particularly important in that they can institutionalize targeted changes in the management process and galvanize management action. Performance metrics serve an important role in providing these linkages.

Without a set of relevant value-focused measures, your organization could find it almost impossible to correlate progress in attaining results tied to its strategies. But if these areas are properly linked through a balanced set of performance metrics, senior executives and managers will find themselves with their hands on all the controls required to implement strategy and achieve objectives.

Performance measurement (and performance management) links value from the top to the bottom of an organization. It takes top-down-driven targets and connects them with company-specific, operational drivers. By identifying these operational, or micro, drivers – examples of which are given in the bottom 'level' of Fig. 7.12 – and linking them to SHV, most companies will develop new insights into their business and new tools to test alternatives.

One of the key messages of value-based management is that SHV is created or destroyed at the point where management decisions are made. So you should be aware, as a member of front-line or middle management, of the SHV implications of every decision that you make – which means that performance measurement and reward processes should reflect and reinforce the creation of SHV.

As Fig. 7.12 illustrates, different kinds of decision are made at different levels in an organization. Matters of strategy, such as the question of which market your company should actually be in, are dealt with by the chairman, CEO and CFO; at the next level down, in strategic business units, decisions about capital expenditure and investment in (for instance) product development or new distribution networks are taken; while at operating unit level it's a question of detailed planning and budgeting. But at whatever level you are working, the principles of value-based management apply: you should establish strategies that are clearly understood, and monitor them by being able to measure efficiently – and reward effectively – the creation of SHV.

These different levels of decision are also reflected in Fig. 7.13, where the levels are identified as strategic, financial and operational, and a number of operational drivers (sometimes referred to as 'micro drivers') are linked with the basic risk/growth/return requirements of the market by the macro drivers. The diagram starts with some broad corporate-level (strategic) goals, which could be the three basic 'imperatives' of risk, growth and returns outlined on page 82 (corporate strategies). The important thing, though, is to go beyond this and establish a link between the macro-drivers and a series of more micro or operational value drivers of the sort described at the bottom of the diagram.

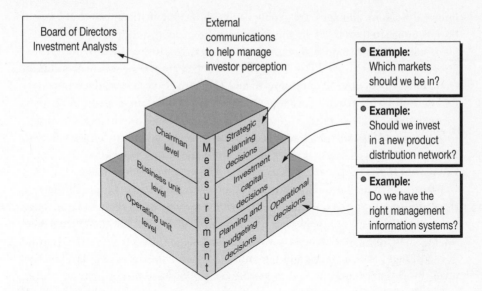

Fig. 7.12 Aligning your processes with SHV

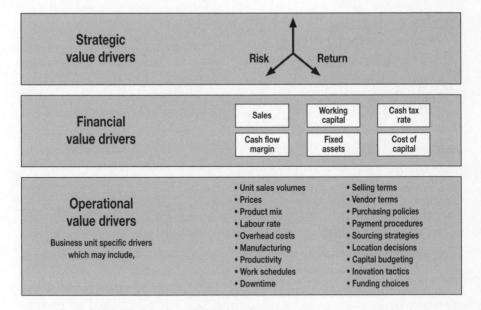

Fig. 7.13 From macro to micro SHV drivers

Using the micro drivers

It can be difficult sometimes to see how the seven value drivers relate to the day-to-day business of your company. As Tom Copeland and his colleagues put it in their book *Valuation*,[6] 'Generic value drivers lack specificity and cannot be used well at grassroots level'.

One way to deal with this is by using econometric business modelling which enables managers to evaluate the SHV impact in individual business units of changes to key operating parameters. This is where you can introduce into your calculations factors such as prices, staffing levels, maintenance, marketing costs, debtors and capital spend.

These operating value drivers can be used to make projections for each business unit's financial status before being consolidated to determine the macro value drivers at a corporate level. Figure 7.13, with its examples of operational value drivers, may have already suggested to you some ways in which the two kinds of driver – micro and macro – provide a structure for evaluating business units. Let us take a closer look to see what action can be taken at the 'micro' level under the heading of each macro value driver.

Here, then, are some examples of initiatives we have observed being undertaken by global corporations to generate SHV. We have listed them according to which of the macro value drivers they affect. (Some of these initiatives will have an impact on more than one driver.)

Revenue growth rate

- Ensure profitable growth that will add value.
- Consider new market entry.
- Develop new products.
- Globalize the business.
- Develop customer loyalty programmes.
- Offer pricing advantage with new distribution outlets.
- Develop focused advertising based on differentiation.

Operating margin growth

- Modernize working practices.
- Restructure including introduction of multi-skilling.
- Cut costs by sharing services and outsourcing.
- Centralize and consolidate back office and finance functions (treasury, tax, corporate finance, financial systems).
- Introduce business process re-engineering with IT systems initiatives including consolidation and integration of billing, customer care, activity-based costing, data warehousing, network management and configuration.

---

[6] Copeland, Koller and Murrin (McKinsey & Company, Inc.), *Valuation: Measuring and Managing the Value of Companies*, pp 106–7 (New York: John Wiley, 2nd ed 1996).

Cash tax rate

- Consider international holding structure.
- Locate and exploit intellectual property and brands.
- Use co-ordination centres.
- Customs duty and transfer pricing planning.
- Minimize foreign and withholding taxes.

Working capital

- Implement working capital reviews.
- Improve debtor management.
- Introduce supply chain management systems and just-in-time inventory methods.

Capital expenditure

- Develop capital appraisal and utilization reviews and project finance techniques.
- Weigh up lease versus buy decisions.
- Develop treasury, hedging and risk management systems.

WACC (Weighted Average Cost of Capital)

- Build management understanding of cost of capital.
- Calculate gearing/leverage optimization.
- Calculate business-unit-specific WACC.
- Consider share buy-backs and demerger of non-core business.

Competitive advantage period

- Improve investor relations by providing predictable and sustainable financial performance.
- Improve business unit cash flow information.
- Return to core competencies.
- Develop executive performance reward schemes linked to share price improvement.
- Give all employees the opportunity to have an economic stake in the company
- Incorporate strong risk management procedures.

Once you have been able to break out the corporate goals into much more specific quantitative (and qualitative) goals such as those listed above, you will have built a bridge between operational decisions on one side, and contributions to

SHV on the other. As Fig. 7.13 illustrates, decisions are best taken within organisations at the level where they can make the most difference.

Understanding the value chain

An important step in introducing an effective performance measurement system is to record the processes which your company goes through to deliver value. This is your corporate 'value chain' – see Fig. 7.14 – which should show the key value functions of your company, each of which must be capable of individual performance measurements. Once you have an agreed value chain, key strategies can be developed and decisions taken to link these strategies to a SHV improvement programme.

The five-stage value chain in a pharmaceutical company, for example, may start with R&D, move to inbound logistics, then to production, outbound logistics and to marketing and sales. In a service organization the five stages may be to identify and develop new services and products; recruit , train and retain professionals; attract clients; run effective marketing and sales operations; and service and retain clients effectively.

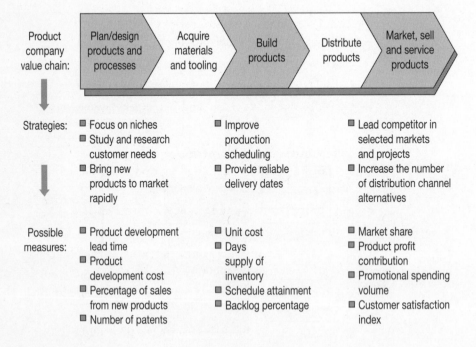

Fig. 7.14 Value chain

Practical implementation

In your initial implementation of value-based performance management, you may focus on a short-term improvement programme that allows quick wins to be realized at the earliest opportunity. But in the longer term, value management must be implemented through a well-executed change programme – see Fig. 7.15.

In summary, you must tailor performance measures for improving SHV to suit each business unit in your organisation, and these measures must be ones that the business unit can itself have some control over. At the same time, these measures must be tied in to the short-term and long-term targets of the business unit – which in turn will be linked to corporate strategy and targets. The performance measures are based on the key macro and operating value drivers of the business unit and combine both financial and operating measures in the value scorecard. We will return to the use of 'scorecards' in the final chapter.

Some performance measures can serve as very valuable early warning signals: customer reports, market share and sales trends, for instance, can be very useful. Other financial measures, however, may only track the past – in which case you may find corrective action will take some time to implement.

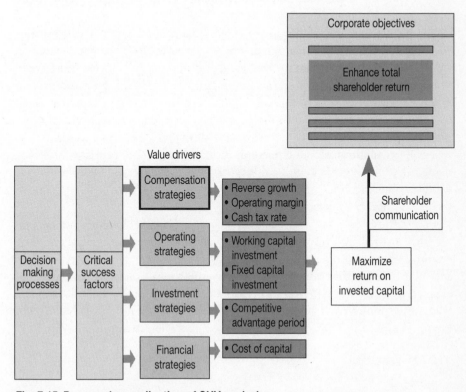

Fig. 7.15 Progressive application of SHV analysis

Compensation

Two elements of Fig. 7.15 have yet to be dealt with: compensation strategies and shareholder communication. For an effective value-based management programme to be fully implemented within a corporation, you will need to incentivize – to link your compensation system to value creation. A successfully directed value-based management programme will, we recognize, make big demands on a management; if you respond to the challenge, you deserve to be rewarded. The linkage of remuneration to value creation will, we believe, promote a culture of performance and ownership that rewards SHV maximization and empowers employees to manage the business as if it were their own. Such a system will ensure that the interests of shareholders and employees are aligned.

The importance of the right kind of corporate culture is emphasized by the anonymous CFO of a large US company:[7] 'In 1995, we established a pay-for-performance plan that went right down to the lowest level employee and was based on earnings growth and return to the shareholder,' he reports. 'So everyone in the company became interested in what was happening to the share price.'

Once senior management has identified the measures that can be managed to create SHV, both executives and employees must be rewarded according to the extent they meet their targets.

No one measure is appropriate for all employees at all levels, nor is one time frame applicable to all people. But any incentive compensation system based on value creation will have certain key features distinguishing it from more traditional plans found in the corporate community today. It will be based on economic performance, which emphasizes cash flow, the amount of capital invested to generate that cash flow, and the cost of the invested capital. It will also use different periods of time to motivate both short-term and longer-term results that collectively lead to value maximization. It may be appropriate for senior managers to address SHV with a longer-range perspective and long-term goals, while people in middle management or on the shop floor will view value through a short-term lens.

By carefully designing a value-based incentive plan that contains an appropriate level of risk and reward, a company can motivate and inspire all employees throughout an organization to work for value creation – to make decisions and take actions that support the value philosophy. (See Fig. 7.16 for an example.) With the right kind of performance metrics, individuals at all levels who are responsible for delivering value should understand what is required of them. To ensure they are strongly motivated, their objectives should:

---

[7] Quoted in *CFO 2000*, p17.

- relate directly to executives' and employees' day-to-day responsibilities
- be balanced between short-term and long-term objectives
- contribute to reaching the organization's strategic goals and SHV objectives.

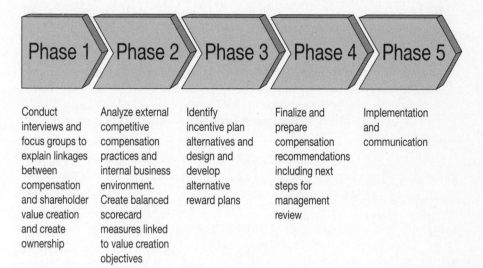

Phase 1	Phase 2	Phase 3	Phase 4	Phase 5
Conduct interviews and focus groups to explain linkages between compensation and shareholder value creation and create ownership	Analyze external competitive compensation practices and internal business environment. Create balanced scorecard measures linked to value creation objectives	Identify incentive plan alternatives and design and develop alternative reward plans	Finalize and prepare compensation recommendations including next steps for management review	Implementation and communication

Fig. 7.16 Five-phase compensation programme approach

There is not the space to go into great detail about the variety of compensation schemes that have been devised – from LTIPs (long-term incentive plans) and share options to performance shares and phantom stock plans – and to what extent they meet the three criteria listed. Suffice it to say that the concerns that have been expressed, particularly in the USA and the UK, over 'excessive' executive pay awards are resulting in changes to the way compensation packages are put together. Rolls Royce, for example, was planning in April 1997 to replace its executive share options scheme with 'a new long term incentive plan ... [that] would involve the grant of shares if targets relating to shareholder return compared with other leading engineering and industrial companies were achieved.'[8]

Value communications and reporting

Although your company may create and preserve value, your investors will not realize this value unless an effective communications programme is in place. Such value communications programmes have both internal and external pur-

[8] *Financial Times*, 11 April 1997.

poses. Internally, they educate the entire workforce about corporate strategies and goals, and have clear linkages both to operations (what they do) and compensation (what they are paid). This education process will teach everyone to think and communicate in the same terms – once again, aligning goals with actions.

Your education process also needs to be able to demonstrate to managers and others within your company why the market matters. As Barry Romeril, CFO at Xerox, has said:

> It's good for investors to meet a broader spectrum of management, but it's probably more beneficial for the broader spectrum of management to understand who are the people making decisions to buy, what's driving their decision, and what their thought processes are.[9]

Equally, investor communications must aim at ensuring that investors understand your company's value-based strategies and goals, and are confident in management's ability to implement those objectives and deliver on them. With the right information, investors can develop an informed view on growth, return, and risk assumptions in assessing value. If investors do not understand or do not believe in management's ability to deliver on these strategies and goals, then your market value will reflect a less informed – or a more pessimistic – view of your company's prospects.

In other words, if you want to ensure that market value reflects the real intrinsic value of your company, you must clearly communicate your strategy and implementation plans. Such communication, combined with a good track record of management delivering on expectations, is critical for investors.

Not only in the USA and the UK, but also in continental Europe, successful companies are beginning to recognize that they must actively spread the news about their targets and achievements if their shares are to be properly valued. Daimler-Benz, based in Germany, saw the importance of investor relations when it sought a listing on the New York Stock Exchange in 1994. It was only then, after meeting US analysts, that it saw that good investor relations could not only raise its profile but also could make it easier to raise capital.

Analysts and institutional investors agree that regular access to the highest levels of management is essential. A survey by the UK's Investor Relations Society found that more than 60 per cent of CFOs and 45 per cent of CEOs spend a 'significant' amount of time on investor relations. This kind of effort is likely to increase as company managements find that developing their presentation and communication skills is essential in today's corporate environment.

In the words of one investor relations specialist:[10]

---

[9] *CFO 2000*, p11.
[10] Bill Stokoe, investor relations specialist at Brunswick.

In Germany and elsewhere in Europe, there is a new generation of managers who know exactly what the international capital markets expect of them. ... They are embracing all the established investor relations techniques – from roadshows to teleconferencing and market research – and are receptive to new ideas.

LINKAGES AND OBSTACLES

All the five core value processes of Fig. 7.9, then, must be addressed if a company is to create long-term sustainable value – and addressed in a way that provides strong linkages between each of them. Compensation structures, for example, must be closely tied to performance management objectives; and investor communications must link directly to corporate value strategies and goals. Strong linkages across the five core processes will ensure that value is created, preserved, and realized just as in Fig. 7.8.

All the same, attaining value transformation is not easy. Throughout the course of a major initiative, a wide variety of issues, challenges, and problems will surface which can sidetrack – often irrevocably – value creation. These obstacles do not generally arise out of any negative intentions, but simply reflect the fact that people initially resist, rather than embrace, major change. You will need to address such organizational and cultural inertia promptly whenever it occurs in the life cycle of a transformation programme. Table 7.1 shows the major stages in a transformation initiative, the typical challenges that may have to be addressed, and the approaches that can be used to overcome resistance.

Table 7.1 Major stages in a transformation initiative

Major transformation stages/challenges	Successful approaches
Evaluate/envision	
• Project does not have support of senior management.	• Reset priorities, have CEO sponsorship.
• Transition management activities ignored in work planning.	• Include in project planning.
• Limited communication of project objectives.	• Formal internal/external communication programmes.
• Full impact on shareholder values not determined.	• Embed value analysis in management processes.
• Performance metrics addressed as afterthought.	• Use value drivers to define metrics.
• Perceived as the consultant's product.	• Joint project teams.
Empower	
• Users are reluctant to participate in change.	• Joint project teams.
• Users have not bought into the value creation.	• Compensation/incentive programmes based on value creation.
• User acceptance is not occurring as rapidly as possible.	• Focus on quick wins, showcase victories.
Major transformation stages/challenges	**Successful approaches**
• Decision and issue resolution is not timely.	• Have identified sponsors/decision makers.
• Turf battles among different teams.	• Install issue resolution system.
• Team members not pulling weight.	• Dedicate best people.
Excel	
• Continuous improvement team meetings are addressing broad/general issues.	• Revisit team charter – focus on specific issues.
• No systematic approach to problem solving being followed.	• Use common language, tool kits, training etc.
• Unfounded assumptions made about what the customer wants or what drives value.	• Refocus team on customer service and/or the key value drivers.

SUSTAINING VBM

Whatever happens, the market overall, and institutional shareholders in particular, will continue to act as judge and jury in assessing how the senior management teams of public companies perform. How well or poorly you and your colleagues develop, implement, and deliver value-creating strategies will be critical to the verdicts that these investors render. This is why an increasing number of CEOs and CFOs are seeking to ensure that all decision making in their organizations is aligned towards an overall SHV objective.

In this chapter we have been talking about value-based management (VBM), which closes the gap between strategy and implementation, the standard mode of business for the entire enterprise. Shareholder value theory provides the framework within which each of the five core processes listed above can be examined, changed, and linked together.

The kind of change envisaged will drive your company's strategy, resource allocation, performance management, compensation, and communications in new directions. For even the most successful companies, implementing this transformation will ensure the institutionalization of decision making processes that enhance SHV[11].

SUMMARY

In this chapter we have looked at how a SHV approach concentrates on sustaining and increasing value at the creation, preservation and realization stages. We did this by focusing on the five core value processes, and show how it is possible to move from a very macro level of analysis into a very detailed agenda of quantitative and qualitative targets which can be applied and implemented at an operational level. We also commented on several obstacles that can prevent the implementation of such an approach.

---

[11]For more detail on value-based management see also Price Waterhouse Financial and Cash Management Team, *CFO: Architect of the Corporation's Future* (John Wiley, 1997).

SHV AT WAR: MERGERS AND ACQUISITIONS

One of the most compelling reasons for taking the concept of SHV seriously is that investors already do. In other words, as we have argued, it is in your interest to see your company the way the market sees it. This is especially true in cases where one company seeks to take over, or merge with, another.

In this book we have already made several references to takeovers – mostly looking at them from the point of view of the victim. When (in Chapter 3) we discussed the importance of ensuring a return for investors above the cost of capital, we implied that it was important to avoid becoming a takeover target – which you could do by delivering consistently high returns to your shareholders. If your assets cannot earn a return higher than the cost of capital, we argued, then investors will eventually withdraw their funds, making your company a takeover target.

This is certainly true in markets where SHV (and value-based management) is taken seriously. But here we want to take a different angle and look at the whole business of mergers and acquisitions (M&A) from the point of view of the shareholder and of the potential acquirer.

As investors adjust their expectations in the light of how a company is performing, so opportunities may arise for buying companies 'on the cheap'. Remember that, using the Q ratio introduced in Chapter 6, both investors and managers can establish which is less expensive: to invest in new assets or to buy up undervalued assets from someone else.

In this chapter we want to show in more detail how you can use the insights of SHV theory for the purpose of acquiring and divesting companies, and we will then use the SHV approach in examining an example of an acquisition. The SHV approach, we believe, offers a superior basis for establishing what the medium-term impact of a merger or takeover will be. Essentially, it can establish whether any merger or acquisition will be in the interests of the acquiring firm's shareholders – a group that has not been particularly well rewarded to date.

THE PROS AND CONS OF TAKEOVERS

Before looking at what can and should happen in the field of M&A, let us consider how effective such operations have been in the past. Shareholder value theory suggests that M&A activity is an important mechanism to keep capital flowing to the areas that need it the most. Capital, it can be said, will seek out the areas of highest return and provide investors with handsome rewards for the risks taken. The question is whether this has happened. The evidence is far from clear.

A McKinsey study[1] of the 1980s concluded that a mere 37 per cent of US acquirers outperformed their peers in terms of total shareholder returns. Early indications of the 1990s show a slightly happier picture. A 1996 survey, carried out in the USA by Mercer Management Consulting,[2] found that of 300 transactions in the 1990s above $500 million, 53 per cent outperformed their peers over the ensuing three-year period – implying that the other 47 per cent either under-performed, or at best were just on a level with, their peers. Which is to say that, from the acquirer's point of view, the success or failure of a merger or acquisition is still little better than tossing a coin.

This leaves a large question mark over the economic rationale for many of these large transactions. If the market is generally fair in its valuation of companies on a stand-alone basis, how does that square with the economics of acquisition, where a premium of 25 to 40 per cent premium is a normal requirement for gaining control? Clearly in SHV terms it often means that the acquirer is passing over the value of the first chunk of available gains to the vendor shareholders. For the acquirer's shareholders to obtain any benefit, the income growth and cost savings have to be considerable.

This is illustrated by one well-known hostile transaction in the late 1980s, when a large US corporate paid a premium of 69 per cent over the pre-bid rumour price for a pharmaceutical company. You did not have to be a genius to predict that the winners would be the target company's shareholders. Certainly the market saw it that way immediately and decimated the acquiring company's share price following the announcement. Although this might be an extreme case, it is by no means unique; the fact remains that shareholders of acquiring companies have not generally prospered, while the shareholders of the acquired companies have.

Shareholders of companies that have fended off unwelcome bids from outsiders have not prospered either. A 1996 study[3] by Scottish Amicable, which looked at 15 UK companies that had successfully fought off a hostile bid

---

[1] In Copeland, Koller and Murrin, *Valuation* (New York: John Wiley, 2nd ed 1994), p 416.
[2] 'Why too many mergers miss the mark,' *The Economist*, 4 January 1997.
[3] 'Backing hostile bids is wise', *Independent on Sunday*, 11 February 1997.

approach in the past ten years, showed that these companies subsequently under-performed the stock market by up to 25 per cent.

These are not comforting figures. They suggest that a lot of M&A activity pays insufficient attention to the question of whether any new combinations will in fact help increase SHV for the acquiring firms – which is the aim of the exercise. Indeed, while the act of taking over or merging with another company ought to raise SHV for the acquirer, the apparent inability of companies to ensure this suggests that M&A is sometimes an obstacle to achieving this goal.

The 'dog in the manger' syndrome

Although it is assumed that acquisitions will add to SHV, in many cases they do not. We think that the main reason for this is that apparently rational people are swayed by a variety of non-rational considerations which often end up by destroying rather than adding to SHV.

While many takeovers are characterized by a desire for greater expansion and power, a fair number of mergers and acquisitions are driven by strategic and defensive considerations. Left to their own devices, many firms would be happy to leave their competitors in peace, or to reject activities in 'non-core' areas as being too risky. But life is rarely that simple. Very often a management will be provoked into action to forestall the threat, real or imagined, of a close competitor acquiring or making a deal with another rival.

This 'dog in the manger' attitude is founded on a belief that to steal a march on rivals by blocking off their access to a new market, or by boxing them into their existing market, will ultimately benefit the acquirer's shareholders. Where the aims of the acquirer are mainly of this defensive type, it seems to us that expectations for the new larger group's performance will necessarily be more diffuse. There may be an emphasis on greater volume and 'critical mass', which will be seen to be at least as important as raising margins and increasing efficiency. Friendly deals may be struck with the management of the acquired firm, allowing existing business practices to continue. With such an agenda, it is not entirely surprising that the acquirer's subsequent share performance is less than good.

Mergers and economic cycles

At the time of writing, we are seeing massive merger and acquisition activity, already surpassing the peak of the cycle in the 1980s – see Fig. 8.1. There are several reasons for this, the primary one being that cash rich companies are looking for other profitable outlets and believe that, either by diversifying into new areas or by increasing their market share in their existing markets, they will prosper further. Cheap finance and buoyant expectations about the future also contribute to these merger waves.

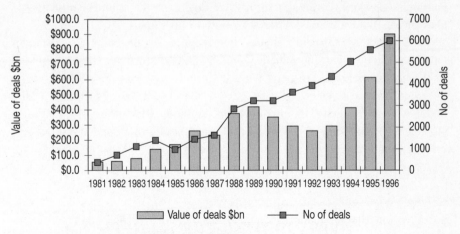

Fig. 8.1 Worldwide M&A activity 1981–1996

The boom of the 1980s has both similarities and differences with that of the 1990s. In both, the background has been one of booming stock markets and high levels of bank lending available to oil the wheels for the required financing. But the underlying trends tell a different story. In the 1980s the fashionable conglomerates of the 1970s were broken up and an often hostile search took place to capture value from under-performing assets. The economics of such transactions were mostly based on driving out costs in the companies that were acquired.

M&A activity in the 1990s, on the other hand, is more to do with the strategic development of core activities, the holy grail of global size and the drive for top-line income growth. This in turn has been sparked off by a shift to a low inflation environment which has made it much more difficult for hard pressed companies to pass on high costs as higher prices to their customers. The aim to drive out costs remains but these are not the costs of excess – which most companies had necessarily to deal with in the leaner years of the late 1980s and early 1990s – but rather of the benefits available through combining similar business activities.

It is perhaps somewhat premature to judge whether the mega-transactions of the 1990s will deliver more SHV than those of the 1980s but they could hardly do worse. Interestingly enough, though, many of the victims in the 1990s are the predators of the earlier M&A boom, such as Hanson. These companies have been truly hoist by their own petard; after initiating many useful initial changes in management, they have failed to deliver the constant improvements in underlying profitability the market now demands. In many cases the earlier predators have learned to their cost the difference between an easily achieved rise in earnings per share and the greater difficulty associated with a longer-term rise in SHV based on strong and consistent growth in cash flows.

While classic M&A theory suggests that corporate raiders should buy up their targets quickly, make deep management changes and then sell these companies to new investors in the hopes of better cash flows to come, the reality is rather different. Many of yesterday's corporate raiders have found themselves lumbered with investments in under-performing industries. One-off changes in management could not hide the fact that the overall growth and cash flow profile of an acquired company was simply not very good, and that its potential for delivering excellent gains in SHV were not great in the medium term.

OVERSHOOTING THE TARGET?

Why do acquirers appear to behave in what looks, particularly to their own shareholders, an irrational manner? Probably we are observing an outcome that is not initially desired by the acquirer, and partly reflects an information asymmetry between buyer and seller. The seller will almost always know more clearly what is being sold, and may have a restricted set of opportunities looking ahead into the future. Purchasers on the other hand have to make guesses about how the acquired company will fit into their plans, and what changes will be necessary in the acquired firm (and possibly in their own firm too). They will tend to under-estimate the difficulties of pushing through changes if the merger or acquisition is to bring any rewards.

Collecting hard information about a possible acquisition can present challenges; inevitably, the amount of data available will vary from country to country, But over time, a fairly full picture can normally be obtained about a particular company from a variety of sources:

- financial statements
- trade sources
- regulatory returns
- market surveys
- internal sources
- broker reports.

As far as publicly available financial information is concerned, transparency varies significantly by industry sector, as Fig. 8.2 sets out. At one end of the spectrum, the utilities sector is highly transparent, with companies often operating in a single country and within a clear regulatory framework. At the other end insurance companies, particularly life assurers, are anything but transparent in the financial information they provide. As a consequence hostile bids for utility companies, of which several have been launched in the last two years in the UK, abound; not so with insurers.

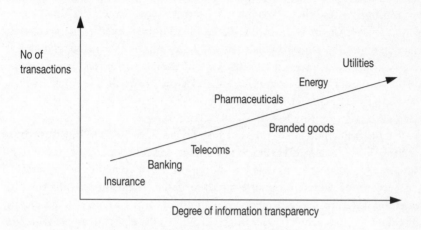

Fig. 8.2 Transparency of information by industry sector

Time pressures

On top of the problems of information gathering, you will have to think about the pressures of time. Establishing the finance and working out the details of a takeover is expensive. It often involves sharing a lot of highly confidential information with advisers, and leads to perturbations on the stock market. It is high profile stuff, especially when there is a hostile and contested bid for the target. In situations like these, the interests of the acquired company's shareholders are relatively straightforward – they simply want to obtain the best deal now. They are rarely in the position of being able to delay; it is quite simply now or never.

The acquiring company, though, can afford to take a longer view. At the margin it is probably prepared to concede more to the seller, once the decision to go ahead with the deal is made. We suspect that this is what principally accounts for the large premiums paid for control of target companies, and takes the underlying valuation of the target some distance from a more soundly based view derived from a hard-nosed SHV framework.

We would like to outline just such a framework. Applying a SHV-oriented approach could, we believe, increase the proportion of M&A successes in the future even if it did so by reducing the flow of deals. It could also be applied as a corrective to the sometimes large egos of CEOs, and to the emotion of 'getting the deal done'.

A FRAMEWORK FOR BEST PRACTICE

The link to SHV

Given the rather mixed record of many takeovers, we would like to delineate a better approach – one that takes the SHV insights you may have gained in this book and applies them to the difficult area of valuing companies in takeover or acquisition situations. In particular, we will focus on the likely impact a merger or acquisition might have on the interests of the acquiring company's shareholders. We think the approach is logical and should provide a very useful guide for any actual negotiations.

It would be too limiting for all M&A negotiations to be based on this type of approach, but we would encourage any potential purchaser to follow this sort of procedure, if only to avoid having to pay fanciful prices for acquisitions of dubious quality. We suggest a simplified transaction value map along the lines of Fig. 8.3 as a means of assessing the effect of alternative acquisitions. (For the purposes of this diagram, it is assumed that neither acquiring nor acquired company has any debt.) Much of what we will go through is drawn from an actual case.

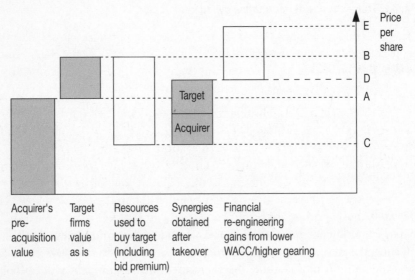

Fig. 8.3 **Simplified transaction value map**

Let us look at the elements of this diagram one by one.

Initial values and resources used

Acquirer's pre-acquisition value

Throughout this discussion our point of view will be that of the acquirer's shareholders, and how the acquisition (or merger) might look to them. To this end, you must try to establish as clearly as possible the current stand alone shareholder value of the company. Following our own earlier definitions, you can take this as being the sum of the discounted cash flow and the residual value discounted at the corporate WACC minus debt, plus net book value of cash and marketable securities. This is equivalent to the market value of equity and, gives rise to a value per share measured as price A in the diagram.

The target: gathering data

You also need to build up an estimate of the stand alone value of the target on the same discounted free cash flow basis as outlined above for your own company as the acquirer. Again, this is calculated by looking first at the cash flows and then at the cost of capital. There may be more uncertainties here about cash flow projections, particularly in the early assessment stage of the project when information is limited, and even more so if the target is a private company. The objective should be to arrive at an approximation of the cash flows which can be gradually refined as better information becomes available. (As we said earlier, information varies from country to country, and from sector to sector – see Fig. 8.2).This value is shown in the second box of Fig. 8.3 and moves the cumulative value of the combined group from share price A to share price B.

The purchase

After assessing how much the acquired company is worth, resources have to be made available to purchase it. These can be treated as debt, thus reducing shareholder claims on the new company and so reducing the share price from B to C in Fig. 8.3. However, this reduction in the value is of a very short-run nature. After all, the reason for buying the target company is the acquiring company's belief that it can generate sufficient additional cash flows not only to repay the debt, but also to generate additional SHV (in other words, the return on capital employed will be greater than the WACC). In particular the acquirer will be looking for synergies, to which we will devote the next section.

Synergies

Synergy literally means 'combined action', and in the context of M&A it is the advantage of combining operations in two or more units that is generally sought. By bringing units more closely together, an acquiring company will be looking to avoid duplication and to pursue economies of scope; a new combined entity should be able to take advantage of having assets in different locations to carry out existing business strategies more effectively.

It is useful to divide such synergies into those that will be gained by the acquiring firm and those that will accrue to the acquired firm: these are shown in Fig. 8.3 (labelled 'target' and 'acquirer'). If these two boxes represent the synergies available to the acquiring and to the acquired (target) firm, the value per share would move from point C to point D in the diagram.

As we have already said, the nature and scope of synergies often tend to be exaggerated, and companies can be too optimistic about when they will be achieved. Our analysis concentrates on cash flows, and it is useful to try and relate all expected synergies to this one measure, since this is going to be the most important way in which they will impact on SHV. Usually two basic sorts of synergies can be identified: cost savings and income generation.

Cost savings ...

Typically, *acquirers* are best at estimating areas for combined cost savings. It is not our intention here to discuss the various areas of cost synergy that should be looked at; they will vary from industry to industry and according to the strategic reason for acquisition. But there are some key points to be made:

- The process needs to look at both the net present value of synergies available within the target, calculated at the target's WACC, and where relevant within the acquirer, at the acquirer's WACC. They will have to be compared to the cost of any incremental resources needed, along the lines of the VROI calculation shown in Chapter 6.

- It is fundamentally important for the acquiring company to involve operational management in its own relevant division or divisions in arriving at any estimates of likely synergies.

- The estimated timing of the available synergies needs special attention. Here a preliminary assessment of the 'softer' areas of possible integration becomes critical. Culture and organizational match and compatibility of systems and processes will all make a difference to the time in which synergies can be realistically achieved. In other words, you need to consider how soon synergy is possible – and how much. This can have a material bearing on gearing levels and on when a group may be expected to hit a predetermined profitability target.

- Equally, opportunities for outsourcing and the disposal of non-core assets or businesses need to be estimated, together with assumptions on the tax effect of any disposals.

... And income generation

Then comes the more difficult task of assessing the effect of an acquisition on income growth. The easier part will be to estimate the opportunities arising from such aspects as technology transfer and access to the target's distribution channels for the acquirer's products or services and vice versa. But there will be more intangible potential effects to be estimated, such as:

- Loss of income in the target or acquirer from customer overlap (e.g. customers who currently dual source from the acquirer and target – the 'cannibalization' effect).

- Competitor reaction to the acquisition negating some of the assumed synergies.
- Intervention by regulatory or competition agencies.

The effect of these, in the assumptions made both in cost and income synergies, will mean that a variety of sensitivity analyses will need to be run at this stage, in order to arrive at a 'most likely' scenario for preliminary evaluation purposes.

By assessing both the cost savings and the likely income generation effects of a merger on the acquiring and the target firm, you can reach an overall estimate of what sort of value the combined group should be able to achieve, after allowing for the costs of getting there. This *combined value* of the new enterprise should include the 'most likely' value of synergies; added together, as we have said, they should move the share price from C to D in Fig. 8.3.

Financial engineering

You can now make a preliminary assessment of financing alternatives. Some acquirers may have little flexibility in the alternatives available – for example, a high level of existing debt may make financing through equity the only possible strategy. But let us assume here that as an acquirer you have full flexibility between equity and debt. The main constraint might be that debt will become marginally more expensive if it causes your overall debt rating to move into a lower category, and that the risks associated with equity will rise when debt exceeds what the market regards as a sensible level. We also need to consider that additional debt will effectively dilute the claims of the existing shareholders.

Obviously, the main aim will be to finance the acquisition at the lowest appropriate cost of capital, sometimes with the secondary objective of creating a more effective finance structure. For example, the financing plans that British Telecommunications announced in its proposed acquisition of MCI Communications Corporation in November 1996 included a part share, part cash offer coupled with a special dividend to its own shareholders, payable whether or not the transaction proceeded. The intention was that BT, a debt-free company before the acquisition, would quite considerably reduce its overall WACC through this financing arrangement. The effect of this on BT's SHV can be arrived at by substituting the lower WACC rate for the original stand alone value.

Along with tax planning, such financial engineering to maximize the efficiency of a company's post-acquisition structure can be a key part of the transaction value map. The impact of higher gearing arising from additional debt is shown as the highest, far right, box in Fig. 8.3. The share price could then move from point D to point E. We can think of this as the combined 'post-financial engineering' value of the company.

STRIKING A DEAL

Using this analysis we can identify the range within which the acquiring company should bid for the target. You might think that if the cumulative value has risen from A to B in Fig. 8.3, then the acquirer should not pay out resources that would reduce the value of the combined entity back to (or below) the initial level at A. Yet in our example the acquirer is apparently prepared to pay more; for a while at least, he will reduce the net value of his stake to level C. This is done on the apparently reasonable assumption that the acquired company will eventually be worth more to him than it is to its current shareholders on a stand alone basis. So, although the purchaser apparently pays too much for the acquired company, the subsequent gain in value through synergies and other economies of scope means that over time the value of the enterprise will rise from C to D, and as we shall see to point E in the diagram.

Life, however, is not always that simple. Many interested parties will be involved in a transaction of this kind, and a valuation reached by applying a fairly rigorous SHV approach could differ quite substantially from, indeed probably be lower than, alternative techniques. If the target is a public company, for example, the purchase price will almost certainly have to fall within the parameters of the premium the market has come to expect – the 25 to 40 per cent mentioned earlier in this chapter has been a reasonably steady expectation in the USA and UK of late. But at what point within these parameters? Leaving aside for the moment any SHV economics, the answer will depend on whether there is already an apparent bid premium in the share price; whether the approach is likely to be friendly or hostile; the form of consideration (cash, shares or a combination); and an assessment of likely alternative bidders.

If the target is privately held, other considerations apply. You will have to assess how likely it is to be available: a German family-owned company with someone from the next generation earmarked to take over control from the father is unlikely to be available at any price, while a division or subsidiary of a highly leveraged company might well be. But initially the principal consideration will be whether the vendor is likely to seek alternative purchasers if an approach is made, in order to introduce competition into the process.

In assessing the SHV economics of any case, we should assume that there will be competition and consequently, as stated earlier, it must also be assumed that the purchase price will need to reflect the improvements any competent purchaser could bring to the target acquisition.

Next it would be wise, particularly in the case of larger acquisitions where the pool of potential alternative purchasers may be smaller, to ask the question: will any other potential buyer be able to extract a greater level of synergies than has been assumed by the acquirer? Given the time involved in progressing an acquisition, it does not make sense to pursue a transaction that will clearly be of a greater value to a competitor. A good example is the purchase, in the UK in 1996, of Peoples Phone by Vodafone. Peoples Phone, with its 400,000 customers, would have been attractive to most mobile telephone companies. But at least three-quarters of those customers were Vodafone users and as Vodafone's chief executive said at the time 'It was more valuable to us than to anyone else.'

Using the SHV model

In seeking to establish a price at which a transaction can be satisfactorily completed, we think that the SHV approach provides a realistic basis on which to identify what the upper and lower limits to a bid should be. You may as a consequence walk away from many otherwise attractive deals – and your shareholders should thank you for your foresight!

However, you might want to use the model in a different sense to ask a slightly different question, one that is too easily overlooked. Given the likely purchase price, what will its implications be for the acquirer's own SHV development? What sort of performance improvement will you have to achieve in order to justify the bid premium? Are the estimated changes in some of the SHV drivers in any sense plausible? If they are not, are you ready to tell your shareholders not to be too optimistic about the likely outcome? In a very real sense, as we have argued elsewhere in the book, the SHV approach can be a highly useful consistency test against which to measure any number of potential purchase prices.

DOWNSIDE RISKS

As we have already noted, many M&A transactions do not appear to have provided much benefit to the acquirer's shareholders. Why? For an answer, we need to focus on a number of messier and 'softer' issues that can hinder the capture of all the synergies so bravely promised on paper and entered into the valuation calculation. Issues of compatibility – of culture and organization, systems, people and processes – can prove to be an acquisition's undoing. The problem is that these difficulties are frequently under-estimated at the pre-approach stage of a transaction, and do not lend themselves to incorporation in quantitative terms into the modelling process of the combined entity.

In such circumstances, the result can be at best a delay in obtaining the assumed synergy benefits – a key factor in itself in the acquirer's SHV. At worst, the process of integration is so delayed that benefits never accrue and SHV is destroyed. Eventually the acquired company is disposed of – an event that occurred in a high percentage of transactions in the 1980s.

To avoid this sort of risk, you must consider closely how you will implement the changes that will be needed after the merger or acquisition has gone through. In our view this can readily be done at the due diligence stage of the merger process.

Due diligence

Those companies that apply best practice see 'due diligence' as being far more than a quick run through of various legal, regulatory and accountancy issues. Most particularly, they see it as an opportunity to test assumptions made at the assessment stage, both quantitatively (confirming the likely synergies available) and qualitatively (general timing and integration compatibility).

For this purpose you can use the matrix shown in Fig. 8.4 to map the probable speed at which each of the individual synergies assumed can be achieved against the SHV driver impact of each.

This matrix should help you focus your initial integration efforts on synergies that appear in the top right box, as opposed to those less critical to delivering SHV. It should highlight those elements of the integration plan whose delay could destroy all benefits the merger was designed to bring to the acquirer's shareholders.

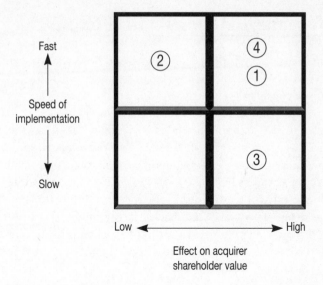

Estimated NPV of synergies

	£ million	
	Target	**Acquirer**
① Head office closure	20	
② Material cost savings	10	10
③ Warehouse combination		30
④ Access to target distribution	40	

Fig. 8.4 Synergy matrix

Practical problems with acquisition models

The risk in applying a structured approach such as the one we have outlined is that the model could be given excessive prominence in the process. It is therefore important to remind all involved that the model is only as good as the assumptions fed into it, and that in the early stages some of these assumptions are by necessity pretty broad. On the other hand, CEOs may see the model as a potential threat to their plans, and regard it as irrelevant when their strategic vision and 'gut feel' is what matters.

A sensible balance lies somewhere in between. The key factor is to revisit the model at all stages of the transaction process and to tie in the underlying assumptions, particularly the key value drivers, with requests for further information at the approach stage and, if discussions proceed thereafter, with the due diligence process as well.

COMMUNICATING TO SHAREHOLDERS

However good your analysis of an acquisition, and however apparently benefi-cial to your SHV, as an acquirer you will gain no advantage if the market is not persuaded of the merits of your case.

The level of information provided in shareholder circulars leaves a lot to be desired in this respect – an opinion echoed by a number of analysts to whom we have spoken. Most circulars provide a relatively brief explanation of the com-mercial rationale for a proposed transaction together with an assessment of the potential effect on earnings per share in the following year, sometimes two. The rest of the document will consist of historical financial information and a mass of procedural detail. This leaves the market largely uninformed as to the eco-nomics from a SHV viewpoint; it is thus left to make up its own mind on the merits of the planned acquisition, and its effect on financing structure.

Track records matter

The acquiring company can certainly make its task easier by clearly articulating the business case for the acquisition, and where possible showing that it already has a good record in managing acquisitions of this type. Make sure this sort of thing is included in a shareholder circular. Managements with a proven track record have a significant advantage in gaining shareholder support.

ScottishPower, for instance, in its 1996 competitive bid for Southern Water in the UK, very much emphasized its experience with a previous acquisition, Manweb, in its shareholder communications – which included the following passages:

> ScottishPower has opportunities to create value for its shareholders from the acquisition of Southern Water which are not available to Southern Electric. Our proposals fully recognise these value opportunities. We are a builder of businesses and have a clearly focused strategy. Our highly successful integra-tion of Manweb proves that our management team has the expertise to reduce costs, improve efficiency and grow revenues. ...
>
> ScottishPower has already announced that it expects to achieve a total of £63 million per annum in cost savings from Manweb. Within the first six months of ownership, the company is ahead of schedule in achieving these sav-ings. The projected savings of £63 million present over 50 per cent of Man-web's controllable cost base.

This was a powerful message which no doubt was a factor in Scottish Power gaining shareholder support.

THE FUTURE

Since we advocate the intelligent application of SHV in financial markets, we believe that there is more scope for applying these techniques in M&A analysis in the future. As we pointed out earlier, this could result in a more 'feet-on-the-ground' attitude to company valuations in both contested and friendly bid situations, as the disadvantages of overpaying for an acquisition become more transparent. Similarly, applying SHV analysis to a given purchase price can be an interesting guide as to what underlying improvements in corporate performance are needed if the combined group is to justify the purchase price. Either way, we think this approach should become more entrenched in the future, just as cash flow valuations have become more common among investment analysts.

SUMMARY

Takeovers, as has often been noted, do not always succeed. Much M&A activity is driven by non-financial considerations, it seems, and potential acquirers can appear to behave in an irrational manner. There is a tendency among M&A transactions to be carried away by the moment and over bid for targets, for which existing methodologies generally fail to establish 'fair' shareholder values. Given this, we have proposed in this chapter a more sensible value-based approach that carefully weighs up the costs. This looks at the initial values of acquirer and target (as far as it is possible to obtain information about the latter); what WACC to use for each; what synergies can be expected in the form of cost savings and income generation; what the final costs will be for advisers, due diligence work, financial engineering and as a result of taking on more debt or creating more equity. By using a transaction value map you can give graphic expression to the likely outcome of a deal and its positive or negative effects on the acquiring company's value. The SHV approach can show what a given purchase price implies in terms of future corporate performance if other goals of SHV creation are to be reached.

For assessing synergies we also recommended a matrix where the strategies most and least likely to improve SHV, and at what speed, could be plotted.

RISING FROM THE ASHES: VALUE RE-CREATION AND SHV

Our economic system requires there to be both winners and losers. When everybody is competing against everybody else, someone is going to come in ahead, and equally someone is going to pull up at the rear of the race. Both are the natural consequences of a system in which risks are taken.

If consistent winners are – as we saw in the previous chapter – in the position of being able to expand their activities, consistent losers may have to consider whether they want to enter the next race at all. This chapter is primarily about the consistent losers, and what might happen to them. We will argue that a SHV approach can be successfully applied in value re-creation situations too – even though in such situations you will have to consider the interests of more parties than simply your shareholders.

All of this means that we will be talking about stakeholders again, and revisiting one of the themes of Chapter 1. This is because when a company is in trouble, it needs to pay close attention to those stakeholders – suppliers, employees and in particular debt holders – who no longer have any incentive to listen to those who nominally represent the shareholders. Frustrated and worried by poor performance, these stakeholders may very well 'take back their marbles' and go off and play with someone else. To avoid such a situation, we will suggest an approach that might succeed in unlocking hitherto untapped sources of value. Let us see how this can be achieved.

STAKES AND SHARES REVISITED

Early in Part I of this book we showed that the longer-term interests of all a company's major stakeholders are similar. All are looking for above average returns – *shareholders* in the form of a good total shareholder return (made up of dividends and capital appreciation); *debt holders* in the form of prompt repayment of principal and interest, so that at the end of the day they make a profit on their loans; *employees* in the form of higher than average wages and salaries and a decent level of job satisfaction; and *customers* and *suppliers* in the form of a steady stream of goods and services either received or sent, at prices and conditions that ensure that they receive good value for the money they have spent. Putting the interests of shareholders centre stage, we have argued, is ultimately the quickest and surest way of satisfying all these constituencies.

But let us look in more detail at these parties, since the more detailed the view, the more disparate the groups will appear. Six distinct interests can be identified: shareholders, debt holders, company management, employees, customers/suppliers, and the community at large. We will consider them in that order.

The shareholders

A company is owned by its shareholders, who provide it with it starting capital. Almost everything a company does is done formally in their name. Their liability is limited to the money put up and converted into shares, and this limits their downside risk, too. The worst that can happen for them is to lose their money. On the other hand, their upside opportunity is virtually unlimited: they participate in gains in asset prices and increases in the intrinsic value or SHV that we have calculated earlier. Although their preferences for receiving their rewards may vary between income and capital gains, their main interest will be in the total shareholder return, a combination of capital appreciation and dividends. As we have said throughout this book, shareholders desire a return at least as great as that obtainable on an investment of similar risk elsewhere in the market.

In the narrow terms of what shareholders are actually entitled to, however, the picture can look a little different. They have a 'right' to a dividend as an income from their shares, subject to management approval. They can ask for their money back when the business is wound up, and they have the power to vote on a board of directors. Their approval for new capital issues is also required. But these powers are really rather remote from a firm's day-to-day operations, and are even more remote from influencing those decisions needed to create SHV.

Indeed, the actual experience of 'traditional' shareholders suggests that their role is frequently even more restricted. As John Plender argues:

> While the property in a company consists of a whole bundle of rights which are spread around the various stakeholders in the business, with the shareholders nominally pre-eminent among them, the reality is the board of directors retains most of the powers of control ... usually associated with ownership, up to the point of hostile takeover.[1]

This means that shareholders mostly delegate their authority and powers to the management team, who make all the operational decisions.

[1] John Plender, *A Stake in the Future* (London: Nicholas Brealey, 1997), pp 134–5.

A short-term bias?

The split between owners and operators has led particularly in the UK and the USA to a hands-off attitude on the part of many institutional shareholders, who typically do not become involved in day-to-day company decision making. What institutional investors always consider is how any one investment is performing relative to others in their portfolio. Poor investment performance will cause many institutions to vote with their feet – to sell their shares in your company and buy those of other better performing companies, perhaps those of your competitors!

Admittedly, this approach is changing very gradually: as we shall see in Chapter 11, investors such as CalPERS in the USA and Mercury Asset Management in the UK are prepared to become more actively involved in management decisions. But this is still relatively unusual. So although formally shareholders have a lot of power invested in them, in general they are poorly placed to exercise it. Indeed, shareholders' claims on company assets are generally last in line in a recovery situation; so before the unmentionable happens, an individual shareholder has every reason to want to be first out through the door.

It is investor mobility, therefore, that acts as an important check on management power. Managements react to this by ensuring their investors are rewarded – action that sometimes leads to the charge of short-termism. In order to appease investors, and particularly those working from an actuarial background, companies are prepared to authorize substantial dividend payments, possibly in excess of what they can realistically afford. In 1994, dividends were over 30 per cent of after tax profits among quoted British non-financial companies, and this pay out rate was even higher in the USA. Companies in Japan and Germany paid out a much lower proportion of after tax profits as dividends. During the 1990s recession in the UK, 60 per cent of companies maintained or increased dividends in the face of falling profits. By contrast, 28 per cent cut dividends, while only 12 per cent of companies missed out a dividend payment. Most evidence suggests that companies have a target pay out ratio for dividends, and aim to maintain this even when business conditions are poor.[2]

Such behaviour may be a case of over-emphasizing SHV, or rather giving it a far too short-term bias. It has given rise to the charge that such generous pay out ratios in the UK, aided and abetted by a tax system that effectively penalizes retained earnings, have sacrificed long-term corporate (shareholder) value creation at the altar of short-term investment portfolio performance. While we would not entirely support this, there is enough substance to it to suggest that tax reforms in the UK, for instance, might even up the balance between distributed and retained earnings.

[2] John Plender, *op. cit.*, pp 58–9.

There is another factor to bear in mind when we consider the shareholders, and before we look at the other stakeholders. This is the simple definition introduced in Chapter 1, where we stated that SHV was corporate value after deducting net debt. It might appear to follow from this definition that the interests of shareholders are inversely related to those of debt holders; *ceteris paribus*, shareholders will appropriate more gains when the debt holder stake is reduced to a minimum. Nevertheless there are occasions when shareholders will prefer additional debt finance to underwrite their expansion plans – as we shall see in the next section.

The debt holders

Debt holders have lent a company money, either in the form of bonds, or as a loan. Lenders have a prior claim on the business's assets, and their main interest is in their lending margin. Able to borrow money themselves at a lower rate (if they are banks), their margin is the difference between the rate at which they lend out and their own refinancing costs. Their primary concern is with default risk, or the risk that they might lose their money. Lenders are quite risk averse, since the loss of just one loan can often wipe out the profits of many other loans.

Under normal circumstances, a company can satisfy the demands of both shareholders and debt holders. All participants will be happy. But a closer examination will reveal that debt holders have a substantially more limited 'stake' in a firm. Shareholders invest because they are looking for substantial upward gains, and they set this against the possible loss of their original stake. Debtholders are much more limited on the upside. All they are ever going to make is the interest margin and their money back. If all goes well, they may then repeat the process, possibly stepping up the amounts involved and so making their profits in that way.

This is what makes debt so attractive for managements, and also for shareholders: it represents a source of finance that has voluntarily limited its participation in the upside. Managements armed with reasonably good inside information as to their likely prospects will see debt as a very useful source of finance. If there is a high probability that an enterprise is going to succeed, and its managers are privy to that information, then it will almost always make sense to raise additional debt, since this will leave more of the gains for shareholders. Furthermore, this same 'information asymmetry' leads to another conclusion: that when a management is not all that sure of the future, it should aim to increase the amount of equity in the business to meet its additional financing needs.

It has long been noted that new equity issues normally form a small proportion of new funds for companies. In the USA rarely more than 10 per cent of total external finance has come from equity, the rest being made up of additional debt or financed from retained earnings.[3] This emphasis on debt as a source of additional finance is entirely consistent with the differences between the amount of information available to managements and what is available to their investors.

Taking this argument further, we can observe that many firms prefer internal finance, and adopt targets for dividend payments which are related to their investment opportunities. These broad strategies at first sight appear to run against the grain of SHV. Dividend payments are necessarily 'sticky' and don't move much year to year; target pay out ratios only gradually change to reflect shifts in investment opportunities. The combination of sticky dividend payments and volatility in cash flows and investment means that there are periods when internal cash flows can exceed the dividend payments; in such circumstances the company will initially build up reserves and pay off debt, and then increase its pay out ratio. When internal cash flows are inadequate to meet dividend payments, many companies will either manage the business for cash (for instance, by selling realizable assets) or raise additional borrowings before lowering its dividend pay out ratio.

All of this suggests a hierarchy in a firm's attitude to finance – a sort of 'pecking order' that puts debt as its first port of call, followed by hybrid or mezzanine debt, with equity as the least preferred part of the financing package. The reason is that managements are keen to protect the interests of existing shareholders, and that additional debt ring fences the gains from any investment and ensures that they flow almost exclusively to shareholders. They share in the upside; debt holders do not.

Debt for equity?

Recovery plans have to take very seriously the interests of debt holders, whose instincts will be to cut their losses and exit from their engagement in a firm as soon as they can. A key issue then may be to persuade debt holders to swap their debt for equity, and so take a longer-term interest in the company.

Recent figures from the UK underline the issue for debt holders. Broadly speaking only 23 per cent of the value of loans was recovered through bankruptcy and insolvency proceedings once a business's difficulties had crystallized into insolvency procedures[4] – which means debt holders have a material interest in trying to make sure none of their companies gets into financial distress.

Management

A company should be run in the interests of its shareholders, who can appoint, or dismiss, its management. Managements are agents appointed to look after shareholder interests. That's the theory – but a considerable body of opinion

[3] See Bealey and Myers, *Principles of Corporate Finance* (1984), Table 14.3 p 291.
[4] SPI Society of Practitioners of Insolvency [SPI], The Sixth Survey of Company Insolvency in the UK, 1995–6.

suggests that in fact management looks after itself first, and the shareholders second. Where there are conflicts of interest, we cannot be sure that management will necessarily put shareholders first. Fragmented shareholdings, or the institutional hands-off policy referred to above, has therefore resulted in considerable power being devolved to management, who can award themselves a substantial part of the value created by the company. To some extent, then, they compete with shareholders, and have to find an acceptable balance between their rewards, the cash the company retains for the future, and what is distributed to shareholders.

It is in recovery situations that the interests of management deviate most substantially from those of the other stakeholders. A company in difficulty is one that has already made a series of poor decisions. In one recent survey (see Fig. 9.1), management failure was cited as not only the second most important primary cause of business failure cited but by far and away the most important secondary factor. And in a 1997 survey of companies that had got into difficulties (but had subsequently achieved some form of turnaround or change of ownership), management foresight or planning issues were regarded as the principal cause of problems by both senior managers and company advisers questioned.[5]

Any management team will probably look for ways to remain in place and participate in a recovery plan. But if the situation already requires the attention of business turnaround specialists, then it is highly likely that the first group to be sacrificed as new policies are introduced and implemented will be the management.

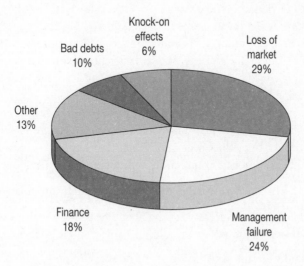

Source: Company Insolvency in the UK: 1995/6, Society of Practitioners of Insolvency 1996.

Fig. 9.1 Why do businesses fail?

[5] Survey by *Business Planning and Research International* for Price Waterhouse.

Employees

Employees represent the core of many businesses and collectively embody the know-how and human capital of the firm. Increasingly, it is a firm's ability to differentiate itself in this area that will create the conditions for successful longer-term survival.

In the short term, the interests of employees are to continue in full-time employment and to receive payment for their services. In the longer term, though, there may be a parting of the ways. In turnaround situations in the UK, typically only 40 per cent of employees remain with the firm once it enters a recovery programme.[6] The issue for the employee will be to balance the probability of a successful future with the firm against an alternative offer elsewhere; meanwhile the management team has to ensure that crucial employees are retained, since their loss can jeopardize a recovery programme.

Customers/suppliers

Customers and suppliers have a 'stake' in a company which can sometimes be supplemented by an actual shareholding, as is often the case in Japan. The extent of this 'stake' is difficult to judge – the depth of stakeholder commitment to the firm (especially customer commitment) will vary industry by industry – but we can identify two more extreme positions where the issues can be clarified. There are some industries where price is the primary determinant of getting business. Price elasticities of demand and switching costs are low, and neither customers nor suppliers have a significant stake in the company. On the other hand there are situations where switching costs and product differentiation are high, while price elasticities of demand are low. It is at times like these that customers and suppliers have significant stakes in the company, and would have a material interest in ensuring its continued survival.

These relationships can be cemented with long-term contracts, and possibly through cross-shareholdings. The stake can sometimes become so high that the customer or supplier buys the other out. When that happens a market transaction is replaced by an internal transaction and the company becomes more vertically integrated.

In recovery situations, it is important that both suppliers and customers are convinced that it is in their interest for the firm that is in difficulties to continue trading. This is easier to do where switching costs are high. A decision by either a supplier or a customer to desert and switch to a competitor can often be the straw that breaks the camel's back. Bearing in mind that around 6 per cent of company failures in the UK arise from the 'knock-on' effects of other compa-

[6] SPI, *op. cit.*

nies' trading difficulties,[7] this is a fate that suppliers and customers need to be persuaded to avoid.

Local community/government

Finally we need to remember the government and the local community or communities in which a company operates. They have a stake, based largely on their role as recipients of tax revenue and providers of infrastructure. In the event of a business failure, they will have to bear the social costs involved in supporting laid off employees, as well as possibly providing support for other companies in the area. Generally speaking, governments and local authorities have more interest in business preservation and continuation than some of the other stakeholders, particularly when the firm in question accounts for a high proportion of total tax revenue.

Even where the fiscal link is less pronounced, at least from the government's point of view, the company will still have legal and social obligations to the local and national community. These extend over a wide range, and include all contracts, support for local initiatives and combined undertakings, as well as compliance with laws on the environment, health and safety.

WHY DO BUSINESSES FAIL?

Clearly, different stakeholders in a company have differing interests, and in the later part of this chapter we will review how these can be integrated to find the best solution to what are difficult business situations. Before doing this, however, let us look more closely at some of the reasons why businesses fail.

As we have seen in Fig. 9.1, the causes of business failure can be broadly categorized. The most common reason given in the case of the UK is that the company has experienced a loss of market – around 30 per cent of all business failures are accounted for this way. This is a shorthand way of saying that the company's information about itself and the market in which it operates has been faulty. It has been caught out by developments, probably unanticipated, that have left it vulnerable to competitors. In more severe cases it could be that the market for this particular specialized good or service has simply dried up. (Although these figures refer specifically to the UK, we think they are reasonably representative for most industrialized economies.)

Although the onset of the crisis may come as a surprise, the underlying situation may well have been affecting the enterprise for a long time before the col-

---

[7] SPI, *op. cit.*

lapse actually came. It was probably the result of weaknesses in strategic thinking, of inefficient operations or of poor marketing. As in Fig. 9.2, the first warning sign is the loss of competitive advantage; this is well on its downward curve
before profits dive and/or costs rise.

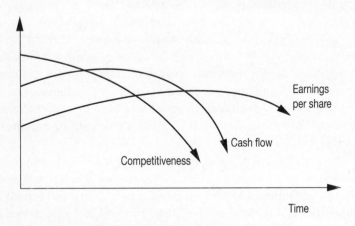

Fig. 9.2 Caught out by a decline in competitiveness

These factors spill over into what is the second most frequently cited primary
cause of business failure, that of management failure. As a 1996 report from the
UK's Society of Practitioners in Insolvency (SPI) says: 'It appears that … businesses still fail because managers lack skill, knowledge, energy or initiative'.

The term management failure (which accounts for around 25 per cent of business failures) covers a multitude of errors, including the sins of over-optimism
and imprudent accounting. But although there are occasions when management
teams or CEOs seem almost wilfully poor, few teams are entirely weak. They
may lack effective leadership and some necessary skills, but in many cases their
real failing is that they lack good information with which to manage. Many of
these factors will be categorized as poor management but such a view could be
too simplistic. A failing business also needs meaningful information just as much
as any other. Indeed, poor management information systems do more serious
damage when companies face crisis and impending failure. In this position there
is little time to take decisions – and good decisions need accurate data. Too often
the available data are old, meaningless or both. A well-designed set of metrics
focused on the important drivers of value (see Chapter 7) would have saved
many a business.

A third factor is unwise acquisitions, or an inappropriate expansion strategy.
This often comes down to a question of timing and finance. With the economy
moving ahead at a good clip, managers may decide to go for an expansion strat-

egy that involves buying up another company. As we have indicated in Chapter 8, a deal might look good on paper but turn out less well when it comes to implementation. Such issues can seriously stretch senior management time, and possibly involve taking on financial commitments in the debt area which leave the new larger company dangerously exposed to an adverse movement in interest rates, or to a slight downturn in the market.

Over-aggressive financing at the end of a business cycle accounts for many company failures. Take a look at the last few leveraged acquisitions in the up phase of an economic cycle, and you will often find the next failures and restructurings as the economy turns down. It is a recurring feature of the business cycle that money chases deals more aggressively as the cycle wears on. A pattern emerges in which market participants will comment on the excessive prices being paid for businesses, while lenders will note that interest rate spreads have vanished. By the time the Indian Summer of the economic boom is reached, industry buyers will often be outbidden by financial buyers, who will focus on growth prospects and efficiency gains to justify a price that seems to exceed the synergy gains that an industry merger might expect.

As the business cycle turns down, or the markets simply fail to deliver forecast growth, cash flow tightens. Business decisions become less than optimal as investment in operating plant or new product development is reined in, and the underlying value of the enterprise is traded in for short-term survival. If management and shareholders do not address such a situation, performance and value will erode. Eventually the business will face a funding crisis and possible failure.

Recent trends in business failures can be seen in Fig.s 9.3 and 9.4, and show very clearly that as the European economies ran out of steam in the mid-1990s, so the number of companies in distress has risen sharply over the levels seen in the boom years of the latter part of the 1980s.

Winning potential

It is our view that many companies in distress still have the potential to become winning players again. Even those that do not have a long-term strategic position may have the capability for improved performance. There are some highly encouraging trends in the UK in this respect; recent figures suggest that nearly a quarter of all businesses that become 'distressed' will be able to make a successful recovery.

Whatever the reason for the distress, to succeed in a recovery, you will need a process for re-creating value, and it is the application of this value process that we will look at in more detail. More extensive application of the value re-creating process will, we think, bring about a further improvement in the proportion of companies able to recover and prosper into the future.

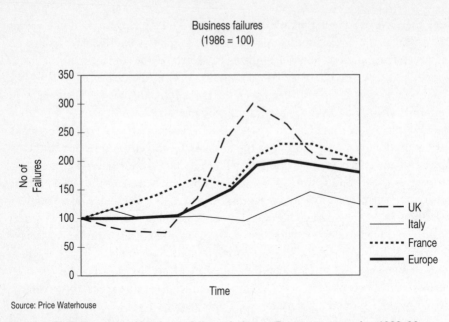

Source: Price Waterhouse

Fig. 9.3 Rising number of business failures in larger European countries 1986–96

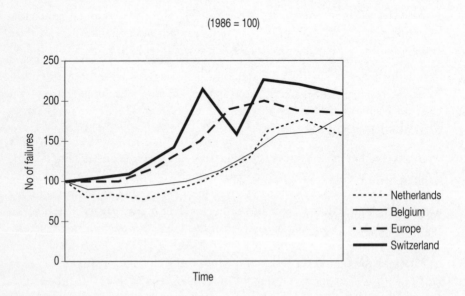

Source: Price Waterhouse

Fig. 9.4 Rising number of business failures in smaller European countries 1986–96

UNLOCKING THE VALUE POTENTIAL OF TROUBLED BUSINESSES

Bearing in mind some of the facts and figures revealed in the previous section, we see considerable scope for developing a coherent approach to restoring, preserving and improving businesses that have fallen on hard times. Quite simply, the SHV approach can offer interesting and relevant insights into the way companies can be turned around. This section describes some aspects of this process.

The SHV approach to businesses or groups of businesses in serious financial difficulty can be very similar to the approach you would take to any operation that is destroying value. There are two important differences, however.

First, there is usually little time available to effect change. More often than not it is a cash crisis that will have brought home to management and stakeholders alike the pressing need for change. The company may be in default of bank covenants, and its borrowing facilities fully drawn with insufficient to meet pending payments. A wave of unpaid trade creditors may be about to break and engulf the business. On the face of it, there will be little or no time to put in place the measures necessary to re-create value in the enterprise. Indeed, at this point the business's whole focus will need to be on survival.

On the other hand, this situation has one real merit. In a time of crisis people – managers, shareholders, employees – will accept the need for change and will probably countenance changes that they would previously have rejected. It is vital to recognize this and take the opportunity to achieve deep-rooted transformation in the business.

Second, the structure of stakeholder interests is always more complex than in a conventional value improvement exercise, because it is not management or shareholders alone who call the shots. Instead, as we have seen, a number of other interests such as bankers, bond holders, trade creditors, employees and even government, all have a legitimate interest in the future of the business. They also have the power, in different degrees, to influence or control the process.

It is important, therefore, for management to be highly proactive in communicating with these diverse groups. They will be impatient for information and progress; much more so than conventional shareholders. They will also be prepared to take unilateral action if they are not comfortable with the steps a company is taking to deal with the crisis.

FOUR OPTIONS FOR GETTING OUT OF TROUBLE

In any but the most hopeless situation, there will be a number of choices open to your business and its stakeholders. Figure 9.5 shows how to set about securing a better understanding of the business and its value potential – after which the four basic options are: to sell the enterprise as it is; to wind down or close it; to go for a short-term performance enhancement strategy; or to undertake a value recovery plan. Fig. 9.6 gives an assessment of these four, ranking them according to their potential for creating value, which, as you can see, corresponds to their risk.

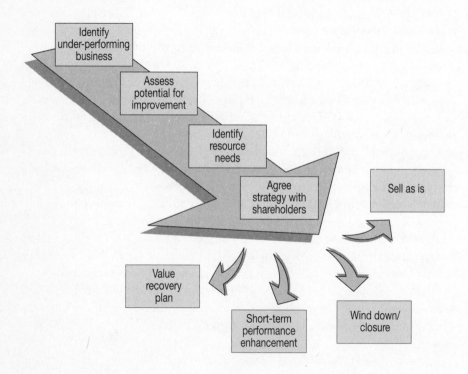

Fig. 9.5 Value regeneration: the diagnostic trail

The first three options

In the case of the first option, to sell the business as quickly as possible – or as quickly as is consistent with obtaining a reasonable value – the lenders may be happy to accept a highly discounted 'fire-sale' price if it secures their position.

Indeed, they may resist any delay or other course of action that offers them only additional risk.

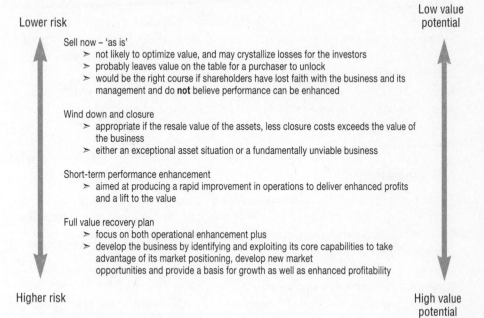

Fig. 9.6 **The value recovery options**

The second option, a liquidation of the assets in the form of a wind down or closure, may be appropriate where the assets have significant value to a purchaser – in effect, a greater value than they have to the business. Such a case might be a factory site with substantial redevelopment value and with an operation which it would be uneconomic to move elsewhere. Although liquidation is not a constructive possibility in terms of business preservation, or from the perspective of the employees, it may be the best strategy for maximizing value – as long as no political intervention is likely, or that legal requirements concerning employee protection are not too stringent.

Some stakeholders may be prepared to take the third option, of short-term performance enhancement. They will accept an element of risk but be unwilling to commit either enough time or money to see through a full turnaround, which they may also see as a high risk choice compared to the relatively quick process of performance improvement leading to a sale. This third option would not involve any repositioning of the business. Rather it focuses only on improving the performance of the existing business, either by raising the effectiveness of business processes or by eliminating poorly performing operations, products or customers.

Allied to tighter controls on working capital and a selective programme of capital expenditure to maintain fabric and competitiveness, such action would enhance performance as measured by the value drivers of operating cash flow and working capital. However, since it will do nothing for business growth prospects, its capacity to enhance value will be limited. It is also a short-term strategy; initial success should not dissuade stakeholders from pushing through a sale when the strategy delivers improved results. To delay may only reveal deeper strategic weaknesses that cannot be resolved in the short term and may undermine selling efforts.

The fourth option

The option of pursuing a full turnaround is the most far reaching approach, with inevitably the highest risk. It will be appropriate in circumstances where the business has a strong strategic position or is capable of achieving one. All phases of the value recovery process set out in Fig. 9.7, from stabilization by way of analysis to strategic repositioning and strengthening of the operations, will be involved. This approach carries with it the greatest upside of the four options, as well as requiring the greatest commitment in time, money and management. Needless to say, the techniques of value management set out in Chapter 7 are as appropriate here as they are in a successful company.

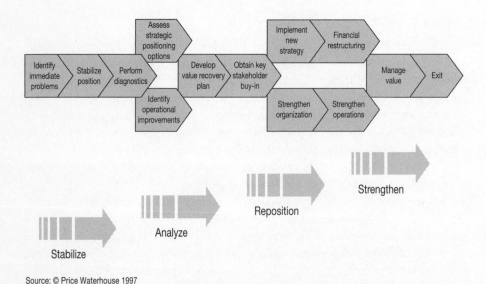

Source: © Price Waterhouse 1997

Fig. 9.7 The value recovery process

Phase one: stabilize

Clearly, the first step in many troubled situations, before attention can be turned to value re-creation, is to stabilize the business. First and foremost, this stabilization phase requires management to become focused on urgency. There is no time for refined analysis: you may have to make some decisions that could damage long-term value. So be it – the alternative is probably failure and unplanned insolvency, which will destroy value much more. The focus in this phase is twofold:

- cash – not maintainable free cash flow, just cash
- reducing the losses and cash demands of the business.

To this end, you must analyze the business quickly to assess how to reschedule payments, reduce working capital needs and renegotiate future commitments. Non-core assets or businesses may have to be sold quickly to generate cash. The purpose of this apparently wild dash for liquidity is to finance the continuing cash demands from trading, and to buy time.

There is no point in regarding these measures as an end in themselves. Their purpose is to eliminate the urgent need for additional cash in the business and to convince sceptical lenders that the business is under control. Only by building credibility in this way can you as management buy time to put in place a proper strategy for re-creating value in the business in the medium to long term. One way of doing this is to consider the following approach, which can quickly identify the main options available to your stakeholders.

Phase two: analyze

If your business cash needs have been stabilized and your important stakeholders have been persuaded to buy into a turnaround process, you will need to analyze the position and prospects of the business. Institute a thorough financial analysis: ask what results the business can achieve, what debt it can support, and what unknown contingencies threaten. There is no point in starting a turnaround only to discover part of the way through the process that additional liabilities are surfacing or resulting from business decisions, and that they cannot be met. Here we would recommend applying many of the techniques we have introduced earlier in this book.

However, your analysis must also focus on the strategic position of the business, and its operational effectiveness. What are its core competencies, and are they being properly exploited? Which products and which customers should be retained and which eliminated? The end product of this diagnostic phase should be a better understanding of the choices open to your business's stakeholders and management – choices that are focused around products or processes offering competitive advantage in selected markets. On this basis, and with the buy-in of key stakeholders, it will be possible to begin rebuilding value. As you will have gathered, such a process will follow the same lines as the ones we proposed in Chapter 7's value transformation programme.

At this stage you should have identified not only the business's value potential and the means of unlocking it, but also what resources you will need. These resources are in time, capital and management. Any programme for rebuilding value has to take all three elements into account. Time may run out, for example, when important contracts expire or losses use up all borrowing facilities. Equally, there is no point in promoting a turnaround plan that will require new capital if the stakeholders are unwilling to commit themselves to it.

The SHV approach, by making several aspects of the situation clearer and more transparent, provides a good informational basis on which to persuade some of the debt holders of the value of holding on – either because they improve the chances of getting their funds back, or because they can convert their limited exposure to the upside into something more concrete by swapping debt for equity. As we have implied earlier, this is not necessarily something the original shareholders will welcome with open arms (since it will dilute their share of any eventual gains). But all the participants will have to be helped to see how, by postponing some of their expected gain, they can nurse the company back to health.

Finally, your management team and its advisers have to be demonstrably capable of delivering the plan. This will often call for additional resources, since the existing management may have already been found wanting. It is unlikely to be able to convince anyone that it can pull off the difficult task of re-creating the value its earlier actions have destroyed. Often a business will be forced into an early sale – and a resulting loss in value – by a lack of realistic alternatives to the current management team. A quick sale may also be unavoidable if the stakeholders are uncomfortable about allowing the time, or putting in the necessary cash, for the business to continue.

Phases 3 and 4: reposition and strengthen

After analysis, the next and most crucial stage will require you to produce a value recovery plan which all major stakeholders must buy in to. Details here will vary with each case, making generalizations difficult, but initially you will have to decide what can be done using existing resources, and what will require additional input from your stakeholders. Once you have acquired time and created a breathing space, it will be up to the new management team, probably aided and strengthened by some outside advisers, to try and produce the tangible new shoots of growth, which will be required if the patience of some of the stakeholders is not to be exhausted.

It is not just the company itself that will face meltdown if things go wrong;

the other stakeholders too are facing the same disaster. But this is a great spur to innovation. Necessity, as they say, is the mother of invention.

A two-part plan: financial restructuring ...

The value plan will need to have two distinct parts. The first will involve some financial restructuring, which means you must take a cool look at your operation from the financing point of view. Any new structure will have to deal with some of the questions of information asymmetry outlined earlier in this chapter. Normally, as we have said, a successful company management will try to bring in more debt when a good outcome is reasonably certain, enabling the upside to be distributed to the shareholders and not to the debt holders. Debt spreads risks, but does not (hopefully) penalize the rewards.

By the same token, a financial restructuring that involves raising more equity is sending out contradictory signals to the market. As arguably the most expensive form of finance in the longer term, equity is something a company will look for only when it knows the outcome of its plans is far from certain. This helps explain why stock prices often fall when a new equity issue is announced – and why existing shareholders are so reluctant to agree to restructuring plans that effectively water down their future returns.

Debt holders too can be faced with unpalatable decisions, especially if they have to convert outstanding loans into equity – in other words, swap a reasonably certain return on debt into much more uncertain equity returns that could stretch into the indefinite future. The existence of a good secondary market for debt can help in allocating the risks and returns involved in debt restructuring.

Once a refinancing package has been agreed, it will be possible to work on the basis of a new target capital structure, and hence a new target WACC. This can then become the new criterion by which to judge whether your new plans are working out or not.

... and reorganization

The financial restructuring package needs to be accompanied by some equally radical measures to strengthen your organization – the second part of your value recovery plan. The options here could include a wholesale replacement of management, a new management structure, and the installation of a new executive remuneration programme that very specifically links rewards to the achievement of several tightly defined targets in the recovery process. You will thus strengthen the operational side of the company and attain improved efficiency levels as a more focused approach replaces earlier and less successful strategies.

By combining a new financial structure with new organizational packages, you will be able to lay down a sound basis for the recovery and recreation of value – very much along the lines described in previous chapters. As the recovery process continues and consolidates, you may ultimately find it possible to find a new purchaser for the company, a purchaser who is willing to pay a good price. We are then taken back into the considerations mentioned in the previous chapter, where we found that it is often the sellers of companies that end up making the greatest profits.

The successful sale of a recovered and preserved company can sometimes be a mouth watering prospect. It is no exaggeration to say that it can ultimately make the trials and tribulations of the recovery process worthwhile – so long as the participants can afford to wait, and so long as the company really has a reasonable prospect of living up to its new promise.

THE VIRTUES OF VALUE RE-CREATION

In troubled business situations, the issues of value management are not different in kind from those facing any business keen to improve its value performance. The potential beneficiaries, however, may be a wider group of stakeholders – some of whom will have to be convinced of the need to work together to build up the value of the enterprise. Not all stakeholders, probably, will have the same appetite and patience for a thorough value recovery effort. In such a situation, you will need to make even more strenuous efforts than usual to communicate your strategy, plans and progress.

The SHV approach we have outlined here is part of a continuum, beginning in Chapter 7, that runs from highly successful groups by way of poor value performers and value destroyers to failing businesses. In all cases this approach is a sound basis for developing strategy and improving performance; indeed, our focus on long-term maintainable free cash flow fits well with the instincts of lenders.

One distinctive feature of troubled situations is the way that an impending failure can inspire change and overcome a management's innate conservatism. Radical change becomes practicable, while a more stable situation would have permitted inertia. This is the key to much of the improvement that can be wrought in a crisis situation.

A value-oriented approach such as that embodied in the recovery process of Fig. 9.7 is a useful tool for ensuring that all stakeholders – employees and creditors as well as shareholders – buy in to the appropriate recovery plan. It combines the pressing need for change and urgent action with a necessary focus on longer-term value generation. It does not prescribe one right way forward. Rather it encourages a proper exploration of the options and the risks that accompany each – providing a basis for taking decisions that optimize the value of a business.

SUMMARY

Our consideration of the uses of SHV analysis for the value recovery process began by going back to the division of interests between shareholders and other stakeholders. When a company is failing, the interests of these others, especially debt holders, come to the fore, and equity is low down in the pecking order. In this situation, a management must strive to communicate as much information as it can to all parties – employees, customers, suppliers, the community at large as well as debt holders and shareholders. After looking at the causes of business failure, we turned to a consideration of the ways that a company can be turned around. There are four options for getting out of trouble: of these, only the fourth, a full recovery plan, will make substantial use of SHV analysis. Such a plan would have, again, four phases: stabilization, analysis, repositioning and strengthening – and ultimately this strength would be based on a combination of financial restructuring and a new organizational package. But as we noted, crisis situations are also moments of opportunity, when doing nothing is not an option and innovation is more likely to be on the agenda.

PART

3

SHV IN
ACTION

SECTOR
APPEAL

L et us begin to narrow our focus. We have backed up our claim that the SHV approach has a wide application by showing, in the three chapters of Part 2, how it can be used not only in normal circumstances but also in mergers and acquisitions and business turnaround situations. Now we are going to move from a generic, global way of looking at companies to a more detailed examination of some of the variety of industries and sectors that make up a modern economy.

This chapter, then, reveals a few aspects of the thinking that has been going on at Price Waterhouse on the question of applying SHV to concrete cases. No two companies are the same, of course, but by developing models for particular sectors such as utilities or insurance, we can identify common factors and the relevant value drivers that must feature in any SHV analysis of a company in that sector.

SHV is not, in our view, a 'one size fits all' solution to the question of performance management. Unlike some SHV advocates, we will argue that there are occasions when the basic approach requires substantial revisions and adaptations; your company may not be best advised to take just any off the shelf value-based management solution and apply it automatically. In areas such as telecommunications, pharmaceuticals, oil and high technology – areas that we will deal with below – we have to look carefully at whether and how the seven value drivers might need to be modified. There are also areas not normally associated with SHV, for instance finance, where we believe the approach can be fruitfully applied. These too we will deal with below.

CASH FLOW AND THE COST OF CAPITAL

Back to definitions

Before plunging into the details, it is worth while pausing to consider the areas where it might be necessary to adapt the basic SHV approach. In the normal model, three main areas have to be considered. These are:

- Cash flow forecasts – is it practical to define a free cash flow number?

- The cost of capital – will adjustments need to be made here?
- Residual value calculations – what assumptions lie behind them?

Defining cash flow

Typically we talk about free cash flow, defined as net operating profits after tax minus changes in fixed investment and in working capital. Depreciation can be either included in its entirety in the cash flow definition, or the replacement part of depreciation can be subtracted from the free cash flow, on the grounds that it is a necessary expense required to maintain the business. In most businesses this is not a big problem, but it does become more important in capital-intensive industries. Here depreciation charges – which are not cash flow items – can substantially boost the EBITDA figure and so make the cash flow larger than would be the case with other earnings-based measures.

Of course it may be reasonable to argue that the depreciation charge is not available for distribution, and therefore should not be counted as being part of the free cash flow. One sector where this is a particular issue is the utility industry, where large investment programmes are required over many years. The size of depreciation allowances, which are tax deductible, can become important. Tax relief on depreciation will lower the effective rate of taxation, and so add to the pool of funds theoretically available to be distributed to shareholders. Which means that EBITDA figures are going to be a lot bigger than EPS-based figures, and the SHV approach will tend to flatter performance in this sector.

Equally, in the financial services sector it can be quite difficult to find a relevant cash flow measure. Large flows of funds occur, but a distinction has to be made between funds that belong the customers – which for sake of argument can simply 'walk out of the door' – and funds that truly belong to the shareholders. SHV analysis requires a clear understanding of the property rights embodied in your company; in the financial services sector it helps to be absolutely clear about what belongs to whom.

The situation can be further confused in this sector by the existence of flows between the profit and loss and balance sheet for all sorts of sensible precautionary reasons. A definition of a free cash flow has to ensure that there is no double counting; to this end it is useful to try to ring fence the enterprise, and like a customs and immigration officer ensure that you only count what goes through this border, ignoring what goes on inside.

Intangible assets and the cost of capital

Even though we dealt with the cost of capital in Chapter 3, there are other aspects that we as SHV practitioners may need to consider. Cost of capital calculations depend crucially on being able to determine accurately the amounts of capital involved in a business. Not only does this require a clear view on current equity and debt, but also how they are going to evolve over time. It is a far from straightforward matter to be able to forecast balance sheets – which is what is required here.

There are further difficulties, of which one of the most important is the value placed on a company's assets. Traditional accounting measures are concerned almost entirely with book values; SHV, however, requires a market value approach, or what can be called a mark to market system. In this approach, you may need to know what the economically useful lives of assets are, a point we raised earlier in Chapter 6.

The value of the assets also has to be adjusted for various intangible items. Here it is helpful to think of four basic types of intangible assets:

- innovation capital
- structural capital
- market capital
- goodwill.

The question of valuing these assets is starting to become a serious macro economic issue. Intangible assets not only form a significant part of total investment, but there is evidence that, as Fig. 10.1 shows, investment in intangible assets is growing faster than for fixed assets. (This point is starting to worry government statisticians.)

How can intangible assets be measured? SHV analysis takes account of the variety of approaches to answering this question, and sets reasonably clear priorities. With *innovation capital*, for instance, current accounting practice is to expense these items. A SHV approach would ideally like to see R&D capitalized, and so included in the company's asset base. Current accounting practice overlooks innovation capital entirely; as a result there are often considerable discrepancies between the book and market value of companies. Recent work by Lev and Sougiannis[1] shows statistically significant and economically meaningful relationships between R&D and subsequent cash flows, and suggests that stock markets take implicit account of R&D investments, regardless of whether they are reported formally in financial statements.

It is important, then, to make adjustments in the balance sheet to reflect investments in R&D assets. Other adjustments need to be made, too, for *structural capital*. Under this heading come items like intellectual capital and knowledge assets. Here, some credit should be given for organizational coherence and

[1] Lev, B.L. and Sougiannis, T. 'The capitalization, amortization and value of R&D', *Journal of Accounting and Economics*. 21 (1996) pp. 107–138.

flexibility – the ability of an enterprise to adapt successfully to changes in circumstances. Elements such as workforce loyalty and skills (human capital) should have a value put on them, too.

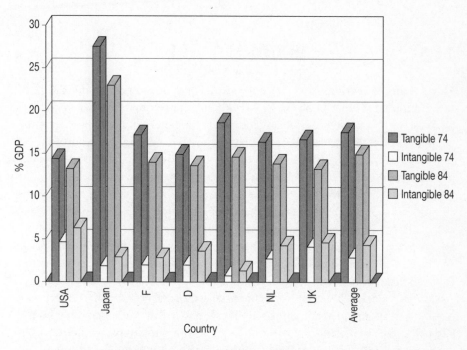

Source: OECD (1992) p 113.[2] Tangible investment: investment in machinery, equipment and non-residential structures. Intangible investments on R&D, advertising and software (training and organizational change not included.)

Fig. 10.1 Tangible and intangible investments

Market capital, our third intangible, consists of established brands, trademarks and other 'mastheads' such as magazine titles in publishing. As useful assets contributing to the success of a company, these undoubtedly have an economic value. Increasingly brands are bought, sold, licensed and managed in just the same way as other businesses. Just like their tangible counterparts, intangible assets need to show a satisfactory rate of return.

Although there are measurement difficulties, we think it is possible to identify brands that are sustainable business assets, often reinforced by high levels of advertising spending. Brand valuation is a controversial issue in mainstream accounting, but in the context of SHV we think it is a useful way of arriving at an improved estimate of an enterprise's assets involved in the business.

2 *Technology and the Economy – The Key Relationship*s. Report on the Technology/Economy Programme (Paris: OECD, 1992).

149

Finally, *goodwill* also needs to be accounted for properly. Here we have sympathy for the way it is treated by US GAAP, where it has to be capitalized. The US rules place a burden on companies to show a return on goodwill above their cost of capital for up to 40 years.

RESIDUAL VALUE

Calculations of residual value are normally carried out to give an indication of the continuing value of a business. As with any approximation, they work better in some circumstances than in others. Our experience of applying SHV includes several industries where special treatment is needed. In resource industries, for instance, particularly oil and gas, we might specifically model a company's value on the expected lifetime of its oilfields, insofar as it is known. But where this remains too imprecise, we can simply make certain assumptions about the discovery of new resources and the depletion of existing ones to work out a life expectation for their given resources. Current behaviour, possibly informed by the company's past record of discovering new resources (and being profligate with those it has), will create an amended residual value, which could vary significantly between companies.

Similar concerns can arise in the financial sector, where for some enterprises income has an annuity type of profile. However, it will still be possible on the basis of today's activities, and with the help of a few simplifying assumptions, to get an idea of the potential stored up business within the firm. Life insurance, an important part of the insurance industry, falls into this category.

Special treatment will also be needed for new start-up companies, often in the high technology sector. Here, short product cycles mean that cash flow forecasts, which in any case are highly uncertain, are also very short – throwing the burden of any valuation heavily onto the residual value estimate. Later in this chapter, we will explore a methodology that offers a solution to this difficulty, and possibly points to one way in which SHV models might move in the future.

We will now turn to particulars. In this chapter's survey of the application of SHV to a selection of sectors we start with finance, where we will look at models that have already proved useful for the banking, insurance and fund management sectors. We will then move on to high technology and pharmaceuticals – industries characterized by fast technical change – before turning to the oil and gas sector. Finally we will examine two industries that share recent experience of privatization and deregulation: the telecommunications and utilities industries.

FINANCIAL SERVICES

An under-performing area

One would have thought that the financial services sector would be more familiar with SHV issues than any other. Indeed, it is – but it is almost entirely with
other people's SHV, and relatively rarely its own, that it concerns itself. The
complications and special treatment that financial services require frequently
lead managements to conclude that somehow their sector marches to a different
drum from the rest of the world, and therefore it should not concern itself
unduly with SHV analysis.

Times are changing, however, and as Figs. 10.2 and 10.3 show, both banking
and insurance have significantly under-performed in European stock markets
for several years. Indeed, they have been the worst performing sectors in the
entire stock market. And although the picture in the USA is better, that has only
come about after several years of very poor performance during the last US
recession at the beginning of the 1990s.

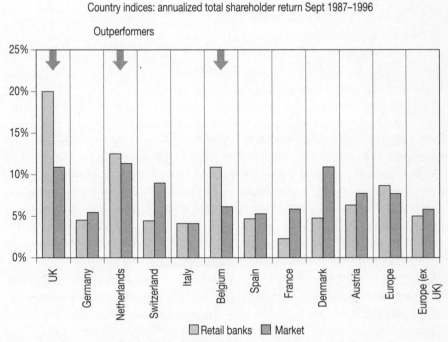

Country indices: annualized total shareholder return Sept 1987–1996

Annualized TSE over 10 years in local currency with dividends reinvested
Source: Datastream

Fig. 10.2 Banking sector TSR in Europe

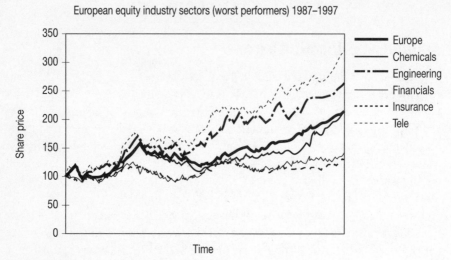

European equity industry sectors (worst performers) 1987–1997

Legend:
— Europe
— Chemicals
—·— Engineering
— Financials
······ Insurance
------ Tele

Fig. 10.3 European TSR by sector 1987–1997

You will recall that we have referred to one financial institution, Lloyds Bank, that has performed outstandingly in SHV terms, and has adopted a strategy that over several years has paid off handsomely. This is to some extent an exception in its field – one organization that has probably pioneered a process that others will have to follow.

So let us now take a look in more detail at how SHV methodology can be applied to the financial sector.

Banking

Our banking model lays out a series of macro level value drivers, and estimates the value of the bank on a free cash flow basis. It can also show the sensitivity of the bank's value to changes in the underlying value drivers. In addition to this it contains benchmarking information so that performance relative to competitors can be established. Like all SHV models, it is forward looking and relates forecast cash flows to current market capitalization, using publicly available information to arrive at free cash flow figures.[3] Initially, it can be based on a relatively restricted amount of external information, but if internal information is available, we can develop the model in much greater detail – but still along the same lines as described here.[4]

---

[3] Free cash flow in a financial institution can be thought of as the dividend paying capacity of the business. This is not the same as cash flow in an accounting sense. The logic for this approach is that banks have specific regulatory capital requirements, and banks cannot, except with special permission, issue dividends to the extent that capital is reduced.

[4] The current version of the model is designed to operate based on the standard format published by IBCA for over 8000 banks worldwide. Previous versions were based on Bloomberg data.

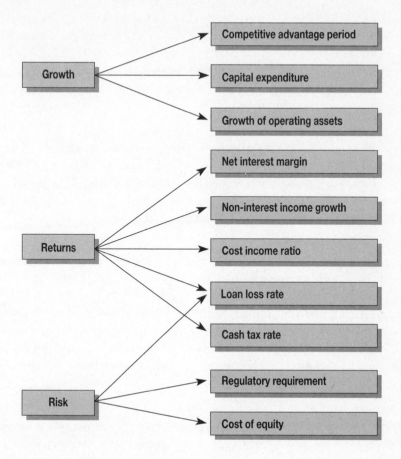

Fig. 10.4 Drivers of SHV for a bank

As Figure 10.4 shows, there are ten key value drivers of SHV for a bank proposed in this model, and these ten can be linked to the familiar three generic value drivers of growth, returns and risk. At the risk of going into technicalities, let us look at the ten drivers.

What the value drivers mean ...

Competitive advantage period

This is the period over which the bank is expected to earn an operating return (net operating profit less tax) in excess of the cost of capital (total economic capital employed times the cost of capital). It is clearly difficult to estimate. The quantitative approach to estimating it could be to calculate the average duration of a bank's assets as a measure of 'locked in' value. A qualitative alternative would be to take a view of how sustainable the bank's competitive advantages are in the marketplace, and base a figure on that – we suggest three to five years,

153

given that banking products are typically easy for competitors to duplicate. Free cash flows are then adjusted to mimic the end of the growth duration period; capital expenditure reverts to maintenance capital expenditure only (default of 75 per cent) to reflect the cessation of new investment as no positive NPV projects exist. Furthermore, growth of operating assets and operating income reverts to a long-term inflation rate.

Capital expenditure

This is the amount spent in the year on new fixed assets, net of disposals. All capital expenditure is immediately charged to the equity holders. We therefore assume that there is an economic equivalence between funding capital expenditure completely from equity, and funding it from both equity and liabilities and then repaying the liabilities as the asset depreciates.

Growth in operating assets

Operating assets are made up of loans and other earning assets. Other earning assets include such items as short-term deposits, loans to banks, short-term investments, government securities, and long positions in securities. A forecast net interest margin on operating assets is used to calculate a forecast for net interest income. Changes in the overall level of operating assets are not considered an equity cash flow item since these are customer cash flows which are financed by depositors. This assumption is summarized by the maxim 'every loan creates a deposit'.[5]

Net interest margin

By this we mean net interest income as a percentage of operating assets. It is used as a proxy for the net interest cash flow margin from the operating asset portfolio. It is often pointed out that interest income includes a large accrued interest component and hence is not a cash flow measure. For our purposes it is reasonable to assume that for a large portfolio of loans with staggered maturities, accrued interest will be a good measure of interest cash flow.

Non-interest income growth

Non-interest income is made up of such items as fees, commissions and trading income. It is forecast using a growth projection. An alternative would be to use a proportion of total income.[6] We also separate out trading income from fee and commission income where we can.

Cost income ratio

The cost income ratio is a measure of the percentage of total income required to cover cash expenses. The cash expenses include depreciation, since this is a

---

5 Consider a simple example of a customer taking a loan for £100 on the same day that another two customers deposit £25 each. The £50 in total new deposits goes towards funding the loan, with the shortfall made up by a wholesale deposit.

6 W D Miller, *Commercial Bank Valuation* (John Wiley & Sons, 1995).

commonly quoted and recognizable ratio. Depreciation is added back in the FCF model.

Loan loss rate

Loan loss provisions are used as a proxy for the cash flow implications of non-performing assets. Once a default is incurred, the bank must repay the lenders, but receives less than the full amount of cash from the borrowers, and thus suffers a cash outflow. This effectively transfers the financing of the dud loan from liabilities to capital (reflected by a charge to the profit and loss account, which reduces shareholders' equity), and is effective as soon as the provision is made, not on the maturity of the loan.[7]

Cash tax rate

This is the actual cash tax paid in the accounting period and normally relates to the previous year of trading. When this figure is unavailable, accounting tax net of movements in deferred taxes can be taken as a proxy. If the cash tax figure is available, then the value driver should be expressed as a percentage of earnings before depreciation and amortization in the previous year.

Regulatory requirement

The regulatory capital requirement for banks and other financial institutions means that cash flows are withheld from shareholders in order to maintain capital adequacy. Our SHV banking model calculates the free cash flow implications of capital adequacy as a function of the risk-weighted assets and targets for the tier one[8] capital and total capital ratios.

Cost of equity

The cost of equity is calculated using the Capital Asset Pricing Model (CAPM) discussed in Part 1. We only look at the cost of equity, the return to shareholders, and not at the return to all asset holders. This is a complex exercise since 'debt' for a bank is similar to working capital for other enterprises. We exclude debt from our analysis here.

... and how to use them

Utilizing these ten drivers, we can then put together a free cash flow forecast model for a bank, as in the example – a simplified view – shown below as Fig. 10.5. While it may look easy, it can be deceptively so. The derivation of some of the forecasts, and the links between some of the figures, is more complex than represented here. You will need a good understanding of banks and their finances, aided by the interpretation of sector experts well informed about current and future developments.

---

[7] See C Madden, *Managing Bank Capital* (Wiley 1996).

[8] Tier one capital capital varies from country to country, but in general it will be made up of equity capital and reserves.

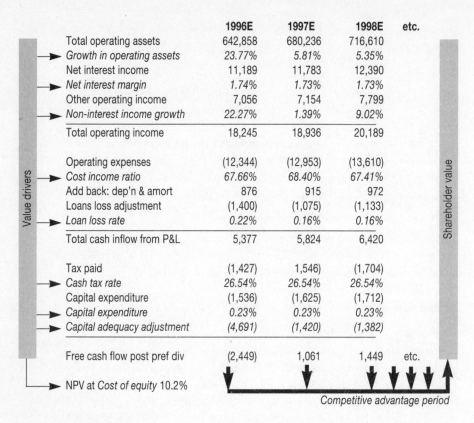

	1996E	1997E	1998E	etc.
Total operating assets	642,858	680,236	716,610	
Growth in operating assets	*23.77%*	*5.81%*	*5.35%*	
Net interest income	11,189	11,783	12,390	
Net interest margin	*1.74%*	*1.73%*	*1.73%*	
Other operating income	7,056	7,154	7,799	
Non-interest income growth	*22.27%*	*1.39%*	*9.02%*	
Total operating income	18,245	18,936	20,189	
Operating expenses	(12,344)	(12,953)	(13,610)	
Cost income ratio	*67.66%*	*68.40%*	*67.41%*	
Add back: dep'n & amort	876	915	972	
Loans loss adjustment	(1,400)	(1,075)	(1,133)	
Loan loss rate	*0.22%*	*0.16%*	*0.16%*	
Total cash inflow from P&L	5,377	5,824	6,420	
Tax paid	(1,427)	1,546)	(1,704)	
Cash tax rate	*26.54%*	*26.54%*	*26.54%*	
Capital expenditure	(1,536)	(1,625)	(1,712)	
Capital expenditure	*0.23%*	*0.23%*	*0.23%*	
Capital adequacy adjustment	*(4,691)*	*(1,420)*	*(1,382)*	
Free cash flow post pref div	(2,449)	1,061	1,449	etc.
NPV at *Cost of equity* 10.2%				

Value drivers · *Shareholder value* · *Competitive advantage period*

Fig. 10.5 Banking model

How does the banking model differ from other sector models? The most significant difference is in the treatment of fixed assets and in the capital adequacy adjustment. A fixed asset account is maintained throughout the forecast horizon based on capital expenditure levels and the rate of depreciation of fixed assets. As Fig. 10.5 shows, the depreciation charge is added back to the free cash flow[9] and capital expenditures are deducted (based on a percentage of operating assets). After the growth duration period, the level of capital expenditure is adjusted to maintenance capital expenditure.

The capital adequacy adjustment is also a special feature of our model, and underlines the point (often neglected by the banks themselves) that there is no such thing as a free lunch. Growing the balance sheet involves ensuring that there are adequate reserves to meet regulatory requirements.

These are not easy to calculate ex ante using external information, but let us assume the bank has target tier one and total capital ratios, and that these targets will be achieved. The bank is then assumed to move, as if in a straight line,

---

[9] Depreciation is treated explicitly in this manner to illustrate its non-cash nature, but also to provide a common definition for the cost income ratio.

from its current capital levels to its targets over the periods specified. Using forecasts for the future risk weighting of assets, we can then infer the amount of tier one and tier two[10] capital from the target ratios and the level of risk-weighted assets. In our view, 'excess reserving' can be treated as a potential reduction of funds available to shareholders for distribution.

In arriving at the forecasts, and in understanding the interrelationship between the variables in the model, some points need to be carefully considered:

- Bank profits from inter-mediation are affected by the structure of their assets and liabilities and the underlying volatility of interest rates.

- Funding long-term assets with short-term liabilities will earn a greater spread in the forward part of the loan when mismatch risk is greatest (known as 'riding the yield curve'). Further, the 'endowment effect' of retail deposits enables banks to widen net interest margins during periods of high interest rates. These factors make it difficult to forecast future income from historic performance.

- Using the cost of equity to discount post-interest free cash flows heightens the sensitivity of this key value driver. This 'equity' approach is necessary to reflect the fact that value can be created on the liabilities side of the balance sheet.

- The stringency with which BIS capital adequacy guidelines are enforced varies between countries. The actual risk weighting mix can also vary sharply from year to year. Complex and changing regulations affect SHV.

- Off balance sheet activity affects SHV and is difficult to forecast.

Even though a model of this kind is surrounded by many simplifying assumptions, we have found it helpful in examining many of the underlying problems of banks and identifying weaknesses. More importantly, when this SHV analysis is combined with a more detailed look at items like value at risk, and risk-adjusted performance measures, we have been able to put together a multi-dimensional diagnostic tool that provides very useful insights into the banking business.

Insurance

From mystification to greater transparency

The insurance sector too is facing major challenges, not the least because recent stock market performance has been less than impressive. Competition for busi-

---

[10] Tier two capital mainly consists of subordinated debt, perpetual preferred stock and long-term loan capital. There are many additional features concerning debt ratings, pre-financing costs, and success resting which, while important, lie outside the model in its current form.

ness is increasing as a result of the deregulation and the crossover into the insurance market of non-traditional providers such as bancassurers, who often have a captive customer base. There is also some convergence taking place, with long-term savings plans operated outside the industry competing with conventional life assurance schemes. The increasing sophistication of customers has sharpened the focus on value creation. Evidence of these changes and challenges comes in the form of a wave of mergers among UK insurance companies (e.g. Royal Sun, Axa UAP).

Financial reporting in the insurance industry is based on the historical development of regulation, financial reporting standards, GAAP, and classical business management and control. Actuarial influences play their part, too. None of this sits easily with SHV.

The operational side of the business has timing complications which are amplified by the need for an effective investment strategy, which requires a long-term perspective. It also makes a difference what type of insurance company is being analyzed. In a 'vertically integrated' composite insurer that controls its own distribution network, additional life policies result in an inflow of front-loaded fees and commissions which are retained within the company. There is thus an incentive to write new business in the short term, even if its profitability later on is questionable.

On the other hand, in a more decentralized insurance group that does not have its own distribution system, the bottom line on writing new business might look rather different. The profitability of newly acquired life business might be negative initially, since commissions to the distributor or sales force are often higher than the premium, and hence the incentive to write new business is rather low, even though its longer-term profitability might be quite high.

Internal management information, then, will not always be sufficient to strike a balance over time that will result in decisions aligned with SHV creation. From outside a company, it is even more difficult to extract meaningful information on its product mix and therefore on the cash flow implications. With such information rarely in the public domain, it is no surprise that the sector is so poorly understood by financial analysts, who are often reduced to recommending insurance stocks entirely on their dividend-creating properties, with little thought to longer-term capital gains

Cash flow basics

Although they are complex, at the end of the day insurance companies are still businesses operating under the same set of conditions as everyone else. They too have to show gains to their investors, and they too will come under the scrutiny of the markets. The model we have developed for the insurance industry therefore follows the basic pattern, where SHV is calculated as business value plus net book value of investments minus debt, where:

$$\text{Business value} = \frac{\text{Insurance cash flows}}{\text{WACC}} + \text{Residual value}$$

There are three basic functions performed by insurance companies, each of which generates its own distinctive kind of cash flows: *Risk cash flows* result from their core business and relate to the evaluation, acceptance and spread of risks. *Investment cash flows* are generated when they act as a financial intermediaries or investment managers. And *service cash flows* occur when they deliver administrative and other services, including for instance risk and investment-related services, for captives. It is also useful to distinguish between the two branches of insurance, general and life.

General insurance

By this is meant insurance for property, theft, fire and other such events. It is generally taken out by a customer for several years. In looking at general insurance, we need first to define an operating cash flow as shown in Fig. 10.6.

Gross premiums written

↓ *less*

Reinsurance

↓ *equals*

Net premiums written

↓ *plus*

Investment income

↓ *less*

Expenses

↓ *equals*

Profits before tax

↓ *less*

Capex

↓ *less*

Cash tax

↓ *less*

Δ *In working capital*

↓ *less*

Solvency requirement

↓ *less*

Claims

↓ *equals*

INSURANCE
CASH FLOW

Fig. 10.6 General insurance cash flow

Investment income belongs entirely to the shareholders in the general insurance industry, and hence should be added to the cash flows. The official solvency requirements are not particularly exacting, even under EU requirements, and most companies hold much larger reserves. As with the banking sector, we can make good estimates of future solvency requirements in the industry.

Investment assets only enter the picture in our model as part of the cash and other financial assets the insurance company has on its books, at market values, and at the start of the forecast period. Since by definition these assets will only grow by whatever the equity market risk premium is, they cannot add to SHV. Some adjustments may have to be made where new business is gained, resulting in more money to invest. As for the cost of capital, in general insurance it is treated in the same way as for other companies, following standard CAPM practice.

There are other value drivers over and above the usual ones that are peculiar to insurance. These include the volume of new business, the ratio of the business retained by the company (related to the importance of reinsurance), as well as factors contributing to claims and losses. They are all to be seen in Fig. 10.7, which is an example of sensitivity analysis in the usual manner (compare Fig. 5.2 in Part 1) applied to insurance.

Life insurance

The subject of life insurance is a complex one, but a simplified view can be seen in Fig. 10.8. It all comes down to 'property rights' – or who at the end of the day owns any surpluses earned on investments but not contractually promised to the client. In our view, life insurance is unlikely to generate much in the way of additional returns to shareholders. In cases where the policy holder obtains what he or she was promised, then there is nothing left over to shareholders. The situation is more interesting when achieved investment performance differs from the promised sum. Where it is less, then the company and its shareholders have a contractual obligation to meet the promised payment, probably out of reserves. Where the sum promised is less than the investment performance achieved, then the difference will accrue to the shareholders. This simple principle highlights the crucial role that the question of property rights plays in understanding how to raise SHV performance in the insurance industry.

% change in market cap. based on a 10% relative improvement on each value driver

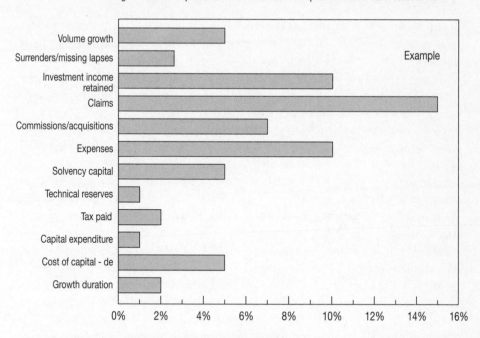

Fig. 10.7 Sensitivity analysis for insurance companies

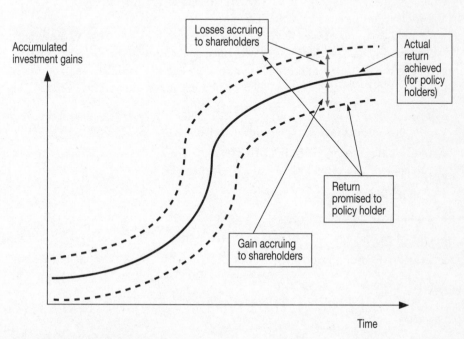

Fig. 10.8 SHV and life insurance

Fund management

The final area in the financial services sector we want to feature is the investment management industry. Curiously, it seems that one of the last things on the minds of fund managers is looking after their own SHV, rather than that of their customers. Where else do you find the strange situation in which a sector's SHV rises faster than the value of a client's money; where a company's own SHV appears disconnected from what it actually does?

Shares in fund management companies prosper in bull markets and under-perform in bear markets. Like the tides, managers think there is little they can do to affect this 'natural' state of affairs – a state all the more alarming when you realize that many banks and insurance companies see expansion into the fund management business as being very desirable in its own right. It will, they think, provide a stable earnings base, just as other parts of their businesses become more volatile.

Publicly quoted fund managers in the UK show strikingly different total shareholder returns. The most impressive return was produced by Perpetual plc, showing a 1731 per cent total shareholder return over the last five years. Other fund managers experienced rather less impressive returns of around 150 per cent over the same period, thus under-performing the FTSE 100. As Fig. 10.9 shows, insurance companies having internal asset management groups per-formed significantly worse than the rest. Figures like these show very clearly that while some managements have very much had their eye on the ball, others' attention seems to have been wandering.

At Price Waterhouse we have begun to look more closely at how fund man-agers actually manage their businesses, once again applying the insights of SHV theory to the industry. There are, we have concluded, seven drivers that greatly influence SHV and which have been combined in a 'Fundbuilder' model. The seven are:

- commission income/average funds under management (FUM)
- funds under management (FUM) growth (average)
- EBITDA margins
- cash tax rate
- capital expendiditure to sales
- cost of capital
- growth duration period

Let us take these one at a time.

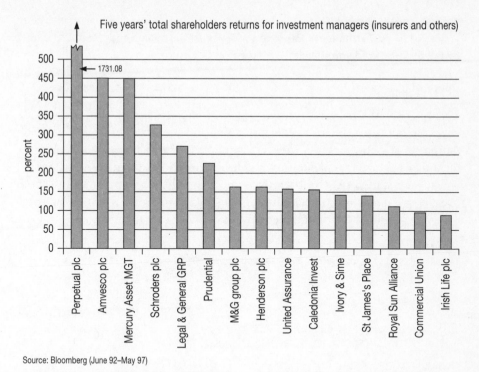

Five years' total shareholders returns for investment managers (insurers and others)

Source: Bloomberg (June 92–May 97)

Fig 10.9 Fund managers' value drivers

Income/average funds under management (FUM)

This gives an indication of how successful a business is in concentrating on activities with reasonable returns. More detailed analysis can show how this differs across asset classes, type of customer and sometimes by geography and market. Although there are different legal compliance costs, the fact remains that there are significant variations in the overall gross margins earned in the industry. While for example retail and wholesale fund management may appear to be similar types of business, managements must understand that the one may be inherently more profitable than the other. In the interests of SHV, choices may very well need to be made.

FUM growth

This is a key driver for the business, since it largely defines the gross income created. Distinctions have to be made between the change in value of the existing funds and the value of new funds and mandates won. FUM growth will also be a function of the firm's perceived success in managing customers' money relative to the competition. These various effects need to be carefully separated out, since better performance resulting from good macro market conditions should

163

be distinguished from better performance resulting from direct management action. SHV performance is improved when both the macro and the micro environments are performing well.

EBITDA margins

This refers to the margin earned by the firm after deducting all its costs and expenses, but before interest tax, depreciation and amortization. It gives a broad indication of a company's efficiency. Figure 10.10 shows that while the investment management companies surveyed have been successful in pushing up revenues, their staff costs have been rising more rapidly, suggesting that EBITDA margins are under pressure. Managing the EBITDA margin is something that companies in the sector find rather hard to do, necessary though it is.

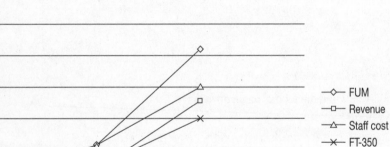

FUM, revenues and staff costs of participants in management survey (95–97) versus FTSE – actuaries

Fig. 10.10 Fund management and other companies

Cash tax rates

This represents a deduction from free cash flow, and varies from company to company in the sector.

Capital expenditure

This is often thought of as small beer, since the numbers are so often dwarfed by others, such as the funds under management. But capital expenditure (capex) can be a surprisingly large drain on company resources; there are very real questions relating to the efficiency with which it is spent. Fund management groups spend large sums on items such as information technology, back office systems and the like, not all of which feeds through to the bottom line in terms of improved performance.

Cost of capital

Most fund managers are effectively debt free, so that this reduces to the cost of equity. This is a more demanding hurdle rate than some realize, especially if returns are being earned in the fixed income markets.

Growth duration period

The period over which a fund management company is expected to create SHV by having a return on capital greater than the cost of capital can in this industry be relatively short, and it is difficult for companies to maintain a sustained competitive advantage for more than a few years.

Benchmarking and flexing

Equipped with information about these seven drivers, we can use our model to use benchmarking and sensitivity analysis to provide a valuation of the company in question and thus see how the company should manage its scarce resources to enhance SHV. As we have said earlier, the objective of benchmarking and flexing is to analyze the financial drivers of the company and so reinforce the message of SHV throughout the company.

Managing companies in this industry is as often based on intuition and feel as it is on cool appraisal. Often there may be a lack of information about client profitability, which can lead to investment managers trying to retain a client relationship even though it is not a profitable one and so destroying SHV.

Another issue is that of staff costs. 'Star' fund managers can be lured away from competitors in the belief that they will improve fund performance and so bring some of their clients to their new company. The SHV model allows a cooler assessment of whether the additional costs caused by employing the star will ever generate sufficient new business to add to existing SHV. Finally, the model enables management to see more clearly where their profits are coming from, and so 'steer' the business to focus more on higher margin products and clients.

Financial services back on track?

This brief overview of SHV models in the financial services sector has, we hope, shown that even in this difficult area it is possible to apply SHV analysis successfully. What we have described here is a methodology that enables financial institutions to be analyzed in a similar way to firms in other industries, suggesting that their problems are very similar.

Banks in the UK have made a start in the right SHV direction, but a large number of big financial institutions in the rest of Europe are very unclear about how they are going to increase their SHV in the future. It is never too late to try!

TECHNOLOGY AND KNOW-HOW INTENSIVE INDUSTRIES

The best way to predict the future is to invent it.
John Scully

Areas of uncertainty

There is certainly something different about technology-intensive industries when it comes to SHV analysis. The uncertainties and risks involved are very high, and the since the pace of technological change is so fast, effective growth duration periods can be very short indeed. Here we will look at two SHV applications. One is the pharmaceuticals industry, where there are quite specific competitive conditions, often limited by current patent law, and by the ease or difficulty with which companies can actually patent new drugs; the other is the more generic high technology area, covering such industries as biotechnology, semiconductors and computer software.

Our look at high technology industries will involve trying to put a value on the options facing a company once a project has reached a certain stage in its life. Since companies in this area are frequently small and in start-up situations there is a close identity between the project and the company.

But for both areas our models will aim to bring a detailed industry understanding to bear on the question of SHV determination. Given the high rate of failure, particularly in the start-up area, we feel it is important that management is given the opportunity to align its polices with SHV.

Pharmaceuticals

Recent trends

The whole issue of SHV is becoming ever more relevant to this sector, and a survey of recent trends helps to explain why. The pharmaceutical industry experienced double digit sales growth rates in the 1970s and 1980s, and significant year on year profit increases, supported by price flexibility and strong sales from 'blockbuster' drugs (commonly defined as those drugs having annual sales exceeding $1bn).

The common strategy of major pharmaceutical companies in the past has been simply to allocate significant resources to R&D with the aim of generating blockbuster drugs. These compensate for underperformance elsewhere in the product portfolio as well as mitigating the effects of manufacturing and other operational inefficiencies – the average rate of asset utilization in the industry is only 20 per cent.

There have been increasing signs that these strategies are no longer working their old magic; the industry's previously buoyant sales growth has now fallen to just 6 per cent a year. Among the contributory factors are:

- Longer and stricter product development processes. Formal phases of development were introduced as a result of the Thalidomide scandal in the 1960s. The length of the development process has now increased to an average of ten to 12 years, costing $400m to $500m.

- Slower rate of discovery of new chemical entities (NCEs), which are the basic fuel for the development pipeline.

- Fewer blockbusters.

- Pharmacoeconomics, which has introduced a need to demonstrate cost-efficiency, in addition to efficacy and safety.

- Generic competition encouraged by US laws, which allow competitor companies to prepare for commercialization of 'me-too' drugs even before patents expire.

The consequence is increasing pressure to manage R&D funds for value and assess alternative sources of revenue with an understanding of the specific drivers of value within the pharmaceutical industry.

This is underlined by the very varied SHV performance of the main players in the industry over the last few years. They range from highly impressive TSRs of over 90 per cent in a year (Hoechst in 1996) to a negative TSR of minus 6 per cent in the same period (Roche, who did nevertheless achieve a much more respectable 30.5 per cent return over the five years from January 1992). SHV also varies greatly when compared to the company's local stock market, with little general pattern emerging.

The SHV model

In line with our practice in other sectors, our model includes several features specific to the pharmaceutical industry. One of the most important of these is the skewed pattern of sales by product, which can tail off quite quickly after patents expire. A typical product life cycle is shown in Fig. 10.11.

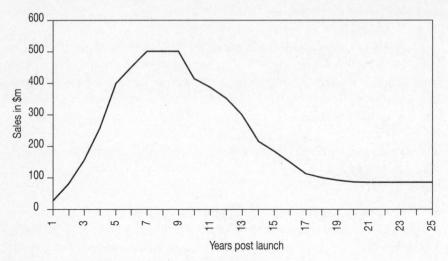

Fig. 10.11 Typical pharmaceutical product life cycle

Under favourable conditions, such a pattern can produce a strong positive cash flow, as marketing expenses fall as the product matures. However, the strength of this flow depends greatly on an ability to maintain sales even after patents have expired, and on customer loyalty strong enough to resist the temptation of cheaper 'me-too' products made by competitors. Neither of these two factors are anything like as powerful as they once were in the industry. The profit generation capabilities of a 'good' drug are described in Fig. 10.12.

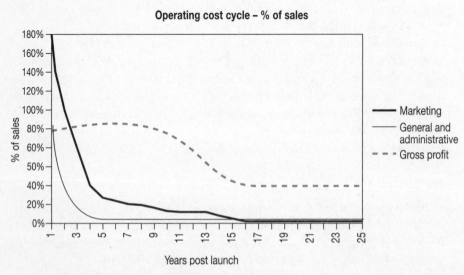

Fig. 10.12 Profit generation capabilities of a 'good'drug

The SHV model for this industry derives aggregate cash flow projections for the existing portfolio of products on the market from:

- the typical pattern of cash flows for an average drug within the operation
- the mix of stages within the of existing portfolio of products.

Figure 10.13 shows the connections between the generic drivers of SHV and the industry-specific value drivers.

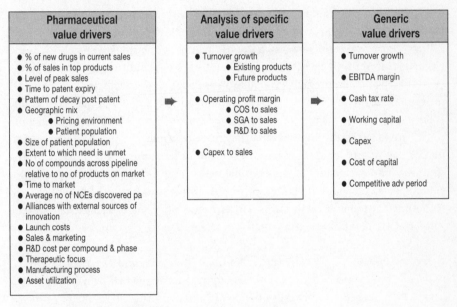

Fig. 10.13 Industry-specific and generic drivers of SHV

Among the listed drivers to consider for each drug are key parameters like the level of peak sales, the speed of sales decline following the appearance of competition from generic products, and whether the product was developed in-house with a higher gross margin. Additional factors such as the time to market and costs of development also have to be included.

Applications

We see our model as being particularly helpful in addressing the question of the SHV implications of important changes taking place in the industry. These can include establishing answers to 'make or buy' questions and 'disintegrating' the value chain, outsourcing parts of the production and distribution process. Considerations can range from examining the usefulness of using contract research organizations who can handle parts of the clinical trial process, through to asking whether it makes sense to have an internal sales force if its functions can be better handled by an outsourcing arrangement.

High technology

Under this heading we subsume technology-intensive industries where innovation is the driving force. They are often emerging industries created through the development of new technology, e.g. the Internet, biotechnology, or pollution control. Or they can be more or less mature industries which continue to show technology intensity such as parts of the IT industry: semiconductors, computer hardware, and computer software or consumer electronics.

Innovation is certainly at the centre of the high technology sector, both as the basis for competition and as the prime determinant of industry evolution. However, there is no comprehensive valuation approach specifically tailored towards technology companies. In its absence, capital markets usually utilize comparable company analysis, market multiples and in some cases discounted cash flow (DCF) to value technology companies. Each of these has serious flaws. Comparable company analysis and market multiples cannot be applied if the company under consideration is unique, as is often the case if novel technologies are involved. Cash flows are notoriously difficult to forecast for high growth technology companies, and fail to capture flexibility. As a result, the market's valuation of technology companies is largely driven by experience and 'gut feeling'.

But we believe that R&D, the technology life cycle, and the valuation technique of 'real options' can be linked within the framework of a SHV model. Under the name 'TechnologyBuilder', the Price Waterhouse model aims to put the valuation of technology companies on a more objective basis and incorporate much of that 'gut feeling' into quantitative valuation.

The two components of high tech value

In dealing with high technology companies we must distinguish between two sorts of value. First that arising from the value of existing assets, and second that from the company's future growth opportunities, over and above those captured in the normal cash flow forecast. This can be defined as:

$$MV = VEA + VGO$$

where MV is market valuation, VEA is value from existing assets, and VGO is the value of the company's growth opportunities.

The first component of company value, that from existing assets, is the value of the capitalized free cash flows (FCF) that are being generated from the firm's current endowment, i.e. a perpetuity of the FCF anticipated for the current year.

To calculate the anticipated FCF, we follow our standard ValueBuilder procedure. This is shown graphically in Fig. 10.14.

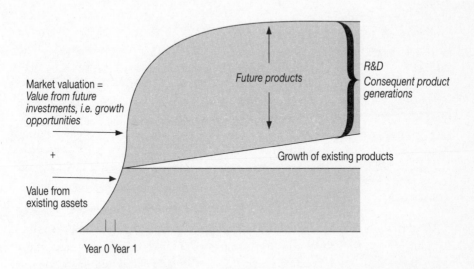

Fig. 10.14 Evolution of FCF, VEA and VGO over time, illustrating a product life cycle

The stock market's current view on the value of a company's future growth opportunities (VGO) can be determined as the difference between the market valuation of the company (i.e. the current market capitalization plus debt) and the value from existing assets. In order to get a feel for the market's perception of the VGO of a number of technology firms, we made the calculations shown in Table 10.1: first, we worked out the value of existing assets (in column 4) as a perpetuity of the anticipated FCF (in column 2), using the company's weighted cost of capital (WACC, in column 3). We then subtracted the value of existing assets (in column 4) from the market valuation of the company (in the first column) to arrive at the market's perception of the VGO (in column 5). In the last column we express the VGO as a percentage of the market value of the company.

171

Table 10.1 Growth opportunity value as a component of total equity value

Companies	US$(m)	Total Co. value (20.2.1997)	Anticipated FCF 1997	WACC	Capitalized value of FCF	Estd value of growth options	% of Total Co. value
Hardware							
Digital Equipment Corp		6,480	(36)	10.5%	(1,264)	6,480	100%
Hewlett-Packard		59,391	2,450	12.2%	26,936	32,454	54.6%
Semiconductors							
Motorola		40,991	1,184	10.6%	12,439	28,552	69.7%
Intel		128,611	4,238	11.9%	42,696	85,915	66.8%
Consumer Electronics							
Thomson		3,934	110	11.5%	1,048	2,885	73.3%
Sony		40,271	789	4.5%	32,311	7,960	19.8%
Philips		22,183	1,711	10.1%	18,842	3,342	15.1%

All of this goes to show that in the technology industry, growth opportunities account for a large proportion of a company's total value, in most cases more than 70 per cent. An interesting exception is troubled Digital Equipment, where the entire company value is based on market expectations that current (early 1997) cash negativity is temporary and can be reversed in the future. Note that the stock market valuation of companies that have never been cash positive, for example British Biotech or Genentech, works on exactly the same expectation. For Philips, however, the market perceives comparatively small growth opportunities of around 15 per cent.

What are the micro drivers?

Using a standard SHV model allows us to perform a familiar sensitivity analysis to find how a company's value might be affected by changes in the seven drivers. And as we have seen earlier, the level of detail can be increased by 'drilling down' from macro drivers to micro drivers. In the high technology sector, these driving forces vary from area to area, so individual micro drivers have to be used.

Take the computer hardware industry, where cost pressures and scale economies are dominant. Since semiconductors now account for 40 per cent of the cost of a PC, chip content is becoming a pervasive SHV driver in this industry. In the semiconductor industry the drivers are related to Moore's Law (which predicts a doubling of processing capability every 18 months) and by book to bill ratios. In the Internet industry we have drivers like churn rate, views per page and so on.

A matter of options

As SHV practitioners we can also look at a company's future growth opportunities (VGO) from a bottom-up company view, based on internal management information, where it is available. The VGO will be based upon the company's internal know-how, which offers a number of options on different future strategies. For instance know-how could have been gained through previous investments in products with multiple product generations or through research and development efforts.

These options are very similar to the options on stocks in financial markets: both are concerned with the right, as distinct from obligation, to do something. In the financial markets it is the option to buy an underlying asset, and in our SHV view it is the option to invest in a project at an anticipated investment cost once the know-how is available. Our model can provide a valuation of these future growth options, and hence verify the top-down approach followed by so many financial analysts. (Share prices in high technology stocks are very sensitive to news flows, and thus to the reappraisal of the value of various options.)

Valuing innovation

As we have seen, our model splits company value into two components: value from existing assets and value of future growth opportunities (VGO). The VGO is the sum of all future innovations. We look at each of these innovations via the four phases of the technology life cycle which follow basic research – invention, innovation, diffusion and maturity – using option pricing.

The key insight behind this approach is that each phase can be considered a 'real' call option on the next phase of the life cycle. Registration of a new patent (invention) offers an option to develop a marketable product, whose market introduction (innovation) in turn offers an option to set the standard in the market (diffusion), which contains an option to become the market leader and reach a certain level of peak sales (maturity). Exercising these 'call options' at any one stage depends on a management's assessment of how profitable of the technology concerned will be.

Alternatively, each phase can be looked at as offering a 'put' option – an option to abandon the development process and recoup some or all of the cost by obtaining a liquidation value if conditions turn out unfavourably. Figure 10.15 maps the 'engine' of the VGO of technology companies, the 'technology tree', against the four phases of a technology life cycle.

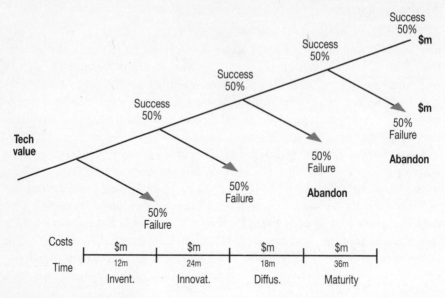

Fig. 10.15 Technology tree

The crucial parameters for valuing the technology tree, the so-called option drivers, are:

- the probabilities of reaching the respective next stage
- the time horizons of the individual stages
- cash in and outflows, namely the expected cash flow in case the target for the maturity phase is reached
- costs (which are saved if the process is abandoned)
- liquidation values.

Although industry averages exist for probabilities, timings, and, to a certain degree, for cash flows, the model allows for individual companies to use their own figures if they differ from these averages.

Sensitivity analysis can show the influence of these option drivers on the value of the relevant technology or project and on company value. Through it, you can, for example, answer questions such as: 'what happens to our company value if we manage to improve the success probabilities of our R&D process for a certain product, or for all products, by X per cent?'. Our model also helps put a value on 'internal flexibility' – a firm's ability to appraise a project quickly, to decide whether to proceed with it and possibly speed up (or delay) the next step in the process.

Our model assumes that after a company's competitive advantage period (CAP) is over, the return on new investment just equals the cost of capital so that no additional company value is created from new investment. In many cases, the length of the technology life cycle determines the length of the competitive advantage period. The terminal value, i.e. the component of the company value that arises after the CAP, is the perpetuity of a percentage of FCF at peak sales. It enters the technology tree together with the FCF that arises during the CAP.

The value of flexibility

Once they have established a track record of innovation – and a commensurate ability to generate sufficient demand for their products – most technology companies are faced with two choices when it comes to new projects. The first is to decide to shoulder all the risks involved by making a full investment and trying as hard as possible to ensure it pays off. The other chance is to evade the risks by doing nothing and waiting for market trends to become clearer – by which time a bolder competitor might have taken the lead. But there is a third possibility: to manage the risks by acquiring growth options. A growth option offers a company the internal or external flexibility to participate in future growth at very limited risk to SHV.

They can, for example, invest in potentially cash-negative joint ventures and strategic networks, i.e. alliances with suppliers and competitors undertaken for the sake of 'being in business' with the right partners rather than for immediate profits. Academic studies have shown that managers intuitively attach a much higher value to such investment opportunities than would be justified on the basis of a DCF valuation.[9] Again, option pricing theory offers ways of valuing this often neglected, highly intangible but nevertheless often significant source of the VGO.

Three option drivers

The two-component approach of the Price Waterhouse 'TechnologyBuilder' SHV model, then, enables valuation to be done using the most powerful information both from the present (cash flows from existing assets) and for the future (success probabilities, timings, cash flows). This valuation is less dependent on free cash flows, which are difficult to forecast, and more on risk, as expressed in the success probabilities of the technology tree, compared to the traditional DCF approach. It explicitly models uncertainty, which makes it both more defensible and accurate.

As we have noted above, the conventional seven value drivers are supplemented by drivers peculiar to this sector – the three option drivers of success probabilities, timings, and cash flows. By explicitly modelling individual phases

---

[9] S D Howell and A J Jägle, 'Evidence on How Managers Intuitively Value Growth Options', *Journal of Business Finance and Accounting*, Spring 1997.

of development, this approach helps to focus management attention on the relatively most important phases. Indeed, it offers a fresh perspective by suggesting that technology companies essentially are managers of a portfolio of options. Its technology life cycle-based approach might well represent the missing piece in the technology valuation jigsaw.

OTHER SECTORS

Oil and gas

The important oil and gas sector is often associated with large integrated companies that control all stages of production from exploration through to retailing. In recent years the emergence of effective secondary markets between each of the various stages of production means that it is no longer essential for an oil company to be present in all aspects of the oil business. As a result, the question of which parts of the oil business create SHV has been given greater urgency.

Our approach to the oil and gas industry is not only to look at the different stages of production, shown in the simplified value chain in Fig. 10.16, but also to give some thought to the connections between them.

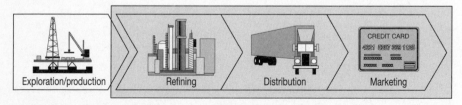

Fig. 10.16 Simplified value chain for the oil and gas industry

Adapting to SHV

Oil and gas companies once used to be led exclusively by professionals from technological backgrounds who, although competent in technical aspects of petroleum engineering, were not always as sensitive to the issues surrounding valuation and finance as they could have been. The wave of restructuring in the form of corporate mergers and takeovers that overtook the industry in the 1980s was to some extent a response to this, as falling oil prices focused attention on the process of value creation.

The oil companies of the 1990s are increasingly being steered by professionals with finance backgrounds; due attention is now being paid to shareholder rights and to communicating to the market about issues that impact on company value. For example, at its triennial investor relations briefing in December 1996, Royal Dutch/Shell outlined its mission as the creation of SHV based upon the themes of profitability and portfolio management, focus on growth and the containment of costs.[10]

Another oil major that adopted and incorporated the SHV focus in its strategy is British Petroleum (BP). Over the last five years the BP management, driven by the mission of delivering SHV, has significantly restructured the company. By proactively identifying value creation opportunities and value-destroying business lines, it has been able to deliver improved performance and provide shareholders with real dividend and capital growth. At its 1996 AGM, Sir David Simon, then chairman of BP, said 'Shareholder return is our key performance measure.'[11] The SHV trend has finally arrived in the industry and oil companies that fail to deliver SHV will become vulnerable to corporate raids in the next phase of restructuring.

Special features of the oil and gas model

Upstream: exploration and production

The features most difficult to include in an SHV model are concentrated in the upstream end of the business. Here, great uncertainties with respect to the size and quality of reserves, as well as the expected life of oilfields, can affect subsequent valuations. The growth duration period, therefore, should be treated as being that of the average life of the oil fields currently owned and operated by the company.

But this is only part of the story. There is also the question of valuing the continuing operations of the company after the end of the forecast period. In our view they can be approximated by referring to the discovery/depletion ratios of the companies. Companies with good discovery rates and relatively slow rates of depletion are going to be 'oil rich' in the years to come; equally, a company that is profligate with its existing reserves, and is not good at discovering new oil sources, will not be.

Other features in the oil industry include a long investment horizon between the pre-licence phase and commercial production that can involve significant capital expenditure – for instance exploration costs, development costs and production costs. There is often little correlation between exploration expenditure and the value of reserves. The major economic value of a field lies in the underlying oil/gas reserves and is a function of estimated reservoir life and US dollar oil price.

[10] Shell triennial investor relations briefing, 16 December 1996.
[11] 'BP sharpening focus on improved SHV, efficiency', *Oil and Gas Journal* Vol 94, Issue 28, July 1996.

The US dollar price of crude oil is one of the key exogenous drivers of value – if not *the* key one – for the upstream industry. It has a major influence, together with production volume, on turnover. Crude oil price is in turn a function of the supply/demand relationship. On the supply side, the OPEC (Organization of Petroleum Exporting Countries) producers, with their huge oil reserves, play a major role in influencing crude prices. On the demand side, oil prices are influenced by several factors such as the individual refined product demand, economic growth, seasonal weather and so on. Furthermore, a company might be producing, in different quantities, several qualities of oil, each with a different price in the market. In overcoming these seemingly complex problems, we need to differentiate between long-term underlying trends and the short-term 'noise' that impacts upon prices. It is the long term that is more relevant in a valuation exercise, although it helps to understand the short-term issues. All of this complicates the forecasting of oil prices into the future.

The main drivers in the model are shown in Fig. 10.17. On the E&P (exploration and production) side, oil companies have very minimal inventory, as crude is transported from well head to refinery as soon as it is produced and so working capital is not a key driver of value.

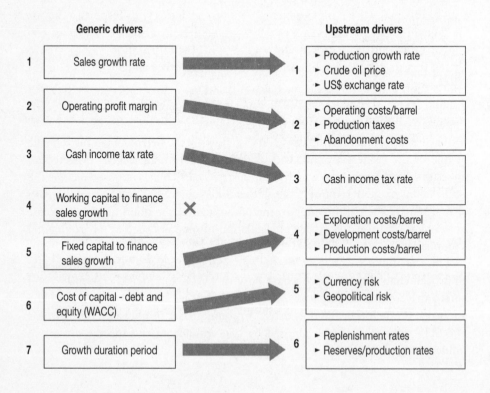

Fig. 10.17 Generic and upstream drivers

Downstream: manufacturing to marketing

The oil and gas industry is an interesting combination of unusual and 'usual' factors. While the upstream part of the business requires some rather specialized drivers, this is not the case with the downstream part of the business. Indeed, we find that the generic SHV model can cope quite well with the downstream end. An oil company's valuation can be based on the familiar seven value drivers. Although the processes involved are extremely complex, externally the refining business is a manufacturing business. The raw material – crude oil – is physically separated and chemically treated to yield a range of saleable products such as gasoline and kerosene. In this respect the refining industry can be compared to the chemicals manufacturing sector which can also be analyzed using the generic models.

Obviously account has to be taken of issues such as environmental regulation and overcapacity (which impact hugely upon the refining industry's margins). Furthermore, there are differences in product demand in different geographic regions; hence the need for geographic and/or market-based segregation of the value drivers.

The transportation and distribution sides of the oil business entail the movement of hydrocarbons from production source to manufacture and from manufacture to end user. We can easily identify the value drivers by examining what impacts upon value of companies operating in the transportation sector. Again, a cash flow valuation can be performed based on the seven key drivers. This is also true for marketing and retailing. Activity here covers the selling of many different refined petroleum products to different groups of consumers – for automotive and marine transport, for aviation, and for manufacturing industry and utilities. Oil and gas marketing have value drivers comparable to businesses such as supermarkets and high street retail chains.

The variety of factors impacting on cash flows in the petroleum industry make it one of the riskiest around, with commensurately high returns expected by investors. Uncertainties to which the industry is particularly exposed include the scale of investment required; the uncertainties in timing and pattern of cash flows; state participation and government influence; the political and economic risks; high taxation and stringent regulation on matters such as environmental compliance.

For the downstream part of the oil and gas industry, then, the generic approach enables us to make a cash flow valuation and identify the macro and micro drivers that are creating or destroying value. The upstream part of the industry, on the other hand, is driven by a unique set of micro drivers; for this the SHV approach can be tailored by conceptualizing the specific drivers of value.

Telecommunications

Under the bright glare of SHV

In the past few years there has been a marked increase in interest in SHV in telecommunications. This has accompanied a global trend away from state-owned monopoly suppliers of a 'plain old telephone service' (POTS) to sleeker, and more profitable, suppliers of a whole range of telecommunications services, many of which simply did not exist a few years ago. An industry previously thought of as dominated by 'natural' monopolies has suddenly woken up to the fact that privately owned companies are probably better placed to be proactive – to increase the supply of services for a public hungry for them, doing so at higher levels of efficiency and at lower consumer prices than state-owned enterprises have generally been able to.

Previously closely tied to the apron strings of government for their investment needs, telecommunications companies now have to raise capital in the financial markets, and reward their shareholders in the same way as other companies. Their great interest in SHV is therefore understandable.

Over the past 15 years an average of US$9 billion per annum has been raised by telecommunications companies across 40 countries. More than two-thirds of this amount has been absorbed by the privatization of NTT (National Telephone and Telegraph) in Japan and BT (British Telecom) in the UK. Deutsche Telekom's IPO and the scheduled privatizations of France Telecom, STET (1998), Telstra (1997), MATAV and Turk Telecom will have boosted the amount of equity raised to over US$35 billion in 1997 alone.

Changes in the regulatory environment have been a catalyst for increased competition. Telecoms operators need to stimulate top-line growth and enhance operating efficiency to retain market share. Over the coming years, the global liberalization process in telecommunications will be shaped by a number of factors – among them EU legislation that *de facto* will open most European markets to competition in basic telecommunications services by 1998; the passing of the US Telecom Bill in 1996; the Japanese government's decision to break up NTT; and successful WTO negotiations in 1997.

So far, fierce competition and price deregulation has led to decreased revenues through market share losses and price erosion. As a result, operators have been seeking to find replacement revenue streams at home from value add services (such as mobile, Internet and VPNs (virtual private networks)) while investing in opportunities outside their domestic markets with perceived higher growth potential. Meanwhile, with some US$30 billion of new equity finance required in Europe alone in the next few years, competition for capital is fierce.

Within this environment, we have found it very helpful to have a SHV model more specifically built up around the concerns of the telecommunications industry. It looks in some detail at both the macro, top-down end of the business, as well as being able to link these broader brush changes to industry-specific micro drivers. This model can support analysis and measurement of SHV at both the strategic and at the operational level. Whether the business unit uses a fixed PSTN (public switched telephone network), a mobile network, cable TV or data network infrastructure, such a tool can be used to determine projections of each business unit's financial status.

Some examples of initiatives undertaken by telecoms operators to generate SHV are given below in Fig. 10.18, under the headings of each relevant value driver. (*See also* Chapter 7 for more general initiatives.) Of course, any new venture may have an impact on more than one driver, and each operator will have different key drivers of value depending on its competitive and regulatory environment.

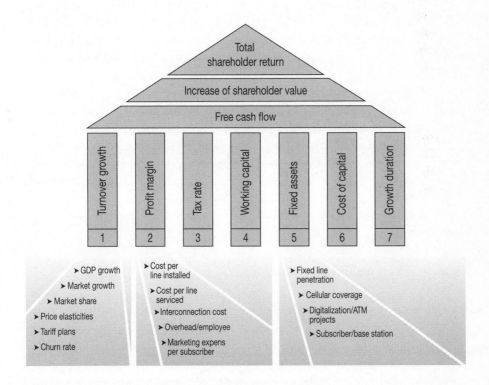

Fig. 10.18 Telecoms operators' initiatives to generate SHV

Under the heading of revenue or turnover growth, it is also worth noting the importance of new IN (intelligent network) services such as premium rate services, chargecards, voice mail, freephone, VPNs, personal numbers and the

Internet, and of the 'bundling' of services. Margins can be affected by such actions as the introduction of shared services (or alternatively, outsourcing); the centralization and consolidation of back office operations, such as some finance functions; and systems initiatives in network configuration and network management. The capital expenditure/fixed capital driver can be cover matters such as asset financing – leasing and sale and lease back arrangements – and, for companies expanding abroad, hedging and risk management. And under 'growth duration period' can come factors such as the role of new entrants versus incumbent advantages; the nature of the regulatory regime; and access to infrastructure.

How do we measure SHV in telecoms?

Many operators have, or will soon have, decentralized their organization through the creation of profit-responsible customer-facing business units. This has been done in order to improve responsiveness and attain closer understanding of customer needs as well as to reduce costs and improve efficiency. Line managers have thereby gained greater responsibility and accountability.

In addition, compliance with regulatory requirements for cost-based charging for interconnection with other operators has created the need for a financial separation between the network and service provider units. This 'line of business' organizational structure brings with it new challenges and issues.

To ensure that management for SHV creation is implemented at every level, virtual business units or value centres can be set up to address this issue. These value centres can be organizational business units, product or customer groupings, or can be project based. An example is the creation of an Internet value centre that serves residential and business customers and uses different access infrastructures.

Transfer pricing and negotiations

Our experience with network operators moving to a line of business structure has shown that the transfer pricing process is one of the most difficult to get right. It is important that this mechanism is well designed and agreed beforehand. Many operators either institute a cost plus 50 per cent mark up on network services – which provides little incentive for service providers to enhance value – or spend an inordinate amount of time arguing about the level of transfer pricing and how it has been calculated. Some of the issues that arise are:

- difficulties in allocating costs of shared network infrastructure
- lack of a framework or 'rules' for commitments and pricing between internal providers and purchasers of shared services
- inability to define internal service level agreements in terms of the required

functionality, quality, cycle time, volumes and cost

- little incentive for internal providers of support services to be more efficient than third-party provider
- customer-facing business units unable to forecast future demand and deliver the volume of commitments made
- the question of whether transfer prices are based on actual costs or are related to market prices – and of what sort of transition plan if starting with the former.

Revenue growth and margins are two of the most important value drivers for telecoms operators. Indeed the two are connected. Most operators need to drive improvements in staff productivity (and other costs) in order to find new resources that can be dedicated to revenue growth or revenue retention activities. So how can a telecoms company make rapid employee productivity gains that will free resources for reinvestment? We give one example focused on a telecoms field force and/or customer service operation.

Performance management

One example where our SHV model has been used is in looking at how to achieve a substantial – 15 per cent – reduction in customer-facing staff costs. (This could also apply to the field/maintenance force). By carefully measuring and managing their activity, it is possible to install initially what is effectively a self-financing pilot study. When successful, this can then be rolled out into the rest of the organization.

Applied to a substantive part of an organization's resources, this could lead to a significant improvement in margins. For instance, taking a telecoms organization which has around 10 000 people in field operations, maintenance and customer support – a 15 per cent saving would deliver some 1500 headcount savings which in turn (using an average $40 000 per annum cost of employment) would deliver approximately $60 million annual savings. (Note that the underpinning framework that is needed to help implement the suggested improvements in margins and growth is based on an activity-based cost management – ABCM – exercise.)

Utilities

Following telecoms into a new world

Utilities, like telecoms companies, have been dragged into the world of SHV and competition by governments keen both to realize cash, in order to ease their deficits, and encourage greater competition and efficiency – leading to lower prices to consumers (most of whom also vote). Even in the USA, privately owned utility companies, hitherto cosseted by reasonably generous rate of return regulations, are experiencing fresh challenges that may well result in more deregulation, and a stiffer wind of competition.

The issues facing most utilities can be summarized under eight headings:

- *Regulatory environment:* introduction of open access to utility systems, stricter environmental guidelines.
- *Competitive pressures:* rapidly intensifying competition – survival of only the fittest.
- *Speed-driven and customer-driven markets:* customers' ever-rising expectations must be met more rapidly.
- *Industry structure:* mergers are concentrating and reconfiguring markets.
- *Technological innovation:* new product and market opportunities are created, requiring more skills.
- *Market globalization:* more diverse customers/suppliers/employees; more complex relationships among them.
- *Information availability:* information superhighway gives customers/competitors instant access.
- *Ruthless capital markets:* private financing and ownership of utility systems; investors demanding focus on SHV.

All over the industrialized world, then, there are moves afoot to introduce SHV concepts into utilities. Once assumed to be unexciting 'pipes, wires and poles' businesses, they are now waking up to the growing influence of investors. The challenges of privatization, market liberalization, the introduction of competition in areas such as electricity generation and power supply, and dynamic changes in generation technology have combined with a tightening regulatory environment and growing investor influence to place huge pressure on utilities looking to increase SHV.

The effect of these changes has been loss of revenues by incumbents as new entrants have won market share by lowering prices; competition and price regulation has not allowed pro rata increases in profits to increases in volume. In the face of nearly static revenue growth, utilities have been trying to substitute revenue streams at home with value added services (such as energy management schemes and customer demand profiling) while investing in opportunities outside their domestic markets with perceived higher revenue growth potential. At the same time, accessing the capital markets for equity and debt financing subjects a utility to the scrutiny of institutional investors. Management decisions on joint ventures, foreign participation, negotiations with the regulator and performance in the domestic market are reflected almost instantly in share prices.

As a result, there has been a high level of consolidation, takeovers and mergers in the utility sector, particularly in the competitive energy markets of Australia, Scandinavia, the UK and the USA. Many utilities in these markets have had to decide whether to acquire and become a global player or to be acquired. For a number of US utilities, the introduction of competition into the electricity and gas sector sectors in the UK has provided useful experience, but the rush to acquire the UK's RECs (regional electricity companies) has been based more on a desire to take advantage of a window of opportunity than anything else.

But what about SHV?

The acquired company's shareholders have certainly benefited from takeover activity. The average gain for shareholders in the UK's acquired RECs since they were privatized in 1990 has been some 300 per cent. This has put pressure on the utilities that wish to remain independent; the recent trend for many of the UK independents to return cash to shareholders through special dividends and buy-backs suggests either a shortage in new earnings enhancing opportunities or a strategy aimed at returning any surplus cash to shareholders.

It does not, however, guarantee shareholder loyalty. In 1995, Northern Electric successfully defended a takeover attempt by Trafalgar House with a shareholder package of some £300 million. In 1996, they faced a second takeover attempt from Cal-Energy and despite offering further payouts to shareholders were narrowly defeated by the bidder's cash offer. As for the acquirers, only time will tell. The share prices of the US utilities that acquired electricity distribution companies in Australia and the UK in 1995 and 1996 did not outperform in 1996 (they fell by an average of 4 per cent against the average utility index), but it seems that the US equity capital markets may be willing to accept a small dilution in earnings in the first year or so as a reasonable near-term price to pay to enter such huge markets.

Utility sector value drivers

Our model has been built up with the electricity generation and distribution industry very much in mind. It basically follows the standard seven-driver approach, but contains greater detail within the main drivers. The main drivers are shown in Fig. 10.19.

In our work with utilities, we have found that to get to the operational decision level requires shareholder analysis at the business unit level. This process has been assisted by the introduction of competition, which has required utilities to unbundle their activities into their principal businesses – for an electricity company these are generation, transmission, distribution and supply.

The next level of analysis is that of the operational value drivers, which in the generation unit of an electricity company would include, among other things:

- production costs measured in terms of p/kWh (kilowatt hour)

- non-production costs (p/kWh)
- load factor
- fuel mix (in megawatt hours or MWh) accounted for by nuclear, coal, gas, hydro or other
- growth in total MWh sales
- average price, which can be linked to forecast pool prices or contract prices.

For an electricity or gas distribution business, the operational value drivers would include:

- operating cost per customer
- operating cost less depreciation per customer
- operating cost per units distributed
- electricity/gas distributed per employee
- distribution operating profit per customer.

For water companies, meanwhile, there is a different but related set of drivers.

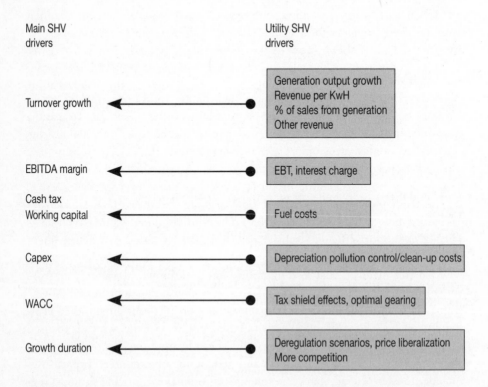

Main SHV drivers / Utility SHV drivers

Main SHV drivers	Utility SHV drivers
Turnover growth	Generation output growth / Revenue per KwH / % of sales from generation / Other revenue
EBITDA margin	EBT, interest charge
Cash tax / Working capital	Fuel costs
Capex	Depreciation pollution control/clean-up costs
WACC	Tax shield effects, optimal gearing
Growth duration	Deregulation scenarios, price liberalization / More competition

Fig. 10.19 Utility SHV

Regulation and SHV analysis

Most businesses are in a position where incremental revenue creates an increase of SHV. This is not always the case in regulated network industries, where a price formula may or may not allow increased volume to be translated into increased costs. In certain instances, increased volumes and revenues can destroy value because costs increase faster than revenue, with some customers served at below cost. This raises a number of issues:

- What is the SHV effect of lost revenues from competition and price regulation?
- Which of the current business units are contributing to SHV, and which are not?
- What is the contribution per customer category or from the major customers?
- What is the potential contribution to SHV from the portfolio of new initiatives?
- Should the same criteria be used to assess green field investments, such as independent power plants – which may not improve SHV in the short term, but can provide long-term revenue and earnings growth – as existing operational assets or companies?
- What cost of capital should be used to assess initiatives?

Transfer pricing

As with telecoms, this is not an easy issue to get right. The transfer prices between businesses are the same prices that allow other companies to use the networks. In the UK, in 1998, the transfer price will be tested in detail as even the smallest domestic customers will be able to choose their electricity supplier. Our experience is that many companies either institute a mark-up on network services, which provides little incentive for service providers to enhance value, or spend an inordinate amount of time arguing about the level of transfer price and how it has been calculated. The underpinning framework that is needed to support effective transfer pricing is activity-based cost management (ABCM).

What this means is that leading utilities around the world are moving from spreadsheet-based cost allocation systems to establishing sophisticated ABCM frameworks and systems that are capable of supporting multi-dimensional profitability analysis. In addition to activity-based transfer pricing, which is focused on the product or service dimension, ABCM can be used for profitability analysis in customer or market segments and geographic market area. Typical uses include transfer pricing, market segment decision making, pricing strategy, regulatory compliance, network investment, business re-engineering initiatives, and financial planning. This can then be linked through value-based management to ensure that the changes and strategies being planned are consistent with the goal of raising SHV.

Our experience with utilities

In the first benchmarking and valuation phase, we have found that in most cases the discounted value of analysts' projections of future cash flows has closely cor-related with the market capitalization. In the one instance where the market cap-italization was significantly below the DCF valuation, the cause was identified as an investor relations issue: the share price of the company rose rapidly soon after this was brought to management's attention by Price Waterhouse.

The most sensitive of the seven value drivers have generally proved to be operating margins and the WACC. As we have observed, revenue growth in a highly regulated utility may not lead to increase in SHV; however, an improve-ment in margins and a lowering of the cost of capital will. Also, in the case of water utilities, fixed capital is an important value driver an importance that reflects the high levels of capital expenditure required to replace, what is in most cases, an ageing infrastructure.

Where operating margins are the most sensitive of the value drivers, a num-ber of utilities we have worked with have carried out a value mapping exercise with their principal business units. We have also developed an electricity-speci-fic spreadsheet model which can value-map its generation, distribution, supply and non-regulated businesses.

As for the WACC, most utility companies accept that the cost of debt is cheaper than the cost of equity – even though after privatization many of the UK utilities were reluctant to take on significant amounts of debt. This is in contrast to the US utilities, which, although investor owned for many decades, have tra-ditionally had gearing levels in excess of 100 per cent. The start of takeover activity in the UK electricity sector in 1995 went some way to changing all this – witness the case of Northern Electric's successful defence against Trafalgar House referred to earlier, where the increased returns to shareholders were financed by taking on increased debt. Most of the other RECs followed suit, and the average gearing level of UK RECs rose from approximately 20 per cent in March 1994 to over 80 per cent two years later.

A partial solution

A word of caution, however. The software packages and sector models for SHV analysis that we have referred to here and in earlier sections of this chapter are, it has to be said, just analytical tools. They do not change culture or behaviour and are, therefore, only a partial solution. More fundamental changes are required within a company if the enhancement of SHV is to become enshrined as the company's principal objective. Value-based management – the process that we outlined in Chapter 7 – is crucial.

SUMMARY

In this chapter we first looked at some of the problem areas that the application of SHV theory might focus on – areas such as the definition of cash flow; intangible assets; the cost of capital; and residual value. All or some of these topics have a bearing on the sectors examined here. We saw how our SHV models varied from the 'basic' standard when applied to a number of sectors: banking, insurance and fund management; high technology and pharmaceuticals; oil and gas, telecommunications and utilities. This has meant identifying value drivers specific to each situation.

SHV AROUND
THE WORLD

Having looked at how SHV theories can be applied to particular industrial or trade sectors, let us now return to the wider global context that has made SHV such an urgent subject. If, as we argued in Chapter 1 and elsewhere, the globalization of markets has increased the pressure on publicly quoted companies for economic returns on the money that investors have entrusted to them, what effect has this pressure had in individual countries? How do the particular conditions of a country – its history, its culture, its traditional ways of doing business – affect the adoption (or rejection) of SHV as a concept?

This chapter aims to put SHV in its international context and will look at the special characteristics of the commercial climate in a selection of countries, taking them one by one. Afterwards, we will devote a whole chapter to Japan, one of the more interesting 'special' cases. Neither that nor the sections on the other countries are intended to be comprehensive guides to these countries' markets – for which we recommend the Price Waterhouse information guides *Doing Business in ...* (available from local PW offices). We will simply home in on some features of individual markets that we think have a bearing on SHV analysis and value-based management issues.

CORPORATE GOVERNANCE

First, however, let us pick up on some of the corporate governance issues that were touched on at the end of Chapter 1. There we painted a picture of a divide between the Anglo-Saxon and continental modes of capitalism. The former have large and liquid capital markets in which more than half of shares are owned by institutions whose priority is to maximize their return. The latter are smaller, less liquid and have a concentration of power among banks, governments and families. How does this have a bearing on SHV analysis? Do different forms of corporate governance have a bearing on share price development?

There is no simple answer to this question – although, as we have noted, the equity markets in general have performed better in the Anglo-Saxon countries than elsewhere. In fact, even this assertion may only be true if looked at in local currency terms. Since many of the European, and particularly the Japanese, economies have performed well, other markets have benefited as a result. If you include the effects of currency changes in any analysis, the position looks rather different. Shares in the less investor-friendly countries have outperformed those in the Anglo-Saxon countries when expressed in dollars or sterling.

Is it then true, as such figures would seem to imply, that the 'stakeholder' approach to investment means that the benefits of corporate action can be felt by a larger circle of participants in society? And can we conclude that the markets currently more hostile to equities will continue to outperform in the future? We don't think so. Rather, we would like to argue that these two variants of capitalism are converging, and that their current differences will diminish as time goes by.

Stakes and shares

Let us look at some of the reasons why stakeholder performance has been so good in the past. We may also be able to find reasons why it may not be so impressive in the future.

The stakeholder approach has worked well in industries that were largely protected from international trade. They may have been either nationalized, or partially nationalized, with the government holding a 'strategic' interest. Or there could have been interlocking shareholdings among the main producers, so that the share price movements of one tended to spill over into the others, regardless of what they did.

In such a protected environment stakeholders could be relatively well served. The suppliers obtained 'protected' prices, often aided and abetted by rules that stipulated that only local suppliers could bid for business. Customers often had no choice, since the producers were effectively in a monopoly. And even where there was more than one producer, price controls might ensure that there was little true competition in the industry. Employees were also well looked after, as some of the 'monopoly' gains were handed out to them as higher wages and salaries. Employees increasingly thought of customers as a nuisance; engineering and 'security of supply' issues took priority.

In the fully nationalized industries, problems arose as investment needs had to be financed by government, or through government guaranteed bonds. Stakeholder companies were often prodigal with capital, which they had no incentive to use wisely or efficiently.

This stakeholder approach might have continued in a relatively untroubled fashion, had it not became clear that deregulation and increased exposure to international competition made it increasingly difficult for governments to maintain these 'cosy' arrangements. As international competition grew, so evidence began to stack up that the stakeholding company was rather inefficient, and had been feather-bedding its employees and suppliers largely at the expense of its customers, many of whom were paying high prices for a distinctly average service – as former customers of the GPO phone division in the UK or Germany's Bundespost telephones will testify.

Government pressures

Two further factors may contribute to the diminished effectiveness of the stakeholder system. One is the growing pressure on governments to reduce their spending deficits and overall borrowing. This has meant that they have been increasingly reluctant to either fill any financing gaps for future investment needs, or to alter the regulatory environment so that these needs could be met by a higher tax on consumers.

A final nail in the coffin has been the changing situation in which the providers of loan capital operate. Stakeholding companies in the past often had access to a pool of relatively cheap funds – bank loans. Not only was the interest on the loans tax deductible, but the banks were ready to lend relatively large amounts of money for long periods of time at moderate interest rates. Again, these rates were often partially subsidized by governments keen on reconstructing industry.

As capital markets have opened up, however, so the relative attractiveness of this pool of long-term capital has declined. Corporate borrowing needs have risen above the capacities of many local banks, and the borrower has been able to go direct to the market and often obtain better terms than the banks could get themselves. Pressure on bank shareholders meant that they were looking more critically at their lending practices – especially as the recession took its toll of several of their larger clients.

There is also evidence that the banks have not been very good at one of their primary functions, the pricing of loan risk, in the recent past. They will have to become more selective about the risks they take on in the future; fewer 'stakeholder' companies will have access to cheap capital, and instead will have to pay more for their funds – thus reducing the advantage that debt has over equity. Finally, by easing certain tax rules governments will make it easier for banks to reduce their 'strategic' shareholdings without incurring high tax liabilities.

The benefits of competition

Faced with these pressures, stakeholding companies are beginning to realize that their future lies in taking a more independent view on pricing and volumes and in better rewarding investors for the capital that they have contributed. When a government is no longer prepared to add funds to an enterprise, but actually wants to end its commitment and receive something back for the investments it has made, change is necessary. Companies have to put 'stakeholding' thoughts behind them and try and arrange their affairs so that they can compete. Newly privatized groups are starting to play close attention to their cost base, and to the process of deregulation.

Judging by the UK experience, it is no exaggeration to say that efficiency gains of between 25 and 50 per cent are possible in a more competitive deregulated regime. The resources released can then be used more productively by society – which appears to be happening.

COULD THE TWO VIEWS CONVERGE?

All the same, we may see a convergence between the two variants of share ownership in the future as pressure for improved share performance increases.

As we have said, the European model will have to change. First and foremost, pressure on banks to perform better could well mean an end to the cosy arrangement of interlocking and 'strategic' shareholdings. Work carried out by Price Waterhouse suggests that on balance most of these strategic holdings tend to reduce SHV, and that the banks could use these funds more productively elsewhere. The growing internationalization of the equity markets is making it easier to place blocs of shares among wide groups of international investors in ways inconceivable only a few years ago.

Privatizations are also changing the equity landscape in Europe, and are opening up shareholdings to a larger range of individuals and institutions than in the past. International investors will be taking a larger role on the new level playing fields, and indeed will be expected to do so. The largest privatization in Germany, Deutsche Telekom, would not have been possible if the shares had only been placed on the German market.

Where strategic shareholdings persist, their owners will look more critically at them, and quite possibly require better performance in the future. This may involve a more activist view on takeovers and mergers. With a more liquid international equity market to tap, it may also involve running down the 'strategic' holdings. These shares will then be 'in play' – making their acquisition by foreign investors easier.

Pressure on public sector budgets will also mean fewer funds will be available for the financing of enterprises on a partnership basis in the future. If a jointly owned company, subsidiary or activity can no longer get additional funds from its shareholders, the temptation will be to turn to the market and get these funds from other, non-tied sources. The more focused interest of shareholders seeking to get increased value from their investments is likely to take the place of the balanced 'stakeholder' view.

More active approaches

Meanwhile, we foresee change in the Anglo-Saxon model of shareholding, too. Long-term investors will probably not be able to take such a hands-off attitude as they do at the moment.

Given the liquidity of the markets, it is easy for an individual fund manager to switch out of one company and find a substitute in the same country or sector. But the larger funds are already finding that alternatives can be surprisingly limited. Some of them have responded to this by handling their investments in a more active way. Instead of simply switching out of companies that under-perform, they are taking the view that they can exercise their influence by adopting a more proactive stance concerning management policies. An institutional investor such as CalPERS in the USA (see below) will in some cases go as far as to seek to replace a company's management rather than simply 'voting with its feet' and selling that company's shares.

This more activist stance could well become more widespread. Institutional investors already hold the balance of power in many contested takeover bids, and their role could well expand as, backed by their own research facilities, they are in a good position to understand, comment on and occasionally criticize local corporate management.

Country values

Let us now look at the state of SHV across the globe, beginning with the 'Anglo-Saxon' markets of North America, the UK and Australia, where the 'equity culture' is at its strongest. We will then work through a number of the more important Western Europe economies. A selection of 'emerging' markets such as Russia, South Africa, and Hungary, follows before we turn finally to Japan, with its own particular idiosyncrasies and challenges, in Chapter 12.

Table 11.1 Shareholders: number and as a percentage of total population

	Percentage	Number (thousands)
Sweden	47.0	4 100
Norway	23.0	968.76
USA	21.0	51 440
UK	15.8	9 000
Switzerland	14.0	1 000
Finland	12.1	600
France	10.1	5 700
Netherlands	5.8	840

Table 11.1 continued

	Percentage	Number (thousands)
Germany	5.5	4 467
Belgium	5.0	500
Austria	4.0	272

(NB Sweden figure includes funds, investment funds and staff shareholders. Figure for direct shareholders is 35.5%. Switzerland figure is direct shareholders only; if indirect ownership of shares is included, the figure is 58%).
Source: Deutsche Bank Group, presentation at 'Factors Influencing Shareholder Value in Europe', Amsterdam, 2 December 1996)

Table 11.2 Pension fund assets in selected countries as at end 1993

	Total (US$ billion)	Percentage of GDP
USA	3 456	59
Japan	1 800	45
UK	717	79
Netherlands	261	88
Switzerland	186	79
Germany	106	6
Italy	12	1

Source: EFTP – EU Commitee/Eurostat

THE ANGLO-SAXONS

USA

Widely considered to be the world's most advanced free market economy, the USA has an established culture of share ownership. The Securities and Exchange Commission (SEC), set up in 1934 to protect shareholders from over-ambitious company promoters and to restrain the power of incumbent boards, presides over a sophisticated regulatory regime that determines the content and timing of financial reports filed by publicly traded companies. The result is that, more than in most other countries, investors are provided with timely business and financial information about the companies they put money into. With a corporate control structure directed towards maximizing value for investors, it is no surprise that it was in the USA that much of the early work on SHV analysis took place.

Stock prices are set on a daily basis around managements' ability to deliver expected returns. The larger institutional investors, who own more than 50 per cent of US equities, are becoming increasingly sophisticated in their equation of expected returns with value; their focus is moving from an extrapolation of growth from accounting-based earnings to free cash flow-based economic models which more explicitly capture risk, growth and returns on investment.

In 1996, Price Waterhouse LLP commissioned a survey of 30 of the largest US equity investment managers to determine their approach to stock valuation. This confirmed that a cash flow-based economic model which explicitly reflects expectations of risk, growth and returns has become central to these investors' outlook. As one analyst put it, 'Cash flow is typically a better and cleaner number ... [it] is ultimately the value of what the shareholder is buying.' Earnings per share, on the other hand, while a 'convenient shorthand', were seen as 'fraught with subjectivity'.

Equity research groups at US securities firms – the 'sell side' – have been slower to develop the SHV approach. Heavy emphasis is still placed on accounting-based earnings, although they are beginning to recognize that EPS growth does not explain value growth in the long run.

As the investment community in the USA has become more sophisticated in its company analysis, so corporate managements have had to adjust – not only by ensuring that they assess investment, operating and financial decisions in terms of value creation for their shareholders, but also by improving their investor communications programmes.

There may still be more to do, however; the survey referred to above also asked the investment managers to report whether they got enough information from companies relating to the seven drivers of SHV. More than 50 per cent reported they did not get enough information on competitive advantage period, cost of capital, and working capital investment. In response to this, companies like Amoco are being much more specific on the competitive positioning of each of their principal businesses, making sure investors are well informed on their competitive advantage periods.

Many companies are also setting explicit debt/equity capital structure targets to manage expectations on the cost of capital and the use of future cash flows. And as far as communication is concerned, a good number of managements are making sure their shareholders know they are applying the same investment disciplines and performance standards throughout their business. To take just three annual reports: in 1996 Coca-Cola stated that 'because economic profit is the most accurate measure of the value the company is creating, we now use it to drive decisions at every level of the business.' RJR Nabisco declared its objective to be 'a total of 20 per cent or better after-tax cash return on common share-holder equity. ... All capital investment decisions will be evaluated in terms of the potential cash return on equity to the individual operating company and in comparison to potential returns from other RJR Nabisco business.' Similarly, Monsanto committed itself to 'a financial metric that would create new levels of share owner value' – one 'that is economically based and tied to cash flows rather than one that is accounting based.'

The pressure for returns

The American investment community's scrutiny (for the most notable example, that of Warren Buffett, see page 75) means companies are looking very carefully at where they are adding value. Using tools such as value chains (*see* Chapter 7), US multinationals are actively analyzing individual product lines as a basis for making decisions on outsourcing, partnering or cross-sharing across product lines to maximize value.

The pressure to deliver superior returns through best practice across industries is rapidly causing companies to focus on core competencies and to divest or outsource areas of their business where value cannot be created. In some cases this can result in downsizing: for instance, Coca-Cola is focusing on selling concentrate, and looking to outsource or set up joint ventures in other areas, for instance in bottling. The chemical industry, too, is asking whether it makes sense to keep all its intermediate stages in-house.

The real challenge to corporate America, however, is to back up their words on SHV with deeds – to take positive steps to ensure that decisions throughout an organization are related to the value they are expected to create for shareholders. Perhaps there have been distractions in the path towards value-based management. The implementation of SHV in the past has been the domain of 'boutique' or strategy consultants, concentrating on senior management compensation plans, while 'metric wars' have debated the best single measure of performance, whether EVA™, CFROI or whatever. Meanwhile the need for fundamental change within an organization has not been stressed.

Another recent area of focus for US companies has been the 'balanced scorecard' approach to performance management, as advocated by Robert Kaplan and David Norton.[1] This is a way of supplementing financial measures with criteria derived from other perspectives – those of customers, internal business processes and growth. But while it has been used to build strategic management systems, it has not generally been tied to SHV strategies at the corporate level.

---

[1] *See* for instance 'The Balanced Scorecard - Measures That Drive Performance', *Harvard Business Review*, Jan–Feb 1992 and 'Using the Balanced Scorecard as a Strategic Management System', *Harvard Business Review*, Jan–Feb 1996, both by Robert S Kaplan and David P Norton. More on balanced scorecards in Chapter 13.

Shareholders as activists

The traditional view of the Anglo-American brand of capitalism is that its large and liquid markets encourage short-termism in investors. The only thing that shareholders are interested in, in this view, is the financial gains that accrue in the near future from their investments. But with the growing concentration of shareholder power within institutions, there are signs that things are not that simple. Take the case of CalPERS, the California Public Employees' Retirement System.

US pension funds are, it has been claimed, the world's largest non-governmental pool of investment capital. They represent the savings of millions of ordinary workers, who have contributed a part of their pay each month in order to assure themselves of a decent income on retirement. The trustees of each fund are responsible by law to their beneficiary members for the prudent management of their savings; they must use the funds entrusted to them for the exclusive purpose of benefiting these members. Hence there is constant pressure on a fund's trustees to increase returns on investment, within the limits of prudence.

At the same time, a fund like CalPERS, with an investment portfolio of over $100 billion and about a million pensioned or still working members, has such large holdings that even a phased sale of its shares in some individual companies could disrupt the market. Further, like many other US funds, it is indexed, so it cannot switch capital back and forth among companies or sectors.

Such a situation has meant, for CalPERS, a more interventionist attitude to the companies it invests in. Where it sees management under-performing it will initially ask for meetings with directors, and seek to get some changes in policy. If private meetings do not do the trick, then it is quite capable of going public with its concerns. Every year CalPERS publishes a list of poorly performing companies, benchmarking them against others in their field. It has also been involved in some very public shareholder uprisings against incumbent management.

As Robert F Carlson, a senior member of the CalPERS board, said in 1994: 'Pension funds are now filling a void in which the management of public corporations had become autonomous and, in extreme cases, unaccountable to the very share owners of the corporations paying their salaries.'

This type of shareholder activism is increasingly becoming part of the investment landscape in the US, where executives and other Wall Street investors have grown accustomed to this hands-on approach. An intervention by CalPERS is generally considered a sign that a company's results will improve. According to a recent study by Wilshire Associated, where companies had significantly under-performed the S&P 500 index in the five years prior to having their shares bought by CalPERS, they went on to outperform the index over the next five years.

Crossing the oceans

In pursuit of value, and in order to achieve the optimum relationship between risk and reward, many US funds have adopted a long-term policy of increasing the international component of their shareholding portfolios. According to analysts, the percentage of their assets held abroad will have to more than double, from 8 to nearly 20 per cent.

As yet there has been little direct intervention by American institutions in European companies' affairs, perhaps because of a lack of familiarity with local 'territory' and the cost and effort involved in obtaining information about continental companies. But it is likely that US funds will increasingly bring pressure to bear for more information and transparency from the companies they invest in. Here again, CalPERS appears to be in the forefront. As William Crist, president of its board of trustees, told European businessmen, 'Outside the US, the traditions, laws, habits, practices and markets are quite different and changing rapidly. We're speaking to directors to seek companies with good internal structures to ask them how they work.'

In other words, one large institutional investor is preparing to select the companies in which it is going to invest on the basis of whether they have a positive view towards shareholders, and shareholder valuation creation, both of which are reflected in having an open and transparent form of corporate governance.

The UK

The UK has had a strong equity culture for years. Buoyed up by equity-financed pension funds, themselves enjoying a favourable tax regime, institutional investors have a stronger grip proportionately on the UK market than anywhere else in the world. Isn't it strange then, you might think, that some of the basic tenets of SHV have not been more strongly in evidence?

All the same, the corporate is generally that there has been too much, rather than too little, shareholder power in the UK. Charges of 'short-termism' have been levelled at the fund management industry as investors chase short term share improvement, and over the years there have been spirited complaints that the supply of long term capital to British industry has been restricted; UK institutional investors, utilizing the freedom to invest globally, have been seen to do so at the expense of domestically based firms.

In our view the truth lies somewhere in between these two poles. The UK equity market is efficient in the sense that it absorbs information quickly and share trading is reasonably transparent. The market is large and liquid, enabling fund managers to transfer their investments out of one company and into another quite easily. This has encouraged a view that where performance of an individual equity suffers, the best strategy for fund managers is to sell out and buy something else. They are not expected to think about using their power as shareholders to directly influence management decisions, preferring to let managers and directors get on with the job.

This sits oddly with the fact that fund managers *en bloc* have been known to take up surprisingly large positions in some companies. They have also been willing to accept less than sparkling performance and yet maintain their holdings, sometimes over several years. There is an impression that performance has to deteriorate quite substantially before positions are closed out completely. This is particularly true if the company is a large blue chip, and is a member of an important stock market index used for benchmarking purposes.

In our view the UK represents an interesting case of a country where all the basic conditions for the application of shareholder value analysis are there, but its application is still relatively limited. It is interesting to explore why this is, and to point to several aspects that suggest that this situation is changing.

The investment community view

UK analysts have for long been great protagonists of an eps-based system of analysis, the drawbacks of which we have already discussed. A lot of their analytical power is spent on trying to estimate next year's earning figures, which as we have seen are poorly correlated with share price movements. A recent Price Waterhouse survey suggests that this is now starting to change. As London's role as the centre of European (and to a lesser extent non-US global) equities has grown, so analysts have become more inclined to used cash flow based measures for assessing corporate performance. One of the reasons for this is that the cash flow methodology escapes from some of the drawbacks inherent in using eps numbers based on different European accounting systems. More recently still, several leading London based investment banks have rolled out equity models that incorporate most aspects of shareholder value analysis. Some, such as Credit Suisse, are making the SHV approach central to their equity analysis. Prodded by competitors in the management and strategic consulting fields, the investment banks have been stung into taking the whole approach much more seriously. Similarly, the buy side analysts, concerned to decipher the sometimes conflicting views of the sell side, have also stepped up their analysis of companies using the SHV methodology.

This has come not a moment too soon, since the corporate market in the UK is also waking up to the possibilities created by using this approach. Again, this has been aided and abetted by the wave of privatizations that have left a swathe of formerly state owned companies in the hands of shareholders. The shock has been considerable as these enterprises, still often staffed by managers used to the more secure environment of state controlled regulation, have had to go to market and lay out their plans to public scrutiny. Freed from the constraints of Treasury spending limits, these companies are having to learn that capital is no longer virtually a free good, and that investors expect their rewards to be every bit as great as they can get elsewhere in the market. This too is creating a more favourable atmosphere for the application of SHV techniques.

What managements are doing

Some UK companies are now starting to embrace shareholder value concepts, particularly when they are faced with a sustained period when their shares under-perform the market. The Rank Organisation, for example, has been reviewing its entire operations at the request of its new CEO in order to see how its traditional businesses are faring and whether the company should be continuing in them. BP is another company that springs to mind as one that took a series of tough decisions several years ago, and by incentivizing senior management on a SHV basis, has been subsequently rewarded by several years of out-performance.

Top management in public companies have usually been incentivized by a variety of share options schemes – or by phantom-type schemes (if private). In the past, the targets that earnings had to reach before executive share options could be exercised were often not very demanding. This contributed in the past to a misunderstanding of what 'shareholder' value meant. Concerns in this area have been partially dealt with by the 1992 Cadbury Committee report on corporate governance, which suggested that there should be far more challenging targets set to management in achieving shareholder value objectives. These are:

- to use relative performance measures (ie comparing other companies in the same sector);
- to use total shareholder returns (ie dividends plus increase in share prices) rather than just an increase in share prices (which could be achieved by a general increase in the market) or raw increases in eps (a figure often subject to manipulation by accounting treatments); and
- to have longer-term performance measures, so that benefits have to accrue to shareholders first over a period of time.

As a result, we are seeing more UK companies keen to put shareholder value measuring systems in place throughout their groups, in order to work out the appropriate yardsticks by which management performance can be assessed before incentives are granted.

Australasia

The pattern of shareholding

While the proportion of shares held by various kinds of investor has not changed much in Australia in recent years, market capitalization has increased impressively in the last five years – from $A198.3 billion to $A347 billion. The most

203

significant change has perhaps been the rise in foreign investment, from 26.1 per cent in mid-1992 to a mid-1996 figure of 32.1 per cent of all shares on the Australian stock exchange, with the USA, the UK and Hong Kong institutional investors comprising over 75 per cent of that figure.[2] International fund investors have been quick to recognize the increased level of liquidity and growth in the Australian equities market.

The lowering of tariff barriers, the partial relaxation of foreign investment restrictions and Australia's proximity to the growing markets of Asia have also resulted in significant levels of foreign direct investment by overseas companies, often through partial and full takeovers.

The proportion invested by life and superannuation (pension) funds has been relatively stable, at around 25 per cent of all shareholdings. However, this proportion is expected to grow. Federal government initiatives will mean increased levels of mandatory pension contributions from employers and more favourable tax arrangements. Superannuation assets are expected to increase from $A240 billion to $A500 billion by the year 2005, largely due to the net inflow of funds as well as the growth in value of the assets.[3] This also means that almost all the working population in Australia are owners of shares indirectly.

Privatization in two countries

One of the leading countries in the trend to privatization has been New Zealand, which early on recognized the need to deregulate its markets. Given its relatively small size, it could not remain prosperous without becoming internationally competitive. In 1986, several government departments were corporatized and converted into state-owned enterprises (SOEs),[4] with a commitment to eventual privatization. In the following ten years, 12 SOEs were privatized and sold for about NZ$8.65 billion, including Petrocorp and Forestry Corp. Several non-SOE assets were also sold, including the Bank of New Zealand.

The trend is gathering force in Australia, too. Privatization, as part of government reform, has occurred at both state and federal level. Recent high-profile examples include Qantas, the Commonwealth Bank, Victoria's utility assets, GIO and the upcoming partial float of Telstra.

These privatized or soon to be privatized entities are quickly trying to develop best practice to allow them to compete more effectively. Many former government departments are now embracing SHV measurements to help link performance with SHV. Probably the most vocal has been Qantas, which uses CVA/CFROI for performance measurement and investment decisions.

[2] *Fact Book 1996 Statistics to 31 December 1995*, Australian Stock Exchange Limited, p 9.

[3] *Securities Institute Education* (1997) p 306.

[4] Drew Stein, 'Deregulation in the New Zealand Marketplace' in Brian Head and Elaine McCoy (eds), *Deregulation or Better Regulation* (1991) Chap 5 p 49.

Going with cash flow

In fact, DCF valuation techniques have been accepted and taught in Australia for many years. The capital asset pricing model, the WACC and related concepts are also widely taught and understood. However, these cash flow metrics in practice focus more on individual project evaluation than the SHV of a corporation.

Price Waterhouse Australasia conducted the first stage of a survey on SHV between November 1995 and February 1996. Its results suggest that equity analysts and fund managers continue to emphasize both accounting (earnings per share) and cash flow measures when seeking to maximize SHV. Interestingly, though, we found that the market as a whole (including the corporate sector) may still favour accounting measures. Indeed, fund managers have been criticized for their undue emphasis on accounting measures – although it should be noted that the critics are themselves selling cash flow 'solutions'.

It seems, then, that equity analysts and fund managers in Australia will continue for the time being to use both accounting and cash flow measures – in part because the accounting information is generally more easily obtained.

A number of well-known Australasian companies have embraced cash flow metrics. These include Qantas, Coca-Cola Amatil, Lend Lease in Australia, and Fletcher Challenge in New Zealand.

However, our experience suggests that other corporations, while claiming to have embraced cash flow metrics, have in fact either a minimal understanding of SHV or have adopted it only at a rudimentary level. Companies that have adopted cash flow metrics and value-based management concepts, and have 'pushed down' the metrics and ideas through their organization are very few in number.

MAINLAND EUROPE

If there is one thing that indicates whether a country's economy is dominated by the 'Anglo-Saxon' or the 'stakeholder' model, it is the liquidity of its stock market. Thus, we only have to look at Fig. 11.1 to see that two of the leading 'stakeholder' countries, France and Germany, are low down in the chart as far as the value of their stock markets is concerned. With little equity-derived finance, then, it could be argued that companies in these countries are less likely to come under pressure from shareholders demanding improvements in performance. (Conversely, it is perhaps no coincidence that the Netherlands and Switzerland have stock markets whose value is comparatively high. These are countries where, as Table 11.2 shows, pension funds hold the equivalent of over three-quarters of GDP.)

Nevertheless, we are looking at a moving picture: no economy is static, and we believe that the ideas associated with SHV are gaining ground in varying degrees throughout mainland Europe. The circumstances that encourage the development of SHV – active institutional investors, increased privatization and merger and acquisition activity, legislation that requires transparency in company accounts and allows share buy-backs – are, as we will see, becoming more prevalent.

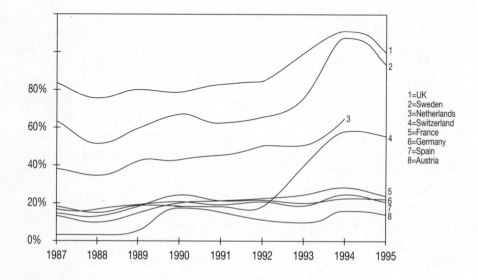

Source: Datastream

Fig. 11.1 Value of stock market as percentage of GDP – European comparisons

Germany

Almost a year after the biggest loss in his company's history, Jürgen Schrempp, the CEO of Daimler-Benz, announced that the new goal would be 'profit, profit, profit'. He was referring explicitly to the fact that SHV was to be the guide for future company action. In Schrempp's opinion, focusing on this approach was the only way to bring the company back into a lasting profitable state. However, his subsequent partial retraction of that policy testifies to the strength of opinion in Germany supportive of a stakeholder view.

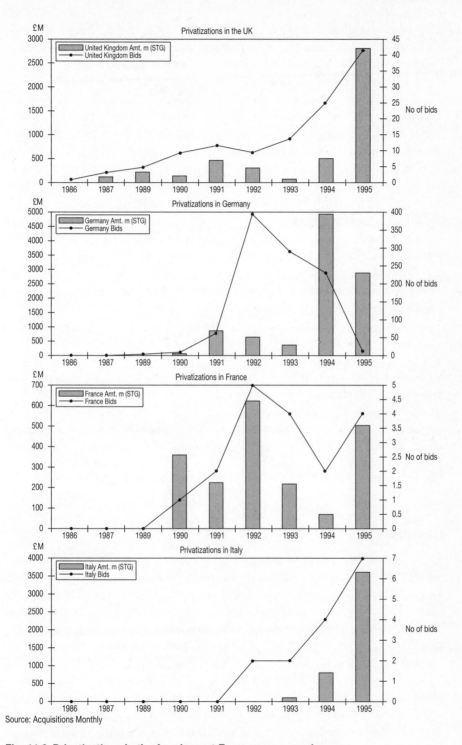

Source: Acquisitions Monthly

Fig. 11.2 Privatizations in the four largest European economies

Nevertheless, the steps taken by Daimler-Benz, the country's largest industrial company, to restrict itself to its core businesses and to dispose of loss-making segments such as Fokker and AEG, have gone ahead, leading to job cuts in these firms – cuts that the unions attribute solely to the drive for SHV.

All of this is a reflection of broader discussions in Germany (and in neighbouring Austria, too, where not only trade unions but also chambers of commerce and the conservative press have expressed their opposition to SHV). Since reunification, Germany has had to deal with slow growth, rising public sector deficits and an alarming increase in unemployment. The discussion around SHV centres on the consequences of concentrating attention on one aspect of SHV at the expense of other parts of the country's 'social consensus'.

Although Germany is often associated with a longer-term view of corporate policy and profits, recent experience suggests that there needs to be more flexibility and adjustment. A company that focuses on SHV will tend to have better cash flows and higher earnings. This in turn will increase job security and create new jobs as it better realizes its growth potential. Restructuring in Germany can therefore release assets which can be put to better use by new owners.

Certainly there are a fair number of companies pursuing the long-term SHV approach now, as it becomes evident that short-term value increases are generally not acceptable. So far, however, shareholders have had little comprehensive or consistent information as to how companies arrive at SHV figures. Very few companies provide figures other than details on dividends.

Of the top 30 companies in Germany, only a handful declare their return on capital. Siemens, Daimler-Benz and the Bayerische Vereinsbank are among those that have set targets for the coming years, while Veba is one of the few firms that has so far determined a risk-adjusted cost of capital for all of its 50 business units.

New accounting?

The disappointing quality of information should not be a surprise. Conventional German accounting practice is aimed at protecting a company's creditors. Hence the required 'transparent' information is not made available to the extent it is in more shareholder-focused Anglo-Saxon accounting procedures. But as the large Germany-based multinationals increasingly tap international capital markets and need to attract large foreign institutional investors, the situation is changing.

For this reason large companies are increasingly issuing their financial statements according to international norms. Bayer and Deutsche Bank are using IAS (international accounting standards), while US GAAP (generally accepted accounting principles) are preferred by Daimler-Benz. In fact Daimler, which became a listed company on the New York Stock Exchange in 1994, was the first

German company to publish accounts under US GAAP, followed by Deutsche Telekom and Veba.

The German legislature is currently discussing whether consolidated financial statements drawn up according to IAS or US GAAP should be admissible instead of traditional legal financial statements. These changes would definitely lead to more useful information (for instance, cash flow calculations) for shareholders, analysts and brokers. Considering the state of the international capital markets and global information requirements, this development has long been overdue in Germany.

The insider environment

It has to be said, however, that in relation to the size of the German economy the number of quoted companies and the market capitalization of these companies is remarkably low. As Fig. 11.1 shows, the country's market capitalization as a percentage of GDP was 27 per cent – lower than France, the Netherlands and even Spain.

Second, the general public has tended to avoid equity investment. Indeed, until the privatization of Deutsche Telekom in 1996, less than 6 per cent of the population owned shares, compared to over 10 per cent in France, nearly 16 per cent in the UK and more than 20 per cent in the USA. Public interest in the Telekom privatization was unprecedented for a placement of shares in Germany; never had so many private shareholders participated before. These and other successful issues should boost equity culture in Germany and thereby help overcome the structural disadvantages of the German stock market, which can be characterized as an 'insider system'. In other words, the multiplicity of cross-shareholdings works in favour of the *status quo* even when pressure from the market might suggest otherwise.

Currently, corporate shareholders own about 40 per cent of listed companies; these funds are largely used to finance the corporations' own pension schemes. Banks and insurance companies are also large shareholders, owning over 20 per cent of the market between them. Deutsche Bank, for instance, holds 25 per cent of Daimler-Benz's shares – a holding that dates back to the 1920s. This leaves a relatively small 'free float' of shares, up to 40 per cent of which is owned by institutional investors.

In this insider environment, loans assume a greater importance in companies' financial structures than equity. (However, retained profits, not bank loans, are the biggest source of finance for German companies.) Banks have played a large role in corporate governance – a role that is not necessarily proactive with regard to management policies. Often a bank becomes active only when it fears there is a risk of bankruptcy and consequently of its loans being written off.

'Unternehmenswertsteigerung'

Many *Mittelstand* companies, which started as family concerns but are now major industrial groups, retain a paternalistic culture that views SHV as a fad. For them, there is too much emphasis on equity investors. Nevertheless, SHV, or as it is often called less contentiously, *Unternehmenswertsteigerung* – literally, the growth in the value of the enterprise – is gaining ground. SHV ideas have had a positive impact in Germany, and have encouraged a closer look at the country as an economic and financial centre.

A recent Price Waterhouse study examined the correlation between the views of investors and the TSR (total shareholder return) of the largest 30 industrial companies.[5] We found that investors were encouraged when a company took a more positive view towards them – and share performance was generally better as a result. The survey showed that in a country not known for providing a good communications service to investors, those that do provide such a service can gain handsomely in terms of a higher share price. (The situation is similar in the comparatively underdeveloped Austrian stock market, where some blue chip companies such as VA Technologies and Wolford have oriented themselves to SHV maximization – resulting in a substantial share price increase.)

It is also worth noting that both stock options and share buy-back schemes, until now frowned upon by the authorities, are soon likely to become acceptable in Germany. In our view the country is one of the more promising territories for the future use and development of SHV.

France

The major feature distinguishing the French system from the Anglo-Saxon model is its differing view of a company's social responsibility. The direction of French listed companies is not determined exclusively by the focus on profitability imposed by shareholders; instead it depends on objectives defined by their owners and managers. This is reinforced by the structure of the French corporate system, in which the public sector has greater importance, and bank loans are preferred to market financing.

The country's 'stakeholder' approach is rooted in the aftermath of the Second World War. During the reconstruction years, entire sectors of the French economy, both industrial and financial, were nationalized. As a result, companies have not focused on wealth maximization as the ultimate financial objective. ROIC and other risk-adjusted measures have been ignored, and profits or sales growth have been the measures of corporate performance and economic profit.

There is as yet no published study on the correlation between cash flow and share price returns on the French Bourse. For valuing stocks, the investment

---

[5] Price Waterhouse and D Hannebohn, *Fundamental Share Analysis and Survey of Investors* (1996).

community mainly uses traditional techniques (earnings per share and price/earnings ratios). Increasingly, however, analysts tend to employ yardsticks like market capitalization or EBITDA – a sign of the growing preference for cash rather than earnings measures. The use of DCF techniques, although not widespread, is increasing.

Insufficient returns

Shareholders, then, have received smaller returns than they had the right to expect from French companies. It is worth noting a ranking of French corporates by EVA™ and MVA in the magazine *L'Expansion*: in 1994, the hundred largest French corporates produced an aggregate negative EVA. This was the case seven times out of the last ten years. Nine of the ten largest companies have been value destroyers; more specifically, the worst five of the hundred ranked were reckoned to have destroyed about FFr 250 billion ($50 billion) – the equivalent of the budget deficit in France or about 15 per cent of France's stock market capitalization.

Some of the factors behind these negative figures include:

- the weight of indirect finance (bank loans rather than equity financing)
- core shareholdings involving institutions where activism is lacking
- the absence of an equity culture
- the large proportion of the French economy in the public sector
- the investment community's lack of understanding, and French companies' limited visibility.

Corporate governance

There are signs of improvement. The French business and financial communities are addressing themselves to matters of corporate governance such as the need for:

- a more representative selection of individual shareholders with expertise sitting on the boards of large companies
- an improvement in the core shareholder system that was established at the time of the 1986 privatization and then expanded
- more effective controls on top management – despite a clear definition of the respective powers that various management bodies have in French *sociétés anonymes* (public limited companies).

This emergence of the concept of corporate governance is a result of shareholder lobbying and scandals related to management misbehaviour. A committee set up by two employers' federations under Marc Viénot, president of the

Société Générale bank, reported in 1995 with a series of recommendations that included a limit on the number of directorships that could be held, and the appointment of at least two 'independent' directors on every public company's board. It also recommended the establishment of committees to deal with board appointments, audit and directors' remuneration.

The Viénot report did not however criticize the practice of cross-shareholding, common in French industry, which has the effect of protecting an incumbent management from suffering the consequences of poor performance, or from takeover. Nor did the report result in any obligations to comply with its recommendations. One observer notes that 'every company I have ever questioned has refused to indicated which [Viénot report] recommendations it has not followed and why.'[6] Nevertheless, recent privatizations have led to a reduction in the strength of core shareholders (*noyaux durs*), the small clique that sits on the boards of virtually all large French groups.

Market pressure in France is also increasingly favourable to shareholders. There are two main reasons for this. The first is the privatization of major financial and industrial firms in parallel with the deregulation of their markets and increased competition. As most of the privatizations have so far been a disappointment – privatization stocks have substantially underperformed in most cases – both the state and the management of the privatized companies need to focus on value.

The second reason for the improving climate for shareholders is the internationalization of the French stock exchange. Foreign investment has increased dramatically in recent years, with approximately one-third of the stock of companies listed on the Paris Bourse now in non-French hands. And these foreign shareholders are asking for more transparency.

Indeed, the signs are that investors are beginning to find their voice and urging businesses to be more responsive to shareholders. And businesses are beginning to respond. In this trend, foreign institutions, which in the past have maintained a low profile, are an important force. Moreover, French stocks have to raise their image as they attempt to widen their shareholder base by diversifying risk and going global.

The pension fund factor

The creation of pension funds is on the agenda now in France. This would bring more liquidity to the market, increase institutional ownership of shares, and force corporate management to focus on SHV creation.

The French parliament recently passed legislation enabling pension funds to be introduced into the private sector. The laws, due to take effect at the end of

---

[6] Sophie L'Helias, 'Corporate Governance Developments in France', presentation to Euromanagement conference on Creating Shareholder Value, Amsterdam, 2 December 1996.

1997, will allow employees to make (tax-deductible) contributions to a pension scheme, complementing the basic state pension allowance. Collected funds will be managed outside the company according to insurance company laws.

A good SHV example

Chargeurs Group recently split its entertainment/media business and its industrial activities into two quoted companies. Previously, Chargeurs had not been looked on favourably, and its strategy was poorly rated. But its spin-off resulted in major value creation for Chargeurs shareholders. It allowed the release of hidden value within the group; the tax effect of the break-up was also minimized. A third advantage was that financial incentives for management and employees were introduced.

The potential for spin-offs, equity carve-outs and share buy-backs as a way of increasing value to French equity holders is substantial. (Buy-backs are permissible under French law, but may have a heavy tax cost for the shareholder.) In Europe, and particularly in France, the number of demergers is likely to increase rapidly, given the large scale of conglomeration. Initiatives like the one involving Chargeurs could have a snowball effect on the rest of corporate France.

Some large corporates also need to resort to equity financing in order to recapitalize in the face of high levels of debt. To attract such equity, companies will have to show their management objectives are aligned with shareholders' expectations.

Switzerland

Institutional investors are, and always have been, very strong in Switzerland. About 60 or 70 per cent of the market's volume is generated by banks, pension funds and insurance companies. The implementation of an electronic stock exchange in the early 1990s has improved the transparency of the market and made it more attractive for foreign as well as Swiss investors. (In 1995, foreigners accounted for 35.7 per cent of all investors.) All of this means that SHV has its attractions for the investment community

In fact, SHV has become a major issue among investors and companies in Switzerland. Partly triggered by a negative article on it by Hans-Dieter Vontobel, chairman of Vontobel Holding, public discussion on SHV has become quite passionate.

Earlier studies from CS Equity Research[7] and CS First Boston analysed quoted Swiss companies on the basis of EVA, ROIC, MVA and other measures. The former found a 76 per cent correlation of EVA with share prices, compared

---

[7] CS Equity Research; 'Economic Value Added und Schweizer Blue Chips – Die Schaffung von Shareholder Value', May 1996.

with a 42 per cent correlation for ROE, 25 per cent for profit growth, 17 per cent for cash flow growth, and 16 per cent for turnover growth.

These studies have focused the public debate on the real issues of SHV. People are becoming aware that this is not simply an Anglo-Saxon political issue but rather a change of paradigm in modern management.

Indeed, executives and boards in Switzerland are increasingly interested. Listed companies are beginning to use value-based measures like FCF and EVA for internal reporting and planning purposes. A survey published in June 1996 in the Swiss magazine *Bilanz* showed that 85 per cent of Swiss blue chip company managements regard SHV as a high priority. Only 45 per cent, however, reported that value-based management has already been implemented.

CS Equity Research ranked a number of Swiss blue chip companies in the order of their past performance in creating SHV. Table 11.3 ranks the companies by indexed EVA from 1991 to 1995, showing the 1995 value of an investment of SFr100 in 1991.

Table 11.3 Companies by indexed EVA – 1995 value of SFr 100 invested in 1991

Company	Value
SGS	317
Roche	268
SMH	162
ABB	150
Novartis	98
Alusuisse	50
Holderbank	24
Nestlé	19
Elektrowatt	11
Sulzer	−41

Source: CS Equity Research

Most of the largest quoted Swiss companies (apart from banks and insurance companies) appear on this list, but two of the top three – SGS and SMH – are not among the top five companies by market capitalization or turnover.

Increasing transparencies

A new federal stock exchange law coming into effect in 1997 aims to ensure transparency and equal treatment for all Swiss investors. As well as setting guidelines for bookkeeping and notification from securities dealers, it includes a requirement for disclosure on the acquisition of a certain percentage of a company's voting rights – at 5 , 10, 20, 33.3, 50 and 66.6 per cent. A minority holding of more than a third will trigger a takeover bid – although there are expected to be exceptions to this.

Italy

The Italian stock market is relatively underdeveloped in comparison to the US and other European stock exchanges. Take the figures for total market capitalization as a percentage of GDP. As at the end of 1996, the figure for Italy was just 20.7 per cent. (Compare the countries shown in Fig. 11.1.) Other facts worth noting about Italian economic life include:

- Only 218 companies were quoted on the Italian exchange (*La Borsa*) as of December 1996. On the same date just 32 companies were quoted on secondary markets (the *mercato ristretto*).

- In the three years 1994–6, there were fewer than 45 new listings on the Italian exchange. (In 1995 alone, there were 600 new listings in the USA.)

- The Italian corporate structure consists of relatively few large businesses and numerous small and medium-sized companies. In 1994 there were more than 3 million businesses operating through various forms and business entities in Italy. Of the 400 000 corporations, only 8000 have revenues in excess of L25 billion (US $17 million) and only 2000 have revenues in excess of L100 billion (US $67 million). The majority of these businesses are family-owned corporations, and obtain financing from commercial banks that provide traditional collateralized debt. Equity is obtained primarily from self-financing and personal sources.

- With the exception of state-owned companies and selected financial institutions, there are very few Italian companies quoted on the Milan exchange with revenues in excess of L5 trillion (US $3.2 billion). Exceptions include Fiat, Mediaset, Pirelli and Olivetti.

- Because of the Italian stock exchange's smallness and lack of liquidity, some of the country's leading companies – such as Fila, Luxottica, Natuzzi and De Rigo – have sought listings in foreign countries rather than Italy. (The requirement that any company looking to be listed on the Italian *borsa* has to have been profitable in previous three years may be another reason for this preference for going abroad.) Others such as Benetton are listed in New York and in other European markets as well as on the Italian stock exchange.

- Trading volume is extremely low compared to other national markets. The 1995 average daily trading volume was approximately L621 billion (US $400 million).

- The Italian market is influenced by large powerful industrial groups and a few banking groups (IMI and Mediobanca) which hold significant cross-shareholdings as 'strategic financial investors'. Control of public companies is traditionally shared by these investors. Hostile takeovers are not common in Italy, partly because a single shareholder (or a group of strategic financial investors) will usually hold enough shares to block unwanted bids.

- The Italian State offers high real interest rates on its debt, thus diverting private funds from equity markets.

- Private pension funds, the largest source of equity funding in the USA and the UK, do not have a significant presence in Italy. On the other hand, there are several other mutual and savings funds in which some L250,000 billion is invested. Of the capital from these funds, the majority (58.7 per cent) is invested in Italian government bonds, but some 10.3 per cent is invested in Italian companies' shares and 8.5 per cent in foreign companies.

- Corporate tax rates in Italy are comparatively high, at approximately 53 per cent.

Cash flow, SHV and the investor

Analysts at selected Italian financial institutions have found no significant correlations between cash flows and the stock prices of Italian corporations. Cash flow analysis is used by institutional investors, but their holdings and those of retail investors are generally minor in comparison to the holdings of strategic financial investors, who employ cash flow analysis as only one element in evaluating investment decisions.

The Italian investment community can be split into three main categories of investors, each having a different perception of SHV.

The first is the large industrial and banking groups (discussed above) which hold a large and diverse portfolio of investments in quoted companies. These investors are more apt to perceive SHV as a function of portfolio performance rather of individual business investments.

The second category is the traditional institutional investor, who perceives SHV (and its maximization) as a factor crucial to investment decisions. Italian and foreign institutional investors are frustrated by the lack of transparency which quoted companies provide to the markets. Information required by institutional investors in pricing equity includes: market performance; statutory financial statements (including cash flow statements); interviews with key management; forecasts (generally used for DCF analysis); working capital and capital expenditure needs.

The third category is retail investors, who represent a minor part of the whole Italian equity investment community. They perceive SHV mostly as a function of a business's earnings performance and dividend distribution policies.

The corporate view

Italian corporations and their management, with few exceptions, do not explicitly focus on maximizing SHV. Management accountability does not require any emphasis on SHV; as is evidenced by the fact that executive remuneration packages in Italy rarely depend on share performance.

The lack of attention to SHV within the Italian corporation is partially attributable to the ownership structure described above. Large companies' priorities are determined by the majority shareholders (either family groups or strategic investors), whose decisions may be driven by factors other than SHV.

Nevertheless, SHV analysis 'does not extend beyond members of the *salotto buono* (high society) to ordinary mortals'.[8] As control of public companies is primarily in the hands of strategic financial investors, business decisions have historically been a function of controlling shareholders' priorities (operational or otherwise) rather than the explicit maximization of SHV. The institutional or retail investor does not yet have enough power to dictate corporate priorities.

A change from the past may come as a result of central and local government privatizations on one hand, and IPOs of medium-sized companies on the other. However, both processes seem to be still slow and unclear.

Belgium

If SHV ideas are gaining ground in Belgium, it is perhaps because of the increasing percentage of stock that is foreign owned: from 23 per cent in 1990 it has risen to 29 per cent in 1994.[9] In addition, a number of Belgian companies are now listed abroad or have embarked upon ADR (American depositary receipt) programmes – which means that they have had to meet a demand for financial transparency on a level with that required in the USA, and for strategic plans that will optimize returns.

Since the late 1980s, when raiders employed ideas of value analysis in hostile takeovers – for instance in the case of Générale de Belgique – many conglomerates have been under pressure to deliver improved and more transparent performance. In the past, information provided in annual reports was limited to statutory requirements, with cash flow, when reported, being simply accounting cash flow (earnings plus depreciation). Shareholders' meetings were deliberately short to discourage questions. Now, though, large international companies provide more transparent information, and are assisted by professionals in drafting annual reports. Indeed, the Belgian CPAs' association advocates the publication of cash flow statement.

Nevertheless, according to a recent survey by CS First Boston, Belgian com-

[8] *Economist*, 7 September 1996.
[9] FIBV figures.

panies in aggregate have destroyed value for their shareholders since 1986, by almost 29 per cent of total market capitalization. Holding companies have performed weakly compared with the stock exchange average, mainly because they have been transferring cash from sound businesses to poorly performing ones.

The investment community view

Belgian analysts use several criteria for measuring SHV. Stockbrokers tend to focus on multiples such as earnings per share. The dividend discount model (DDM) – a method of capitalizing dividends – is still widely used by the local community for company valuations. But it has not reflected the potential value of companies.

Cash flow-based alternatives to DDM were introduced in the late 1980s and early 1990s, mainly by Anglo-Saxon investment banks and brokers advising on large cross-border deals and privatizations, or simply following local stocks for international investors. International consultancy firms have also advised large company boards or top executives on what drives SHV. As a result, cash flow-based approaches are being used more and more for valuation purposes and in assessments of creditworthiness. Such approaches have shown better correlations with value than other methods. Increasingly, investors call for transparent financial information, an indication of company strategy and future prospects as well as information on products and services and distribution channels.

In Belgium, as in much of the rest of Europe, institutional ownership is growing in importance. But unlike (say) the USA, where the fund business is a separate industry, funds in Belgium are essentially another product line in a bank or insurance holding company and can hardly be expected to take strong positions against banking interests. Shareholder control over companies' activities is minimal today – but can be expected to increase with the development of institutional ownership.

The corporate environment

Although, as we have noted, many heavy industrial groups and major conglomerates in Belgium have destroyed value, retailers and medium-size companies – which are more focused – have generally performed rather well. Names like Barco (a now well known example of a share initially overlooked by Belgian investors) and Deceuninck in particular have by far outperformed the market.

One can observe an acquisition trend in Belgium, driven by low financing costs and future cash flow prospects. The merger between the Crédit Communal and Crédit Local de France to form Dexia, and Cera's purchase of 80 per cent of Banque Indosuez Belgium are recent examples.

In general, though, efforts towards implementation of value-based management are at an embryonic stage. Models for calculating SHV creation division by division are being developed by corporations in the manufacturing and financial services sectors, but these are often confined to top management levels.

Denmark

It is perhaps inevitable that a small European country like Denmark should have to adjust to the external factors that make SHV so important internationally. The country is increasingly moving away from its traditional 'patient' investment, illiquidity and low dividend regime to a more value-oriented economic environment.

Historically, the Danish stock market has been characterized by 'friendly' investors, modest dividends and low trading volumes. Pension funds and other institutional investors have traditionally not been greedy in terms of demanding a return on their investments. In fact, the average dividend yield on Danish stocks for the last ten years has been some 17 per cent of net profits – compared to 49 per cent in the UK.[10]

One explanation for the country's historically low dividends is a tax regime that favoured capital gains over dividends (capital gains on stocks were tax free after a three-year grace period). In 1993, however, tax regulations were changed, treating capital gains as well as dividends more equally from a tax point of view. In theory, this should mean that dividends will increase. (Share buy-backs, while possible, are rare in Denmark, as investors are taxed at a higher rate in such circumstances.)

Another factor in the low level of dividends as well as the low market liquidity is ownership structure. Many companies are dominated by large investors who are either families, trust funds or institutions. In fact, institutional investors – pension funds and financial institutions – control not far short of half of all shares in Danish listed companies, and also hold shares in a large number of non-listed companies. (Pension funds and insurance companies, however, are allowed to invest only two per cent of their liabilities in non-listed shares.) The figures for proportions of shares held at the end of 1996 were: pension funds 18 per cent, trust funds 16 per cent, strategic holdings 15 per cent, foreign investors 15 per cent, insurance 8 per cent, banks 4 per cent.[11] (A further 0.5 per cent of listed shares are held by companies themselves – under Danish law a company can hold up to 10 per cent of its own shares.) Studies suggest that if strategic holdings are added to institutional investments more than half of all shares on the market are accounted for.

[10] Uniboers, Dagbladet Boersen, 18 April 1996.
[11] Figures from Aros securities.

Increasing foreign ownership

The pattern of low dividends seems to be changing, however, and several larger companies have actually changed their dividend policy in an attempt to attract foreign investors. Thus, on the request of international investors, Carlsberg increased dividends to 22 per cent of profits – still far from the dividend levels found in other European stock markets.

Foreign ownership now accounts for some 15 per cent compared to a mere 5 per cent just a few years ago, but it is still concentrated on the 20 largest listed companies. US institutional investors especially seem to be active in the Danish market, claiming that Danish shares are cheap by international standards. This increasing foreign ownership will, it is thought, not only put pressure on companies to increase return and payout ratios, but also increase market liquidity.

According to the CEO of a large Danish bank, 'as professional investors play a still bigger role among shareholders, we will have to meet these higher demands. Also, the banks have become more international, and as investors and analysts operate on a global basis, we will have to live up to the demands of US investors as well.'

Certainly a new generation of fund managers and investors seems more responsive towards cash flow-based valuations than price/earnings figures, and research among analysts suggests that cash flow-based models are becoming more widely used. Denmark's Association of Chartered Accountants is in favour of the DCF model, and has demanded that it be used for valuations in connection with mergers and acquisitions. Nevertheless, simplistic and short-term valuation measures such as p/e ratios and EPS are still favoured by most Danish analysts, because these measures are easily applied and well understood by the market.

The role of the institutional investor

Danish institutional investors (and with them family trust funds) have been protective towards conservatively managed – and in some cases even poorly performing – companies, thereby avoiding takeovers and boardroom revolts. Such investors have played an active role in supporting and restructuring industries, on occasion saving larger companies in trouble in order to preserve jobs. In some cases the institutions have helped Danish companies avoid foreign takeovers.

In recent years, however, their role has been changing. The director of one large institutional investor put it this way: 'We will have to focus on the issues important to shareholders – i.e. the issues creating wealth for shareholders – even if the management of the company does not approve.' Coming from a traditionally 'patient' investor used to playing a somewhat defensive role, this is a rather bold assertion.

Sweden

It is a familiar story in Sweden, where the country's better-known multinationals are in most cases controlled by one of a few groups of owners, the most prominent being the Wallenberg group. Shareholders holding normal shares with less voting power than those held by groups can 'vote with their feet' by selling and buying, but do not in practice have any other opportunity to influence company policy through board membership or representation.

Partly thanks to the Swedish tax system with its double taxation of dividends, private shareholders have become significantly less important over the last decade. Their place has been taken by institutions and investment funds, which the tax system treats more favourably, and by foreign investors. These institutional investors are pressing more and more for their views to be considered in the election of board members: in 1995–6 the biggest insurance company in Scandinavia, Skandia, published a policy on how it would act where it is a major shareholder in other companies.

A trend towards focusing on core business activities, started in Sweden during the early 1990s, can be seen as an attempt to improve SHV. Many companies are now analyzing their remaining divisions and investments from a value creation point of view, and restructuring is continuing in the name of SHV. Examples are the breaking up of cross-shareholdings between quoted companies, refocusing on growth sectors, acquisition of major new operations and so on.

Recent adoptions of SHV have, perhaps unfortunately, begun with a focus on top management bonus systems, which of course could be tied to value creation. In a booming stock market this has looked like a good way to trigger increased bonuses. Astra, the pharmaceutical company, for example, has introduced a management bonus system based on value creation without disclosing any details. Meanwhile, the real challenge of implementing management reporting systems focused on the value drivers, although it has attracted interest, is only being taken up slowly.

Reporting to shareholders

A couple of years ago a number of mainly poor performing companies felt the need to improve their share price development on the stock market. The SHV concept became a tool for top management to communicate its aim of improving performance in the interest of shareholders. Most Swedish investment companies holding major blocks of shares in other companies were at this time quoted at 20 to 40 per cent below adjusted net equity, reflecting the stock market's view that blocks of shares were held for reasons other than earning profits for shareholders – such as controlling voting within certain spheres of interest, and even as cross-holdings between different quoted companies.

In their 1995 annual reports, several major Swedish companies began to talk in terms of the SHV concept – a trend that has gathered pace in 1996 reports. There are, however, significant differences as to the extent to which Swedish companies report having established monitoring systems for SHV. Mostly they describe their systems and application of the value concept in very vague terms.

SCA, the major paper company, has declared its aim is to achieve a certain yield on investment for its shareholders, mentioning SHV in this context. It has also stated that different entities in the group are assessed on the basis of generated cash flow that will increase the SHV. Incentive, a key medical and investment company in the Wallenberg group, has also gone a long way towards introducing SHV: during 1996 it developed its own model for monitoring SHV. The model is cash flow based, with increases in SHV being assessed by a combination of profitability, growth and free cash flow.

Other European markets

While we believe SHV concepts are gaining ground in Europe, their take-up varies from country to country, as we have seen; often it can depend on particular tax and other legislative environments.

For instance, if a company's cash flow figures are readily available, SHV analysis may be easier to introduce. Such is the case in **Spain**; there, cash flow information became compulsory in annual reports from 1990 onwards, making it common to evaluate company performance by means of cash flow analysis. All the same, the level of cash flow information varies in quality depending on the particular industry or sector. SHV has been introduced in some major Spanish banking and electricity companies – although only in terms of the share price.

Particular markets may have particular characteristics relevant to SHV. Take **Norway,** where the Oslo Stock Exchange is the home for the equity of extensive shipping and offshore construction companies. These industries, as well as the oil and gas industry, are extremely capital intensive and naturally have large non-cash items in their accounting records. Because of this the Norwegian marketplace has long recognized that earnings multiples are of limited use. The historically low relative market capitalization of technology and service and trade businesses, and the relatively high relative market capitalization of capital-intensive industries has forced institutional, private financial and strategic and industrial investors to focus on relevant cash items rather than accounting information.

In **Finland,** as elsewhere, increased internationalization has meant that the price formation of many of the country's central stocks is exogenous to Helsinki Stock Exchange. Companies are more likely to consider the opinions of shareholders when they have large numbers of international investors. For instance, after Nokia's management announced it did not intend to sell off the company's

TV business division, despite its dismal performance, growing outside pressure forced Nokia to concentrate on its core business. The company divested after all, and Nokia stock soared on the announcement.

The Finnish stock market is notable for the large number of companies with dual-class share structure. It is not exceptional for shareholders with, say, 14 per cent of total stock to have 80 per cent of votes. Not surprisingly, hostile takeovers are a rare phenomenon in Finland. But new legislation will increase the power of minor shareholders by requiring a majority of votes in every share class at shareholders' meetings.

EMERGING MARKETS

Hungary

Stock markets in Hungary and other developing market economies in Eastern Europe are very small, very young, and illiquid in nature. In the case of Hungary, there were just 43 listed companies at the end of 1996, when the Budapest Stock Market had been working for only five years. The correlation between cash flows and share performance, therefore, cannot be assessed on a statistically reliable basis.

All the same, institutional investors are increasingly influencing the character of the market, which is controlled and moved from London via various funds and investment banks. These investors do not simply invest in the market overall, but on a case by case company basis, relying on their investment banks' contacts in Hungary and brokers' reports for their decisions. Such reports contain in-depth industry and company analysis of the kind found in the West, including significant cash flow-based analysis. It is clear from discussions with various banks and brokerage firms that cash flow measures are considered both by analysts and in investors' final decisions.

Certain other factors, however, such as political country risk, industry risk, and a need to make money primarily on the capital gains side (not dividends and capital gains) seem to carry a much greater weight than in Western markets.

Inflation and debt

A few other special factors need to be taken into account. Inflation in Hungary was around 25 per cent in 1996. No long-term debt finance is available; there is only short-term local currency funding at close to 30 per cent. This usually means that most companies view equity as cheap, and debt as extremely expensive, even if the corporate tax rate of 18 per cent reduces the cost of debt. The usual argument that debt is cheaper is not entirely true under these circumstances.

In Hungary, then, in the short term, equity funding is the less expensive choice (if the company can obtain it through the stock market or elsewhere) since most investors do not look for immediate dividends and capital gains but hold to a longer view of the region and the company. While debt funding carries 30 per cent interest rates, and requires cash payments quarterly, equity funding represents long-term cheaper funding from the company's point of view. In the end, the 'normal' model – in which debt is cheaper and equity funding more expensive – will prevail, since investors will eventually require a higher return in both dividends and capital gains.

Under such circumstances, creating SHV needs to be based upon the notion that debt is indeed more expensive in the short run. The short-term/long-term conflict is much more important in economies such as Hungary's, as is the financing – the mix of debt and equity within the total capital structure – from a company's point of view.

SHV in the investment and corporate communities

Increasing SHV is, in itself, an acceptable notion in Hungary. The link to specific cash flow-oriented analysis and future cash generating capacity is more questionable. While cash flow analysis and liquidity (sources and uses of funds) are generally accepted methodologies, and most significant companies provide substantial amounts of information on these matters, locally investors are still biased towards earnings. Perhaps this somewhat 'German' orientation is because many of Hungary's accounting rules and regulations are based on the German system. Discounted earnings and price-earnings multiples are the most common methods of evaluation.

As for managements, they are just beginning to wake up to the idea that SHV is their key goal. It is interesting to note that while DCF analysis is a widely accepted methodology for specific individual transactions, it is harder to take this approach in managing the business. Convincing managers that they must take account of the cost of equity in their internal measures of 'profitability' will probably be a major issue in the future.

But given most companies have spent the last five years in transition from an economy where production was centrally planned to one where profitability measures predominate, the concept that businesses should be managed to concentrate on cash and SHV will be a bigger step forward than for most companies in the West.

Russia

During the decades of Soviet control, economic competition was eliminated from the Russian marketplace. Through state ownership and central economic planning, the government effectively dictated the activities of business management. Furthermore, there was no need for investors or financiers within this system of state sponsorship and control. Production alone, rather than market share, cost controls, long-term business development or other activities which would increase SHV, was the primary goal of Soviet economic policy.

Beginning in 1992, in an effort to develop a market economy, the Russian government embarked on an ambitious plan to privatize the nation's wealth on a scale that had never been witnessed before. Although the state retained significant control in most major companies, privatization resulted in the transfer of a great deal of the nation's wealth into the hands of individuals.

After decades of operating within the centrally planned Soviet economy, these newly independent Russian companies were immediately faced with the need to restructure and modernize in order to compete effectively and survive in the global market economy. However, faced with a shortage of domestic capital, they began to look outside Russia, typically to the West, for the investment capital they needed. Analysts, traders and business partners have since struggled with methods to arrive at fair and proper shareholder valuations of these Russian enterprises in order to assess their business prospects.

Missing information

With an initial lack of meaningful financial information, companies were primarily valued on the basis of physical assets alone. Natural resource reserves were of particular interest to the investment community given the availability of international commodity prices. Since these humble beginnings, information has continued to improve, with some companies now even providing Western financial statements, business plans and cash flow forecasts. Such information, when available, has proved helpful in the valuation of the underlying Russian economy.

For example, in valuing oil and gas companies it would be important to consider the relationships between market capitalization, Russian proved and potential natural reserves, current and anticipated production, revenues and net income for the company, and compare these relationships to those of their Western counterparts. Other considerations might include the company's overall financial position, the competitiveness of functional business units, production costs, the status of existing assets, future investment needs, market position, and corporate structure and strategy.

However, as is often the case, where information such as this is still not available, basic independent research is necessary. As well as analyzing the available information, such research must consider information on comparable Russian companies, industry trends, individual companies' strategic plans, and the general political situation. Furthermore, the Russian business environment of today can best be characterized as a maze of regulations surrounded by political and economic uncertainty. Potential investors must attempt to find their way through this bureaucratic puzzle, on their way overcoming cultural barriers too. These intangible factors can also affect the perceived valuation of enterprises.

SHV has a role

Given this lack of quality information, the lack of an efficient stock market, as well as the current general political and economic situation, any correlation between cash flows and share price is not easily determined. The prices of Russian companies are deeply discounted and are trading at a fraction of their theoretical value (although if they are listed overseas, they trade at higher prices). However, this does not mean that cash flow analysis and its impact on SHV has no place in Russia.

Russian companies are being forced to scrutinize SHV and cash flow by the following factors:

- Due to the government's privatization efforts, ownership of a significant portion of Russian industry now rests in the hands of business managers and employees, as well as international investors. Understandably these people have an interest in seeing the value of their investment improve.

- As Russian companies struggle to shake off the vestiges of Soviet era economic policies, they are increasingly looking outside Russia for additional investment capital. The business partners and financiers sought by these companies will also certainly have an interest in SHV.

- As the environment inside Russia continues to improve over the coming years, shareholders and potential investors will undoubtedly focus increasingly on SHV as a gauge of management performance.

Re-engineering begins

Now that Russia has embraced the ideals of a market economy, SHV must be considered a priority throughout the country's business community. Only by demonstrating their ability to increase long-term SHV will companies be able to attract investors and obtain the needed capital that will enable them to compete in the global marketplace. Although not universally, Russian business managers have started to recognize this need and to implement processes of re-engineering the way that their companies operate. They are focusing their efforts on identifying and eliminating old and inefficient practices, replacing them with those of proven effectiveness and reliability. In this, they are able to rely on the advice and expertise of Western advisors and companies that have implemented such practices.

The production-driven economic policies of the old Soviet system still have deep roots within today's Russian business community. However, due to privatization, managements now have a stake in seeing SHV increase. Furthermore, they recognize the need to attract investment and to obtain financing so that their companies can survive in the global market economy. The growth opportunity of SHV is the key that will attract the needed capital.

South Africa

For years, South Africa was politically and economically isolated due to its internal policies. In order to conserve foreign exchange the government embarked on an ambitious but economically wasteful programme of import substitution. To protect so-called 'infant industries' a wall of tariffs and duties was erected to discourage imports and to provide price advantages to the local producers. The result of this policy was an inefficient, uncompetitive and tax-payer/consumer-subsidized industry which increasingly displayed classic symptoms of oligopoly.

At the same time South African residents, domestic companies and to a lesser extent non-residents were subject to foreign exchange controls that effectively prevented them from investing abroad.

In such a captive market, most people's savings in the form of pension fund contributions and insurance premiums found their way via institutional investors into the Johannesburg Stock Exchange (JSE), which offered better returns than both bond and money markets. In some years during the 1980s, real interest rates became negative – which of course fuelled inflationary spending. The results were there for all to see: a misapplication of capital and a disregard of SHV. Interestingly enough, the big institutional investors did not complain, as they were trying to allocate their cash to an ever decreasing number of investment grade companies, the so-called 'shortage of good scrip'. The JSE, thus, became one of the most illiquid stock exchanges in the world – less than 7 per cent of the total market capitalization was traded there in any given year.

With 1994's new democratically elected government and the peaceful transition from apartheid, a renewed interest from foreign institutional investors began. The country's risk has been assessed by major international agencies such as Moody's and Standard & Poor's, and South Africa has begun to be included in emerging market indices. The foreign exchange controls on non-residents were first relaxed and have now been completely abolished. It has been estimated that the inflow of foreign funds, most of them earmarked for the JSE, amounted to R22 billion [US$6 billion] in 1995.

Local circumstances

A further peculiarity of the South African market worth noting is the restriction on share buy-backs. Companies cannot buy their own shares except in special circumstances – a law that observers see as inflexible and out of touch with current international practice. The indications are that the current situation will change, however, and it is possible share buy-backs will be permitted by 1998.

Companies' financing arrangements are also somewhat different in South Africa. Traditionally, they have relied on direct loans from banks; the bond markets for private corporate debt, in contrast to those for government and utilities, are rather underdeveloped. Nevertheless, things are changing. Listed private sector companies acquired R2.2 billion (US$500 million) of funds through rights issues of fixed interest securities (including convertible preference shares and debentures) in 1996, compared with R900 million (US$200 million) in 1995.[12]

The chance of obtaining funds at below banks' prevailing lending rates was perhaps the single most important reason for the increased popularity of fixed interest securities among private sector companies in 1996. Table 11.4 has some recent statistics from the JSE.

Table 11.14 The overall performance of the JSE using the All Share Index – ALSI (%)[13]

	1992	1993	1994	1995	1996
Return ALSI	(5.4)	50.3	19.9	6.2	6.9
Dividend yield	3.6	2.4	2.2	2.3	2.5
Overall return	1.8	52.7	22.1	8.5	9.4
Avg R/US$ depreciation[14]	(3.3)	(14.6)	(8.7)	(2.2)	(18.5)
Return to non-residents[15]	(1.5)	38.1	13.4	6.3	(9.1)

Source: *PW South Africa* (using BFA Database)

A changed focus

The real economy has mirrored the developments taking place on the capital markets, with trade liberalization and a phased-out approach towards the dismantling of tariffs. South Africa became a signatory to GATT, further committing itself to free trade. The focus of the economy has changed from import substitution products to export-led ones. An additional factor is the govern-

---

[12] Source: *Quarterly Bulletin South African Reserve Bank*, March 1997.
[13] The returns have been calculated using the calendar year period.
[14] This is the year on year depreciation in the average R/US$ exchange rate.
[15] This is the return on ALSI held in US$.

ment's firm commitment to scrapping all remaining foreign exchange controls, thus enabling institutions such as life assurance companies, which are repositories of private savings, to invest abroad.

The obvious consequence has been an upsurge of interest in SHV, led by foreign investors. In the face of increased international competition, there is little doubt that the country's business community is paying more attention to wealth and SHV creation. Change is being accelerated by such factors as: the proposed commercialization and privatization of government enterprises; 'unbundling' by large privately held conglomerates; and the rise of black-owned and highly geared enterprises.

With some big institutional investors among the converts to SHV in South Africa, we believe that bodies such as pension funds will increasingly use the tools of SHV to appraise their current and future investments and demand better returns from their portfolios. A number of recent developments support this trend. First, the law now allows the Public Investment Commissioner (PIC) to invest in publicly held companies – previously investments were confined to government stock and some parastatals. Second, a relaxation of exchange controls means that institutional investors can invest up to 5 per cent of their net inflow of funds abroad.

There is also evidence that the pension funds are getting more proactive in the management of their investments and are not averse to championing a potential acquirer if they are convinced that incumbent management is incompetent and is causing their investments to perform poorly. This role, as change agents, is bound to continue growing for South African institutional shareholders, who at the time of writing hold more than 70 per cent of issued share capital on the JSE – a figure that is likely to increase.

These developments have not been lost on the investment community, which sees the latest concepts of economic value as a basis on which to offer valuation services to companies. One stockbroking firm has grafted the EVA concept onto the database of the University of Pretoria's bureau of financial analysis, and has reportedly tested the system and modified formulae to suit South African reporting standards and local conditions.

While EPS is still a tool widely used by both analysts and institutional investors in South Africa, the SHV concept receives ever more attention in financial magazines. Table 11.5 shows the market value added figures of the three best and three poorest performing sectors on the JSE, which are now being published annually.

The concept of SHV has been enthusiastically embraced by some executives of the major South African companies. It is worth noting that most managers have become exposed to economic value through consultants who have tried to align top management pay packages with the market value added objectives of their companies' shareholders. The result has been a proliferation of the incentive schemes for top management. Big companies using the tools of SHV to assess performance include, among others, South African Breweries, Murray & Roberts, Sentrachem, and Nissan South Africa.

Table 11.5 Market-added – selected from top 200 companies on JSE (Rm)

Sector	MVA	MV	TC
Top 10 companies (mostly mining beverage and industrial holdings)	139,407	281,822	142,415
Middle 10 companies (mostly food, hotel and electronics)	3,377	12,590	9,213
Bottom 10 (mostly steel, motor and textiles)	(17,463)	58,581	76,044

Source: The *Finance Week 200*, 17–23 April 1997

An interesting aspect of SHV creation when one analyzes the results presented in Table 11.5 is that the South African market displays the same characteristics as most US and European markets – with the possible exception of mining, which historically has occupied pivotal role in the economy. The textile, steel and allied, and motor sectors have been the biggest destroyers of shareholders' wealth in the country; traditionally, they enjoyed the highest protection from international competition.

SUMMARY

So far, then, we have looked, in varying degrees of detail, at the economies of a number of different countries and their potential for SHV. There is one more economy which is starting to adapt itself to SHV concepts, and which presents an interesting study in the adaptability of capital markets. That country is Japan, and we shall devote the next chapter to it.

JAPAN: A SPECIAL CASE?

For most of the last 40 years, the Japanese economy has been regarded as a flourishing one by most commentators. Its successes in a variety of fields have been held up as a positive example of the 'stakeholder' model and as a pattern for less 'successful' economies to follow. Now, however, things seem less straightforward.

The collapse of the bubble economy – a period in the late 1980s in which Japanese equity and real estate prices appreciated rapidly due to a liquidity boom by the Bank of Japan (see Fig. 12.1) – caused many Japanese financial institutions to suffer substantial losses on their real estate and equity portfolio holdings. Due to these losses and to foreign competition, Japanese financial institutions today face tremendous pressure to increase returns on the assets they manage. At the same time, Japanese companies are increasingly raising capital in global financial markets just like their foreign competitors, and as a result are becoming exposed to investors who demand a satisfactory return on investment. It is no coincidence that a number of Japanese corporations have in recent years begun to target return on equity as an important measure of performance.

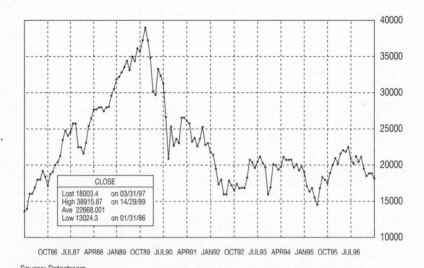

Source: Datastream

Fig. 12.1 Monthly closing prices of the Nikkei 225 index (January 1986–March 1997)

The fact that the Nikkei 225 index is still 50 per cent below its 1989 peak, as Figure 12.1 shows, has heightened Japanese concern as to whether the country can continue to grow along the lines of its post-war economic model. We see a consensus beginning to emerge; a belief that significant changes are required if Japan is to resume its growth.

The pressure is on, therefore, to deregulate and internationalize Japanese financial markets in order to maintain Tokyo's role as a global financial centre. The situation is epitomized by the proposals Prime Minister Ryutaro Hashimoto made in his New Year's Address at the beginning of 1997, for a 'Big Bang' to liberalize Japanese financial markets.

HISTORICAL BACKGROUND: WHO ARE THE OWNERS?

In Japan, historically, corporations have not focused on the goal of creating value for shareholders in the same manner as corporations in the USA or even in Europe. To understand why, it is necessary to look at the country's share ownership patterns.

It was only in 1996, for instance, that foreign shareholdings in Japan exceeded 10 per cent of the market in terms of value for the first time.[1] As of 31 March, 1997, 11.9 per cent of shares were held by foreign investors.[2] Interestingly, this marked the first time that the percentage of shares held by foreign investors exceeded the share held by Japanese life insurers (11.1 per cent).

Nevertheless, at first glance share ownership patterns in Japan appear similar to those of other major international stock markets. As elsewhere, the percentage of stocks owned directly by Japanese individual investors has declined throughout the post-war era (*see* Fig. 12.2) and has been overtaken by a corresponding rise in the percentage owned by financial institutions. In 1949, individual shareholdings made up 69.1 per cent of the Japanese market; this declined to 22.4 per cent in 1988, before recovering to 23.6 per cent in 1996. (The level remained static in 1997). At the same time, shares held by Japanese financial institutions (mainly banks, trust banks, life insurance companies) have risen from 9.9 per cent of the market in 1949 to 46 per cent in 1989 before falling back to 41.5 per cent in 1996. As a result, the share of the stock market held by financial institutions (domestic and foreign) now exceeds 50 per cent. This shift closely mirrors the trend in other major capital markets noted earlier, but there are differences.

---

[1] Survey of shareholding as of 31 March 1996: National Conference of Stock Exchanges.
[2] *Ibid.*

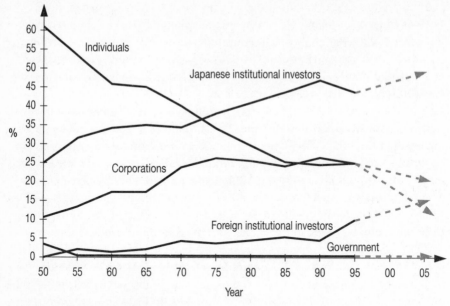

Source: National Conference of Stock Exchanges

Fig. 12.2 Owners of Japanese shares

What's different about Japan?

The principal owners of Japanese shares other than financial institutions are corporations, which owned 23.8 per cent of the market at the end of March 1997. Corporate ownership rose from 5.6 per cent of the market in 1949 and peaked at 27.5 per cent in 1973. This large-scale presence of corporations marks a major difference between the share ownership model in Japan and other countries.

As has been well documented,[3] cross-shareholding or *mochiai* originated after the earlier *zaibatsu* (industrial groups such as Mitsubishi, Mitsui, etc.) were disbanded under the American occupation immediately following the Second World War. The purpose of the cross-shareholding system is to promote stability and to protect the companies from takeover. *Mochiai* shareholding patterns usually involve bank-financed purchases of newly issued shares. As the proceeds from issuance are generally used to purchase new shares or to repay bank borrowings to purchase shares in another group, there is no equity capital raised by the transaction. These patterns became more common in the 1960s due to a combination of two factors: the desire for protection from foreign competitors following the opening of the Japanese economy when it joined the OECD in 1964,

---

[3] Yukihiro Asano, *The Stock Market from Investors' Viewpoint (Toushika kara mita kabusiki shijo)* (Chuo Koron, 1996).

and the need to support equity prices during the brokerage recession of 1965.[4]

Over time, cross-shareholdings have increasingly come to define reciprocity in business relationships, with their level increasing or decreasing according to the intensity of those relationships. This system has contributed significantly to the closed nature of the Japanese market. Thus, life insurance companies or banks purchasing shares can expect to receive business in the form of insurance sales or loans from the companies in which they invest. Members companies of Japanese industrial 'groups' (Mitsui, Mitsubishi, etc.) can expect to receive financing in the form of bank loans for strategic rather than economic reasons. Some analysts have gone so far as to suggest that financing costs related to such investments should be considered selling, general and administrative expenses. More significantly, member companies of Japanese industrial groups such as Mitsui and Mitsubishi could expect to receive financing in the form of loans from the group bank for strategic rather than economic reasons.

The success of these practices can be gauged by the lack of competition in the market for corporate control – and in the relatively low level of dividends paid by Japanese corporations. It is also significant that a substantial majority of public companies hold their annual general meetings on the same day, in order to prevent shareholders from attending. On 27 June 1997, for example, 2355 listed corporations had annual shareholders' meetings. This represents 88 per cent of all companies that scheduled meetings in June, the most popular month for such meetings.[5]

Nevertheless, the general consensus, while somewhat difficult to quantify, is that cross-shareholdings have declined over the last few years – from upwards of 60 per cent to probably a little below 50 per cent of the Japanese equity market[6] (see Fig. 12.3). This is partially the result of an increase in the number of corporations seeking to raise capital through direct access to the financial markets rather than through bank loans. As a result, floating equity has now come to represent approximately 50 per cent of the market. There are thus two divergent types of shareholders now: those who hold shares for relationship or strategic purposes and those who hold shares in order to obtain an economic return on investment.

The role of the banks

Japan's banks, too, play a role somewhat different to that in most Western countries. This has its origins in the post-war occupation, when American administrators, in their efforts to break up the *zaibatsu*, sought to enhance the ability of Japanese corporations to raise capital through direct financing activities (i.e. the

[4] *Ibid.*
[5] Nihon Keizai Shinbun, 27 June 1997
[6] Asahi Shinbun, 18 August 1996.

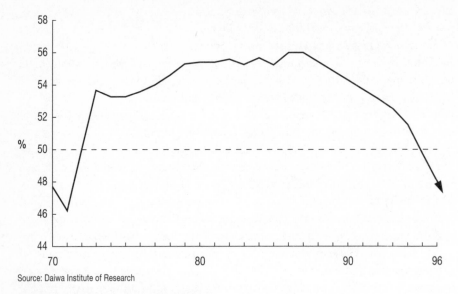

Source: Daiwa Institute of Research

Fig. 12.3 Japanese cross-shareholding

issuance of bonds and equities). The markets at the time, however, were confused and functioning ineffectively, and banks were in a better position to attract
money. Having incurred losses during the war by buying government bonds,
people preferred the safety of bank deposits to the potentially high return of
equities. Rather than investing directly in the markets, they put their money in
banks, which as a result became the leading providers of corporate funds.[7]

The primacy of banks has continued to the present. For example, between
1990 and 1994, on average, 80.3 per cent of the external financing for Japanese
corporations came from bank borrowings, followed by issuance of equities (8.9
per cent) and bonds (7.1 per cent) and payables (3.7 per cent). In large corporations however, the ratio of bank borrowings to total external financing is
much smaller, at 55 per cent.[8]

Fall-out from a decline

The 'bubble economy' collapse, however, seriously eroded the capital base of
most traditional sources of indirect finance, especially banks. Many of these
institutions had relied on unrealized profits from long-term securities holdings
and/or real estate to provide a capital base for their loans. Additionally, the
traditional method of providing loans was based on collateral asset valuation,

---

[7] Summarized from Nihon Shokenshi, *History of the Japanese Securities* (Nihon Keizai Shimbun).
[8] Japan Development Bank report, June 1995.

primarily real estate. As property prices have continued to fall, bad debts have risen, further deteriorating the capital base.

The consequence was that many Japanese firms faced a credit crunch during the 1992-1994 period because their traditional sources of indirect finance were unwilling to provide funds, despite low nominal interest rates. This has led to a search for new sources of direct finance and a call for the expansion of the domestic bond Japanese market. We believe the long-term trend is for direct financing activities, such as issuance of equities and bonds, to increase.

The other major fall-out from the decline of asset prices has been a collapse in the returns that life insurance companies and trust banks have been able to receive on the funds they have invested for corporate pensions. As Japan's population ages, corporations will be required to increase returns on pension assets or make further provisions. Furthermore, the proposed deregulation of the investment asset management market will open the door to foreign asset managers who can achieve higher returns than traditional Japanese pension managers, simply because their investment policy is based on forecast return on investment rather than relationship investing. In fact, observers now point to the recent success of foreign asset managers as one of a limited number of foreign successes in prying open the Japanese market.[9] Competition from these outsiders will increase as a result of the proposed 'Big Bang' reforms and may significantly alter the investment strategies of Japanese institutional investors.

As we have seen elsewhere in this book, a major factor behind the drive to maximize SHV in the West is the move from individual share ownership to investment by institutions. But in Japan that trend has been offset by corporate cross-shareholding, where the need for a return on investment is not explicit. Instead of achieving returns in the form of capital gains or dividends, the return sought has been one of stability and increased business ties. It has also been offset by reliance on indirect rather than direct financing.

Shareholding versus stakeholding

To illustrate the difference in management focus in the *mochiai* (cross-shareholding) system and in the global capital markets environment, Figs. 12.4 and 12.5 compare the performance of a leading Japanese diversified heavy electrical manufacturer (company A) with General Electric Co. of the USA under both stakeholder and shareholder return criteria. We take employee headcount as a measure of stakeholder interests and begin by comparing headcount for the ten-year period from 1987 to 1996.

From the employee and, by proxy, stakeholder perspective, it seems clear that company A has clearly outperformed General Electric, which has dramatically

---

[9] *ACCJ Journal*, March 1997.

reduced its headcount during the first part of the period as part of a major restructuring programme initiated by CEO John F Welch, Jr. On the other hand, when we compare the performance of the two companies from the shareholder's perspective, the results are starkly different. Figure 12.5 presents an indexed total shareholder return comparison for the ten years from 1987 to 1996 (total shareholder return is defined as dividends + capital gains). On this measure, General Electric has clearly outperformed its competitor Japanese company A.

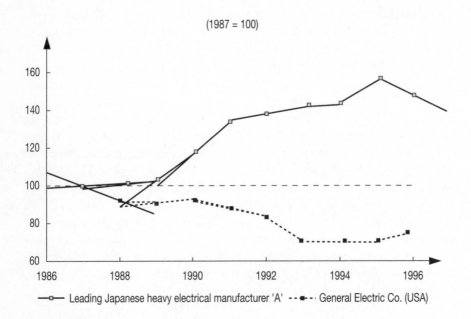

(1987 = 100)

Source: Company reports

Fig. 12.4 Indexed headcount comparison

Success is defined differently in the *mochiai* system and in the global capital markets environment. Consequently, we believe that one's view about the state of SHV in Japan will be shaped by the degree to which one foresees a further breakdown in the system of cross-shareholdings. Our view is that in order to compete in today's global economy, Japanese companies will have to raise capital in global financial markets through direct financing activities. Over time, the vagaries of individual markets will come to matter less and less as global institutional investors assume an ever expanding role. While it will take time for Japanese companies and financial institutions to adjust, we believe that the trend is clear.

(March 1987 = 100)

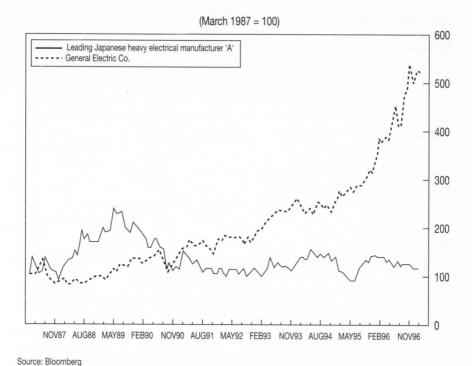

Source: Bloomberg

Fig. 12.5 Indexed total shareholder return comparison

VALUATION TECHNIQUES

Valuation techniques utilized in the Japanese market depend on what kind of investment policy is being pursued – relationship investment or portfolio investment. At a simple level, portfolio investors must make some assessment of the value of a stock before buying; relationship investors, on the other hand, purchase at whatever is the current price. As we have noted above, an estimated 50 per cent of Japanese shares are held for relationship purposes, rather than for securing a return on investment. Although this has negative implications for shareholders, as we have seen, this percentage does not have a significant influence on stock prices as these shares are not regularly traded

Prices are determined by daily buying and selling, and more specifically by the views of the marginal investor. In today's markets, the marginal investor is generally an institutional investor or portfolio manager. Price Waterhouse interviews with buy-side investors have indicated that they consider a number of factors in deciding whether to purchase stocks; one such factor is cash flow.

239

Accounting rules

As we have seen in Chapter 4 and elsewhere, one reason for preferring a DCF model over an earnings-based model to assess value, is that earnings are subject to manipulation. This is true in most countries, of course, but the problem is particularly acute in Japan due to lax accounting rules – notably in relation to consolidations and the treatment of unrealized gains and losses (both on and off the balance sheet).

At present, Japanese regulations do not permit the filing of consolidated tax returns. Consolidated financial statements are not required for uniform commercial code purposes. Due to this, and to their historic goals of growing the scale of their businesses, Japanese managements appear to have focused on aggregate parent company pre-tax earnings results rather than on consolidated net income on a per-share basis. Furthermore, there is flexibility for Japanese group companies to determine which subsidiaries are to be consolidated – thus allowing them to record losses in unconsolidated subsidiaries.

This problem is further compounded by the accounting treatment for unrealized gains and losses, i.e. a failure to mark to market. Readers of the financial press will no doubt be familiar with the topic of problem loans at Japanese banks. Commentators have questioned whether the amount of unrealized gains on securities holdings (*mochiai*) or land purchased many years before will be adequate to cover estimated losses related to bad loans. Due to the difficulty of obtaining true figures, a number of foreign investors have stopped investing in Japanese bank stocks despite the fact that they represent over 20 per cent of the stockmarket's value. Japanese life insurance companies are now taking the same view, too: recently, they announced they will not purchase additional shares in banks that are seeking to shore up their capital position until they address the problems of bad loans by reducing risky assets.

In addition, Price Waterhouse experience shows a number of significant differences between the accounting treatment prescribed under Japanese GAAP and US GAAP, the *de facto* global standard. Differences may arise in the following areas: pensions and employee benefits; leases; consolidation versus equity accounting for investments; financial instruments; and business combinations. There are also other differences in accounting principles which may have a significant effect for individual companies.

Analyzing stock performance

As a result of such differences and the subjectivity inherent in financial accounting data, recent research about the Japanese stock market by a number of securities firms has shown that cash flow-based analysis may prove to be a better predictor of stock price performance than earnings-based measures. For example, in a frequently cited study, Kenji Uno of the Daiwa Institute of Research concluded that the concept of CCR (cash flow/cost of capital return) had a correlation with return on investment about three times higher than did the growth in EPS.[10] Similarly, analysis by the Nomura Research Institute (NRI) has concluded that traditional measures such as the price/earnings ratio or the price/book ratio are not strongly correlated with earnings-per-share growth or return on equity. According to NRI, cash flow analysis provides a more complete evaluation and reflects factors such as cost of capital, capital structure, timing of return on investment, and so on.[11]

Work by Western investment banks and consultancies supports these conclusions. In 1994, for example, SBC Warburg analyzed the returns of stocks in the Nikkei 300 index and classified them in five portfolios: cash generating - growing; cash generating - slow growing; cash absorbing - growing; cash absorbing - slow growing; financials and other. This analysis, as summarized in Fig. 12.6 (excluding financials and other), tends to indicate that there is a link between cash flow generation and total returns. This conclusion is supported by a 1993

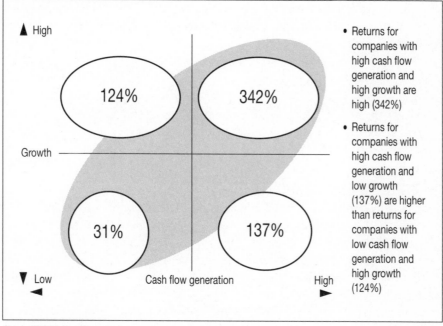

Source: SBC Warburg Research

Fig. 12.6 Nikkei 300 index total return on investment by portfolio type: 1985–94

---

[10] Kenji Uno, 'Corporate Analysis and Investment Method by CCR, Management & Investment Measures from Shareholders' View', *Security Analysts Journal*, April 1995.

[11] Nomura Research Institute, *Comparison of Shareholder Value of Leading US and Japanese Companies through Free Cash Flow Valuation (Furi Kyashhu Furo Baryueshon ni yoru NichiBei JuyouKigyou no Kabunushi Kachi Hikaku)*, (1992).

valuation and analysis of 28 Japanese companies by McKinsey & Company, which concluded that there was a high correlation between market value and discounted cash flow value, after non-operating factors such as excess real estate and marketable securities holdings were taken into into account.[12]

These studies notwithstanding, it has to be said that this aspect of the Japanese market has not been subjected to the same breadth or depth of research and analysis as have other markets. It would therefore be premature to conclude that a definitive correlation has been established between share price returns and cash flow for Japanese equities.

Several reasons can be offered for this lack of comprehensive research. Three are: that the major portion of the stock market invests on a relationship rather than portfolio basis, as we have seen; that there is much less disclosure in the financial statements of Japanese corporations than in most foreign ones (especially US companies), making analysis difficult to carry out; and that cash flow models are a relatively recent innovation in Japanese financial institutions. Nevertheless, securities analysts have told us that the attitudes of Japanese corporations towards investors have dramatically improved in the last few years. As companies grant more access and better information to analysts, and as cross-shareholding ties begin to unwind, we believe it is likely that cash flow will show an increasing correlation to ROI.

TOWARDS MANAGING FOR SHV

A consensus emerges

In the view of many observers in the financial community, corporate managements have begun to pay attention to shareholders in the last two or three years because share values have fallen dramatically. (The Nikkei 225 index peaked at 38 915 on 29 December 1989, plunged to 14 309 by 18 August 1992 and is around the 19 000 level at the time of going to press). A consensus has evolved that it is no longer possible to ignore shareholders.

As a result, we have seen a trend for companies to develop investor relations programmes or departments. This is supported by a 1996 survey of investor relations activities in 576 publicly listed Japanese firms by the Japan Investor Relations Association (JIRA), which found that approximately two-thirds of the non-JIRA members were performing investor relations (IR) activities. Including JIRA members, approximately 72 per cent of the companies in the sample performed IR activities (*see* Fig. 12.7).

---

[12] *Valuation: Measuring and Managing the Value of Companies* (McKinsey & Company, Inc., 2nd ed 1994).

information is relevant when prepared. In time, they will become capable of assessing the value of their business units on a global basis in a timely manner.

The holding company arrives?

A law that permits holding companies was among the reforms that Prime Minister Hashimoto's administration passed in June 1997. We believe that we will see corporate groups consolidating their core elements and selling off their cross-shareholdings in entities not deemed to be part of the core (*see* Fig. 12.9).

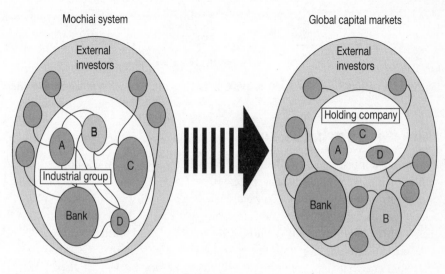

Fig. 12.9 Anticipated Japanese industrial group capital structure transformation

Elimination of cross-shareholding patterns will also make the relationship between shareholder and management more explicit. It will also lead corporations to seek a new class of stable shareholders. Increasing exposure to global institutional investors – a major available source of capital – will require changes in corporate attitudes, and in improved corporate governance practices. Hopefully, these would include outside directors and more responsible scheduling and conduct of annual shareholders' meetings. But ultimately, the major change will be an increased focus on SHV. Once this point is reached, large-scale financial restructuring, similar to that observed in the USA in the 1980s, should follow (*see* Fig. 12.10).

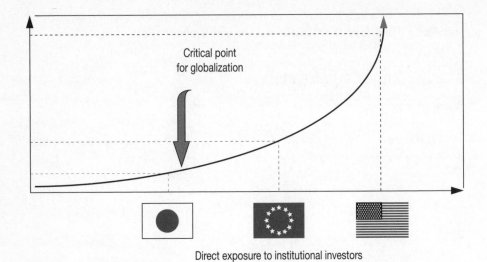

Critical point
for globalization

Direct exposure to institutional investors

Fig. 12.10 Emphasis on SHV rises as institutional investors become more important

More stock buybacks, too?

As managements come to understand which elements of their groups create and destroy value, we anticipate that there will be a significant increase in the volume of mergers and acquisitions. Companies will seek to dispose of, or swap, assets to increase returns. Recent announcements of a merger between Mitsubishi Oil and Showa Shell, and of acquisitions of Mazda, Hokuriku Seiyaku and Nakamichi shares by non-Japanese corporations, suggest this trend has begun. We anticipate that the recent trend towards stock buy-backs will also continue. This trend is due to a relaxation in restrictions towards treasury stock which has made it easier for Japanese corporations to buy back their own shares.

Further legislation to permit share repurchases when authorized by a board of directors may soon be in place, too. Further liberalization to permit share repurchases authorized by boards of directors was approved by the ruling political coalition in May 1997. The importance of this is that many Japanese corporations increased the number of their outstanding shares through rigorous equity financing during the 'bubble' era. As a result, capital efficiency decreased for most Japanese companies and, in many cases, the weighted average cost of capital increased due to the inadequate use of debt referred to above.

To improve returns to shareholders, about 30 corporations, including the Toyota Motor Corporation, Mitsubishi and Mitsui had announced plans to buy back their own shares as of the time of writing.[17] As illustrated in Fig. 12.11,

[17]Price Waterhouse research.

248

such plans have had a very positive effect on Toyota's share value – a valuable lesson for other Japanese corporations, many of whom are likely to have huge volumes of cash in hand after disposing of their shares in non-core group companies. Failure to return this cash to shareholders or to invest it in high-return projects would have the unfortunate effects of either raising the weighted average cost of capital through less than optimal use of debt or destroying value.

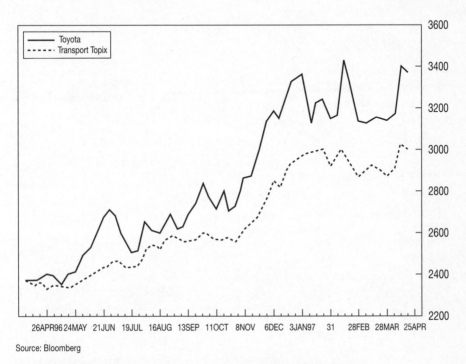

Source: Bloomberg

Fig. 12.11 Toyota Motor Corporation versus Topix Transport Index
(April 1996–April 1997)

JAPAN AND THE DECLINE OF STAKEHOLDER POWER

The evidence from Japan points to a financial system that is clearly under pressure. Content to march to a different rhythm than the rest of the financial world for many years, the country is now undergoing a process where the entrenched interests of stakeholders are being gradually eroded. Pressure on banks to become competitive means that they are having to take a progressively more critical view of the value of their strategic shareholdings. As these get put into 'play', so outside investors will become increasingly influential and demand more accurate and timely information.

Faced with these pressures, globally focused Japanese companies are likely to respond more quickly, while more domestically oriented firms will move more slowly. Nevertheless, we think that a clearer trend towards emphasizing SHV can be seen in Japan.

PART

BRINGING IT ALL TOGETHER

4

REPORTING ON THE FUTURE: THE BLUEPRINT

Reporting on the future? The title of this chapter may seem paradoxical – after all, we normally report on the past and predict the future – but there is a point to it.

As we have said throughout this book, creating value is the central imperative in today's business environment, where globalization, the computer revolution and the free flow of capital are combining to demand as much information as possible about company performance. What's more, the performance information that investors need is not simply *historical* information; they – and the managers of the companies they invest in – need information that is oriented towards the *future*.

Of course, information is available, to some extent. The closely regulated obligations of annual reports, prospectuses, proxy statements and other formal documents ensure that there are data about company performance out there to be studied. But a gap has always existed between these facts and figures and a management's own information. Some part of that gap can be explained by the confidentiality that any commercial enterprise needs – and anyway, market analysts will often fill part of the gap with their own reports and projections. Information about a company's plans will eventually reach the public domain when its financial statements have to reflect changes in circumstances. But it's not a systematic matter. Future-oriented information, reflecting financial management and investment policies, is not subject to disclosure requirements.

However, because of the rise of SHV, we believe it is in managements' interest to make their companies more transparent. A new kind of reporting is emerging that focuses on long-term cash flow and other key financial performance metrics.

This chapter, then, is about *Value Reporting* – the new kind of reporting that will increasingly be demanded as SHV imperatives take hold throughout the world. To help explain what it all means, we have drawn up a value report for a fictional company, Blueprint Inc., (Appendix 1) at the end of this chapter. But first, let us go back and remind ourselves of the market forces that are causing a shift in emphasis from point in time reporting to value-oriented financial reporting.

WHAT MAKES VALUE REPORTING NECESSARY?

As we have shown throughout this book, today's executive management and directors live under the 'perform or perish' scrutiny of investors. Increasingly, the intelligent shareholder is not content to rely solely or even primarily on a company's annual report for his or her information. The world financial markets are examining other factors, including specific business areas that previous generations of investors left unexamined. As a result, some large shareholders are becoming more aggressive than ever before, pressuring managements to achieve better results faster. (The example of CalPERS, touched on in Chapter 12, is a case in point.) In some cases, investors are keenly interested in influencing strategic decisions.

At the same time, cash flow is becoming the key performance metric for judging company performance. With intangible assets such as intellectual property or brand recognition on the increase as a proportion of a firm's total value, and with the amount of long-term, non-liquid assets declining, there is less of a correlation between book value and market value. So when financial markets value your company, they pay more attention to free cash flow as we defined it in Part 1. If you provide sufficient cash to stockholders through dividends, or invest it in ways approved of by investors – in new technology, products, brands, or new management structures – markets typically show their gratitude by increasing your share price.

Advances in computer technology have dramatically reduced the expense and time that scenario assessment – procedures such as the sensitivity analysis outlined in Chapter 7 – needs to be effective. These new capabilities make it possible to do in a few hours what previously would have taken weeks of work, or would not have been undertaken at all. Sophisticated analysis will, we believe, become commonplace for companies as they look for new strategies to maintain or enhance shareholder wealth. Given that historical financial information is just a jumping-off place that tells you little about the future, value reporting, aided by increasingly powerful (and portable) computers, will become much more important.

WHY ASK ACCOUNTANTS?

This book has been written by people who work for a firm best known for its 'core competence' of accountancy and auditing; yet so far we have written as if that activity is only marginally involved in the transformations that we foresee. In fact, the fates of corporations, investors and professional services firms such as Price Waterhouse are intertwined.

In the new business climate, corporate management and investors are increasingly hungry for information that bears on the future of a business. Investors will exert more pressure on businesses, who will look to their service providers to help them address these demands in various ways. Identifying areas where value can be built, and supporting management's subsequent reporting on that value, is emerging as an important focus of professional services firms.

We believe that value reporting (VR) promises to have extraordinary power, and that power lies in its twofold potential: first, to integrate the principles of traditional financial reporting, investment reporting, and management reporting, and second, to help professional firms' services evolve so that they provide even further benefit to the investment community, company boards of directors, and company executive management. Helping management focus on areas in which to build value and reporting on it is emerging as the central focus of professional services firms in the business marketplace of the next century. Meeting company needs in the coming years will require new professional services – and VR will be at the centre of these.

The public accounting profession is keenly aware of the potential impact of the changing business environment on its ability to meet the needs of companies and investors. The profession's thinking on these issues is being led by the AICPA (American Institute of Certified Public Accountants) Special Committee on Assurance Services, established in 1992 to consider the relevance and usefulness of financial reporting and the ways in which it is changing to meet today's business requirements. Its view is that:

> financial reports are losing their significance because they are not future oriented and do not provide value-based information. ... To meet users' changing needs, business reporting must: provide more information about plans, opportunities, risks, and uncertainties, focus more on the factors that create longer-term value, including nonfinancial measures indicating how key business processes are performing, [and] better align information reported externally with the information reported internally to senior management to manage the business.[1]

THREE AREAS OF ACCOUNTING MERGE

VR will be made possible through the convergence of the three important areas of accounting noted above: traditional or historical financial reporting, investment or shareholder accounting, and management accounting.

---

[1] *Preliminary Report of the Special Committee on Financial Reporting* (New York: American Institute of Certified Public Accountants, July 1992).

Traditional financial reporting

We can be pretty certain that external reporting of financial results will always exist in some form. Governments will always require accurate financial reporting as a basis for levying taxation; in fact, more external reporting may be demanded as investors ask for more frequent communication, and in more areas, regarding management's stewardship. Such communication will be made possible by the ubiquitous nature of communication technology.

Investment accounting

A critical driver of corporate market wealth is the market's perception of how long the cash flow a company is generating can be sustained to benefit investors. If the market concludes that the cash flow will not last, investors will leave skid marks in abandoning the stock. This perception of how long the company can reasonably expect to have good times ahead is exceptionally important; the market is judging the company's actions in such areas as new technology, new products, patents, and long-term strategic planning. Historical financial reporting is just one key element of communication.

Management accounting

Management accounting is directed toward the analyses that managers need in order to make important business decisions. This branch of accounting relies on internal and external information in areas such as revenues, cost, pricing, budgeting, and profits. For example, management accounting information would indicate margin by product line, inventory value at current standard costs, and anticipated internal rate of return of a capital expenditure. An important part of management accounting is assessing the capital planning and control process in order to gauge how the company will make decisions that are strategically relevant to its future performance.

We predict that in the business environment of the future, these three areas of accounting – traditional, investment, and management – will come closer and perhaps even combine to some extent as companies make the changes necessary to meet the new requirements of the marketplace, their business partners, and investors.

THE SEVEN CORE COMPONENTS OF VR

The value reporting approach consists of seven core activities that a professional services firm, working with company executive management, will incorporate into its work. It will:

- *Perform a preliminary evaluation of the financial drivers of the company – the levers of SHV:* especially in the USA, and increasingly in Europe, management has already performed this type of analysis. VR incorporates this analysis and the assumptions that have gone into the evaluation.

- *Determine how management has embodied these drivers in the corporation's objectives and how these drivers are shaping business operations:* for instance, the company's objective might be, in numerical terms, a 10 per cent free cash flow improvement, a 15 per cent share of the market, and 30 per cent of revenues from products less than five years old.

- *Understand how management has developed the strategies to achieve these objectives:* e.g. by raising prices for slow-moving items, concentrating on large customers, investing more in new products, and streamlining the R&D process.

- *Determine whether these objectives and strategies are supported by performance measurements, and assess the quality of the measurement data provided to management:* the financial drivers should be linked to a 'balanced scorecard' of financial and non-financial metrics (*see* p. 263) that reinforce the SHV message at all levels of the company. These metrics will need to be reviewed periodically to assure management that the information they receive is accurate.

- *Assess whether management processes foster value creation:* such processes would include goal setting, capital planning and acquisitions, budgeting, strategic planning, product/service planning, management forums, and executive compensation. Is the value-creation message being communicated effectively to the individuals who are responsible (and accountable) for all these corporate processes?

- *Draw up the 'big picture' from all of the foregoing, and select the most relevant points to communicate with the investing public about value-creating strategies, processes, goals and results:* in some companies, such management communication has in itself enhanced the stock price – because as the management's actions have become more transparent to investors, so investors perceive there is less risk. Naturally, management must deliver on its expectations. This would mean giving the investor information about whether the company's strategies and processes are effective. In some companies, such management communication, by itself, can enhance the stock price.

- *Review, on a rotating basis, how effectively the major processes of the company are functioning, and fix what needs to be fixed:* processes here would again be things like capital planning and acquisitions, budgeting, strategic planning, product/service planning, management forums, and executive compensation.

EXTERNAL REPORTING

A significant benefit of VR is that it enables you as a manager to communicate your VR conclusions about company strategies, measurements, and processes to the external business and investment communities – perhaps, in the case of measurements, accompanied by an opinion from an independent accountant. Such external reporting makes sense only if several criteria are met: that your investors desire additional information; that your proprietary information can be protected; and that effective 'safe harbour' rules are established to protect you from lawsuits. (Forward-looking information may lead some investors to expect more positive results than you subsequently deliver.)

Topics for external reporting that might be useful include: product development; market share for major lines of business or products; average cost of capital (and investment hurdle rates); additions to intellectual capital; and customer satisfaction survey highlights. These might be organized around a 'Statement of Shareholder Value Achieved' template, an example of which is shown in Table 13.1, which is based on the publicly reported information of a US company, supplemented by some estimates.

In general, you should take a balanced attitude to external reporting – particularly the commentary associated with such reporting. You should give weight to earnings per share while also emphasizing the statement of cash flow, SHV achieved, cash flow return on investments, and the primary drivers of long-term financial success. These could include such things as information on product development, number of new patents being obtained, changes in market share, percentage of revenues from products less than five years old, new technology, and industry-specific factors that affect shareholder wealth.

Table 13.1 Statement of Shareholder Value Achieved

	1996	1995	1994
Sales and other income	7,058	6,331	5,754
Cost of product sold	4,212	3,866	3,633
Gross margin	2,846	2,465	2,121
Selling, general, administrative, and other expenses	1,213	1,137	1,073
Other operating expenses, net of other income	95	72	36
Operating earnings before interest, taxes, etc. (EBITDA)	1,538	1,256	1,012
Capital expenditures required for normal operations (Note 1)	352	335	350
Net operating profit before taxes	1,186	921	662
Cash taxes (Note 2)	401	286	314
Net operating profit after taxes (NOPAT)	**785**	**635**	**348**
Capital charge for invested capital			
Net receivables and operating cash	1,351	1,291	1,109
Inventories @ FIFO	941	886	893
Current working assets	2,292	2,177	2,002
Accounts payable and accrued expenses	(1,104)	(1,034)	(921)
Net operating working capital	1,188	1,143	1,081
Net property, plant and equipment	2,835	2,742	2,787
Other operating assets, net of other liabilities	27	54	82
Net operating assets	4,050	3,939	3,950
Weighted average cost of capital (WACC) (Note 3)	11.3%	11.5%	11.0%
Capital charge (on beginning asset values)	**445**	**454**	–
Shareholder value achieved			
Net operating profit after taxes (NOPAT)	785	635	–
Capital charge (on beginning asset values)	445	454	–
Economic profit/shareholder value achieved	**340**	**181**	–

Note 1: Depreciation and amortization from the Statement of
Cash Flows has been used as an approximation.

Note 2: Cash taxes on EBIT (adjusted for non-operating items)

	1996	1995	1994
Effective income tax rate	*38%*	*38%*	*43%*
Interest expense	*85*	*86*	*103*
Non-operating <income> expenses	*(162)*	*(20)*	*15*
Tax effect of interest and non-operating expenses	(29)	25	51
Provision for income taxes	480	325	236
Decrease <increase> in deferred taxes	(50)	(64)	27
Cash taxes	**401**	**386**	**314**

Table 13.1 continued

	1996	1995	1994
Note 3: Weighted average cost of capital (WACC)			
Cost of equity			
Expected return on US equities market	11.3%	11.7%	11.3%
Risk free cost of capital (US ten year treasury bond)	6.6%	6.9%	7.3%
Market risk premium for US equities	4.7%	4.8%	4.0%
Beta for company			
(Measure of risk adjusted for financial leverage)	1.13	1.11	1.08
Cost of equity			
(Return for business and financial risk of shareholders)	**11.9%**	**12.2%**	**11.6%**
Cost of debt			
Marginal cost of debt	7.9%	7.8%	7.8%
Tax adjustment	–3.0%	–3.0%	–3.4%
After tax cost of debt	**4.9%**	**4.8%**	**4.4%**
Total market value			
Total shares	291	291	145
Share price	45,750	37,125	75,875
Total market value	13,313	10,803	11,002
Total debt outstanding	1,221	1,144	1,129
Total value of invested capital	14,534	11,947	12,131
Weighted average cost of capital			
Equity percentage of total capital	91.6%	90.4%	90.7%
Debt percentage of total capital	8.4%	9.6%	9.3%
Equity contribution to WACC	10.9%	11.0%	10.6%
Debt contribution to WACC	0.4%	0.5%	0.4%
Market cost of capital	**11.3%**	**11.5%**	**11.0%**

Source: Illustrative, based on publicly reported information of a US company and estimates

APPLYING VR: A HYPOTHETICAL CASE

How could your company make use of and benefit from VR? To begin answering this question, let us take a hypothetical company undergoing a VR analysis in conjunction with its independent accounting firm. This process differs from an annual financial audit, although it can draw on some of the knowledge gained in the traditional practice, which will be still be carried out.

Identifying the value levers

Since most companies' top goals include enhancing SHV, this is the first area that the VR process addresses. To identify the levers of SHV in an organization, the VR approach develops a thorough understanding of the company's processes, and thereby identifies key SHV areas, including those that may not be included in annual reports today. Some of these matters may have an associated degree of attestation.

Areas that could affect the company's future, and therefore interest investors, may include: tight definitions of product development – the total amount the company is really spending; the percentage of revenues coming from 'younger' products; the number of patents being obtained; and the company's market share. In addition, VR activity would identify industry-specific SHV factors that may help investors in making judgements about the company's future.

Value reporting also demonstrates how the company resolves its most important strategic issues. Generally, these issues might include acquisitions, divestitures, investment in new products and establishing new plants. These are the kinds of matters which could be the basis for informed recommendations concerning:

- how to improve the business's internal processes relating to such areas as revenues, costs, working capital, and capital expenditure planning
- the impact of possible decisions and actions on SHV
- event-related matters such as how the company should set about merging the cultures and systems of a new acquisition.

During the first year of the VR process (which would be conducted on top of regular financial auditing work), the VR project team's initial operational steps would include developing a thorough understanding of the factors that enhance SHV and influence strategic decisions in this particular organization. First, the project team, in conjunction with management, would assess the company's key financial indicators in relation to those of its competitors, to obtain an external benchmark of how this company is performing compared to others. This effort might include learning about such areas as revenue growth, margin growth, cash tax rates, how the company absorbs its working capital for its incremental dollar sales, capital expenditures, and so on. Additionally, since most large corporations have many divisions and an array of product lines and markets, the team may want to expand the benchmark efforts to encompass all of the company's individual business segments.

The project team would then proceed to pinpoint the locations of the company's areas of financial strength and weakness – the value levers of the organization. The team would convey this information to executive management, and suggest that the accounting firm should continue using the VR concept in this attestation function for the next several years.

At this point, the team – and the company – would be well placed to move from a primary focus on diagnostics to value creation through performance enhancement. The aim would be to understand which factors within the company improve the drivers of financial success; for example, what improves revenue generation, what improves margin, what improves working capital utilization, how capital expenditures are authorized, and so on.

Creating a metrics scorecard

Equally important, the project team would want to learn whether this company had performance-measurement metrics in place that could help determine whether its value objectives and other strategic goals were being achieved. If work is needed in this area, the team would help the company link its financial drivers of SHV with a 'balanced scorecard' of performance-measurement metrics as it proceeded with the VR work. The metrics would not be abstract algorithms but would be straightforward and meaningful to employees at all levels. They would tell them what counts.

In creating this metrics scorecard, the project team would work with management to select a balanced set of performance measures designed to achieve goals at the corporate level – goals that it would then 'drill down' into its business units. Some of these measurements would be financial, others would be related to customer service and other factors, but all would be expressed in quantitative terms and have a common focus on long-term sustainable value. They would include such matters as: average time to market for new products, new product development expense as a percentage of sales, product return on investment, new product sales dollars as a percentage of total sales dollars, product quality and margin, and customer satisfaction (Fig. 13.1).

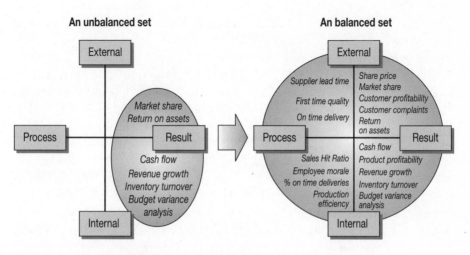

Fig. 13.1 Example of balanced scorecard

263

Testing reliability and effectiveness

Towards the end of the first year, or possibly in the second year with this hypothetical company, the VR team would ask: How effective are the organization's existing processes and its systems for reporting performance measurements? Is the system bringing about positive changes in the drivers of SHV? At this stage, the project team would probably select one or two of the company's key processes – for example, the capital spending process, or the R&D effort – to test of the reliability of the information derived from the metrics. The VR team would plan, in future years, to test processes for effectiveness in such areas as budgeting and planning, purchasing, and customer acquisition.

In some situations, the company may decide that it could benefit from VR through creation of a continuing role for the accounting firm as external reviewer and adviser. This role would have two parts: on a recurring basis, each year, the firm would ensure that the metrics were providing the correct information, and on a rotating basis, the firm would 'audit' or test the company's key value-driving processes to ensure that they were functioning effectively. And of course, the firm would comment on the reliability of such information and processes for executive management.

Senior executives may want to enlist their professional advisers' help in looking down through the layers of middle management to understand better what is really happening in the company. Top executives value objective, dependable information about how well the company's processes and metrics are working, brought to them by an external party who has free access to all parts of the organization.

In later years, a value reporting team might turn to examining other processes within the company, seeking areas in which to improve efficiency and reduce costs. These might include the processes for strategic planning, customer relationships, product delivery, quality assurance, environmental affairs, and risk management. In each of these areas, the team would issue a report with commentary for management. So many people will be involved that reviewing these processes will not be easy; field guides, process descriptions, and training will be needed. Nevertheless, such an activity, even though it involves areas not traditionally addressed by accounting firms, is not substantially different from understanding whether a company's accounts receivable process is working effectively.

In essence, the long-established skills and worldwide trust enjoyed by leading public accounting firms would act as a security for any company that decided to apply value reporting; after all, what they do now is conduct independent testing of data and report on the quality of processes that produce the data. With VR, a firm will have to test different bases and examine different processes to see whether they are effective – but the principles are the same.

Communicating to investors

At the appropriate time – probably not before the second year – executive management may want to share publicly certain information (such as market share or new products/services) that could help investors gauge what the company is doing to ensure shareholder wealth. Obviously, it is critical that such information should be reliable; this is where attestation becomes important.

In line with the investing public's expectations of reporting, a shift away from commentary regarding earnings per share and towards a Statement of Shareholder Value Achieved as in Table 13.1 may be in order. Attestation by the independent accounting firm as to the reliability of such information becomes important here.

During the second or third year, management may consider modifying the information given in the annual report, by starting to emphasize cash and SHV. This approach could include a substantial amount of commentary; for example, the management and discussion analysis (MD&A) could include analyses of the outcomes of new performance measurements, thus enabling investors to judge how today's actions will enhance future value.

Subsequently, based on the accounting firm's assurance that the key metrics were reporting accurate information, management and the board may consider expanding the company's communication of SHV information to investors. By now, management will be more comfortable with this information, whose reliability will have the additional assurance provided by the attestation work of external accountants.

All of this is something close to an ideal in investor communication, providing information of this type sets your flag on impressively high ground. As a company you will send the message that you are changing, that you have put new metrics in place, and that you are doing much to monitor their progress. This type of communication will, in itself, start changing the investor's view of your company.

THE FUTURE OF VALUE

The area of value reporting holds exceptional significance for corporations, the investment community, and public accounting firms and other professional services providers worldwide. We anticipate that investors will continue to pressure companies for more disclosure of performance measurements, possibly including an annual statement of SHV achieved or even a more detailed annual value report. This is the demand that our hypothetical 'Blueprint Inc.' model (*see* Appendix 1) has been draw up to meet. It may seem to some readers to be somewhat extreme in terms of types of disclosures made; but the reporting environment of (say) the year 2005 could be strikingly different.

VR, then, is the consequence of the SHV imperative which has been with us in this book from the beginning, and is an integral part of 'value realization' – the last step in the value transformation process that we met in Part 2.

As we move forward into the next millennium the thirst for value will not abate. The causes of this thirst – globalization, the information revolution and the mobility of capital – are not easily satisfied and are increasing in momentum. Scope and scale, the competitive drivers of this century, are being augmented by speed and knowledge management.

As we have described it in this book, the creation of value is a synthesizing process of analysis, action and communication. It requires the reconciliation of the strategic and economic with accounting approaches to analysis; it necessitates the co-ordination of changes in culture and mindset with new measurement systems; and it demands the integration of now separate management, investor and financial reporting practices.

To rise to the challenge of value creation, to understand it and improve on it, is no easy task. But all around the globe, it is a challenge that investors, managements and their advisers are focusing on. We trust we have helped you focus on it too.

To go on from here ...

If you would like further information about the shareholder value services that Price Waterhouse provides through its ValueBuilder™ process, contact your local Price Waterhouse office or telephone 0181 939 3000 in the UK (+44 181 939 3000 elsewhere).

APPENDIX 1
Blueprint Inc.[1]

The following report is an illustration of the possible structure and content of corporate reporting in the future. The extent to which this type of information will be disclosed publicly may be difficult to assess today. What is clear, however, is that this form of analysis should be at the heart of any company's internal reporting and measurement systems because it links value analysis to measurable performance indicators.

Company executives may be wary of demands for more disclosure. But as institutional investors master SHV analysis, their ability to scrutinize and probe publicly quoted companies will improve. Indeed, executives may see a considerable advantage to be had by improving the flow of relevant information to the market.

Blueprint Inc.

Mission statement

The key to our corporate success is cash generation. Our ambition is to build value by exploiting our core competencies to achieve this goal. We must identify those pulses that contribute to the long-term enhancement of cash flow – customer satisfaction, employee satisfaction, growth and innovation. These and all value-achievement matters must be embedded in our business processes and our actions.

---

[1] For the purposes of this book, the name 'Blueprint Inc.' is fictional and does not (and is not intended to) relate to any real entity, product or service.

Letter from the Chief Executive Officer

I am pleased to report another successful year in which the Company 's value has been further enhanced. Our progress in creating value has contributed significantly to the Company's successful performance in the areas of productivity, competitiveness, revenue growth and profitability.

Set out below are the key features of our value reporting model. Developed last year, it provides the structure of our value report for the year ended 31 December 1996.

The Company's main mission is to maximize long-term value. We will achieve this by consistently delivering superior performance relative to our competitors year after year. We measure value in terms of both financial and non-financial indicators, reflected through their effect on past and future cash flows.

The financial measures we use are based on the drivers of past and future cash flows and are not the traditional earnings-based indicators. The non-financial measures help to assess the value of several critical areas, which are emphasized in our mission statement: our customers, employees, growth and innovation, and internal processes. Only by improving these indicators continuously can we improve financial performance and, hence, value.

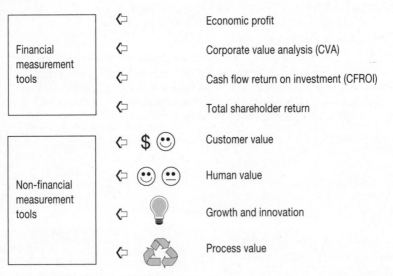

All financial measurement categories consider the extent to which value has been increased or decreased in the financial period. The non-financial indicators are the activities which underpin historic financial performance and which, if managed effectively, provide the basis for sustainable growth in value.

Blueprint Inc. Value drivers

Value drivers are the framework we use to analyze the free cash flow in the business and to understand which levers will have the most effect on corporate value. The cube below illustrates the fact that all drivers, whether financial or non-financial, are interrelated.

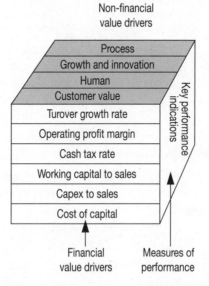

The table below demonstrates which non-financial value drivers have an impact on the financial value drivers.

	Customer	People	Growth and innovation	Processes
Turnover growth rate	✓	✓	✓	
Operating profit margin		✓	✓	✓
Cash tax rate		✓		
Working capital to sales	✓	✓		✓
Capex to sales		✓		✓
Cost of capital		✓		

In operating the company, we need to be able to focus on the activities which provide sustainable growth in value. We have accordingly developed a series of performance indicators which we believe ensure that the management team and the rest of the organization commit their time and resources to the key value-adding activities.

On the next few pages, we consider some of these primary performance indicators. We have not significantly changed the indicators in the last 12 months, although improvements have been made in the way performance is measured, particularly in the area of 'people value', which we believe will be the most important factor in the Company's long-term success. This conclusion is clear if one analyzes the relative impact of each value generator on the financial drivers.

Blueprint Inc. Financial Value Drivers

	£million					
	Actual			Projected		
	1994	1995	1996	1997	1998 ...	2006
Sales and other income	5,754	6,331	7,058	7,868	8,770 ...	20,914
Free cash flow						
Operating earnings before interest, taxes, depreciation and amortization (EBITDA)	1,012	1,256	1,538	1,636	1,824 ...	4,350
Depreciation and amortization	350	335	352	365	371 ...	424
Operating earnings before interest and taxes (EBIT)	662	921	1,186	1,271	1,453 ...	3,926
Cash taxes on EBIT (note 1)	314	286	401	496	567 ...	1,531
Net Operating Profit After Tax (NOPAT)	348	635	785	775	886 ...	2,395
Add back depreciation and amortization	350	335	352	365	371 ...	424
Gross cash flow	698	970	1,137	1,140	1,257 ...	2,819
Less: reinvestment of cash flow						
Increase in working capital		34	18	(92)	129 ...	307
Capital expenditures		356	454	388	395 ...	451
		390	472	296	524 ...	758
Free cash flow before dividends and scheduled debt repayment (FCF)		580	665	844	733 ...	2,061
Net assets						
Property, plant and equipment						
Original cost – balance at January 1	6,158	6,042	6,163	6,464	6,572 ...	7,503
Capital expenditures	293	356	454	388	395 ...	451
Gross retirements	409	235	153	280	285 ...	326
Original cost – balance at December 31	6,042	6,163	6,464	6,572	6,682 ...	7,628
Accumulated depreciation – balance at January 1	3,187	3,255	3,421	3,629	3,714 ...	4,446
Depreciation and amortization	350	335	352	365	371 ...	424
Accumulated depreciation on retirements	282	169	144	280	285 ...	326

		Actual		Projected			
	1994	1995	1996	1997	1998 ...	2006
Accumulated depreciation – balance at December 31	3,255	3,421	3,629	3,714	3,800 ...	4,544
Net property, plant and equipment	**2,787**	**2,742**	**2,835**	**2,858**	**2,882 ...**	**3,084**
Operating cash and equivalents	112	62	106	116	129 ...	308
Receivables	997	1,229	1,245	1,388	1,547 ...	3,690
Inventories at LIFO	683	687	738	822	917 ...	2,186
Adjustment for FIFO	210	199	203	0	0 ...	0
	2,002	2,177	2,292	2,326	2,593 ...	6,184
Accounts payable and accrued expenses	921	1,034	1,104	1,230	1,371 ...	3,270
Other current assets net of other current liabilities	82	54	27	27	30 ...	72
Net operating working capital	**1,163**	**1,197**	**1,215**	**1,123**	**1,252 ...**	**2,986**
Invested capital	**3,950**	**3,939**	**4,050**	**3,981**	**4,134 ...**	**6,070**

	Actual		
	1994	1995	1996
Note 1 – Cash taxes on EBIT			
Effective income tax rate	43%	38%	38%
Interest expense	103	86	85
Non-operating (income) expenses	15	(20)	(162)
Tax effect of interest and non-operating expenses	51	25	(29)
Provision for income taxes	236	325	480
Decrease (increase) in deferred taxes	27	(64)	(50)
Cash taxes	**314**	**286**	**401**
Note 2 – Weighted average cost of capital (WACC)			
Market value			
Total shares	145	291	291
Share price	75.875	37.125	45.750
Total market value	11,002	10,803	13,313
Total debt outstanding	1,129	1,144	1,221
Total market value of invested capital	12,131	11,947	14,534
Cost of debt			
Marginal borrowing rate	7.8%	7.8%	7.9%
Tax adjustment	3.4%	3.0%	3.0%
After-tax cost of debt	4.4%	4.8%	4.9%
Cost of equity			
Expected return on US equities market	11.3%	11.7%	11.3%
Risk-free cost of capital	7.3%	6.9%	6.6%
Market risk premium for US equities	4.0%	4.8%	4.7%
Beta	1.08	1.11	1.13
	11.6%	**12.2%**	**11.9%**

▶

		Actual	
	1994	**1995**	**1996**
WACC			
Equity percentage of total capital	90.7%	90.4%	91.6%
Debt percentage of total capital	9.3%	9.6%	8.4%
Equity contribution to WACC	10.6%	11.0%	10.9%
Debt contribution to WACC	0.4%	0.5%	0.4%
	11.0%	11.5%	11.3%

Financial value drivers

We use a number of cash flow-based financial measures. All of these are linked and the source of data from which they are calculated is shown above.

1 Economic profit

The operating profit created during the year in excess of the cost of invested capital.

		£million	
	1994	**1995**	**1996**
Net operating profit after tax (NOPAT)	348	635	785
Less: Capital charge (WACC x opening invested capital)	(428)	(454)	(445)
Economic (loss)/profit	(80)	181	340

As indicated, in 1994 the cost of capital was not covered by NOPAT, which resulted in a loss of value. The following two years, however, saw a period of positive growth; value reached an all-time high of $340 in the current year. The economic value calculation above looks only at each year in isolation. The projected economic profit can be discounted at the cost of capital to give a value for the Group.

Present value of economic profit at cost of capital	8,232	8,949	10,737
Add: Invested capital	3,950	3,939	4,050
Less: Value of debt	(1,129)	(1,144)	(1,221)
Internal value	11,053	11,744	13,566
Market capitalization	11,022	10,803	13,313
Over/under valuation	(51)	(941)	(253)

The value of the Company in 1994 was very close to its market value despite loss of value in that year, showing that the value and market value reflect the Company's prospects.

2 Free cash flow (FCF)

The free cash flows discounted to a net present value at the company's cost of capital, less company debt.

		$million	
	1994	1995	1996
Present value of free cash flows discounted at cost of capital	12,182	12,888	14,787
Less: Value of debt	(1,129)	(1,144)	(1,221)
Internal value	11,053	11,744	13,566
Market capitalization	11,002	10,803	13,313
Under-valuation	(51)	(941)	(253)

In 1995, because our implicit value was significantly in excess of our Company's market capitalization, management embarked upon an extensive series of road-shows to more fully explain our strategy and future plans. We believe that this has been reflected in the reduced under-valuation.

3 Cash flow return on investment (CFROI)

The discount rate at which the net present value of the inflation-adjusted cash flows are available to capital holders equals the value of invested capital. The value of capital invested is adjusted for depreciating assets and the residual value of non-depreciating assets such as land and working capital.

	1994	1995	1996
CFROI	6.5%	9.8%	11.0%
Assumed investors' required real rate of return	7.0%	7.0%	7.0%
(Discount)/Premium	(0.5%)	2.8%	4.0%

In 1996, the Company again a cash flow return on investment in excess of the assumed real rate of return required by investors. Based on our internal projections, we believe this position is sustainable provided we continue to invest carefully in technical innovation and human capital.

4 Total shareholder return

The total return available to the equity shareholder. This represents any dividends paid and movement in the share price.

	1994	1995	1996
Share price	75.88	37.13	45.75
Share price movement (%, adjusted for stock split)	15.18	(2.14)	23.22
Dividend per share	1.04	1.12	1.18
Total shareholder return	17.72%*	0.075%	26.88%

In 1995, there was a stock split resulting in an adjustment to the share price. Coupled with market uncertainty, the share price fell 2.14 per cent. In 1996, the share price recovered to $45.75, showing an improvement of 23.22 per cent on the year, which together with the full year dividend gave an overall shareholder return of 26.88 per cent.

* The figures in the tables above are for illustrative purposes only.

Market share

We have continued to maintain our global market share while many of our competitors have lost theirs to new entrants from the Pacific Rim. We believe our position as market leaders has been secured through our customer care programme and our focus on product innovation and quality.

Share of customer

We have been building strong relationships with our customers over many years, and once again have maintained our average percentage share of their spending on consumables. Our acquisition of Jupiter, Inc. will enable us to expand our current product list, and we believe it should enable us to increase our share of customer spending in the future.

Customer satisfaction

Our latest annual customer satisfaction survey undertaken by Price Waterhouse showed room for improvement in certain areas but, overall, a promising result. We have already commissioned a review of our pre-sales service and our ability to deliver on time. Furthermore, the results of our two-year project into the redesign of our core 'K' product will address the 'value for money' concern expressed by our customers.

1	☺☺☺	Overall satisfaction
2	☺☺	Pre-sales service
3	☺☺	Overall fulfillment
4	☺☺☺☺	Product quality and innovation
5	☺☺☺	After-sales services
6	☺☺	Value for money

Product defects

Product defects continued to fall, and we are now close to achieving our 'six sigma' target set two years ago. We continue to invest in new technology and procedures, and have been particularly pleased with the input provided by our workforce around the world through our 'Kreative' ideas initiative introduced in 1996. Further, we have introduced a 'no quibble product guarantee' in which any defective product is replaced within 12 hours with no questions asked.

"NO QUIBBLE GUARANTEE" — 12 hours

Blueprint Inc. People value

Employee survey index

Having been disappointed with the poor results of the 1995 employee survey, we invested heavily in 1996 to address a number of the key weaknesses. In particular, our increase in investment in training has been reflected in an above-average score on skills building, and our move to greater teleworking, our 'time out' and 'children at work' initiatives have significantly improved the Company 's overall lifestyle rating.

☺☺	Overall assessment
☺☺	Job satisfaction
☺☺	Career development
☺☺☺	Skills building
☺☺	Life style
☺☺	Rewards

Intellect index

We continue to measure and monitor the intellectual capacity of the Company through our 'Global Intellect Index', which is based on qualifications held and relevant experience of all our employees. We are pleased to report that the investment in recruitment made in 1994 is already having a marked effect

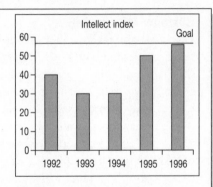

on the level of innovation and creativity at the junior management level. Further work is required in this area if we are to achieve the levels of performance currently recorded by competitors in Singapore and South Korea.

Resources and cultural balance

We have continued to invest in our programme to realign culturally and numerically our human resources with the markets we serve. This has resulted in $30m being spent on recruitment in the Pacific Rim and $20m on cultural training for our senior executives in North America and Europe.

	% of world population	Company resources
North America	5	30
Europe	11	20
South America	10	8
China	54	25
Russia	5	5
Africa	14	6
Australasia	1	6
	100%	100%

Training

We continue to invest heavily in training and have, in the current year, achieved a per-capita expenditure on training equivalent to 49 percent of wage cost. This puts the Company in the top quartile of global companies, and will be surpassed next year as a result of the introduction of the sponsored MBA programme for middle managers, to be delivered via the Inter-

net. Funding for this development is made possible by our ability to close two global training centres no longer needed in the new telecommunications environment.

Blueprint Inc. Growth and innovation

Research and development

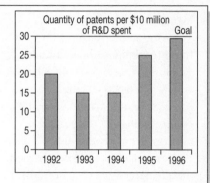

Our long-term strategy has been to invest heavily in Research and Development and in the intellectual capacity of the business. These investments are now providing valuable payback in the form of market leadership. The Company is in the top 10 percentile of all companies in number of patents obtained in 1996 for every $10 million spent on R&D. One disappointing event in the year was the negative outcome of our litigation against Pluto, Inc. over the 'Q' patent, which we believed we had secured.

New product pipeline

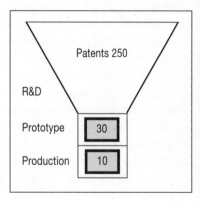

Our new product pipeline remains very healthy although we have been disappointed to have brought only 10 products to market in the last 12 months. We are currently reviewing the speed with which we test quality and market demand in order to reduce significantly our future development time. Sales of our new K2 product suffered in the year due to a major competitor's achieving a market launch one month earlier.

Structured thinking

We set a target of 18 percent for structured thinking in the Company in 1994. After two years we have achieved 17 percent through our scenario planning, product innovation, employee development, and process reengineering programmes. This level of performance is still considered unsatisfactory, and further initiatives are being introduced to encourage structured thinking time and to protect staff from low value-creating activities.

Brands

The company's brands continue to be strong despite tough competition from our main rivals. We have in particular seen a strengthening in our brand positioning in the developing economies in which we have increased our marketing and promotional activity in the last 12 months, and have started to build the pre- and post-sales infrastructure present in the more developed OECD markets.

Each square represents the relative strength to competitors of our brands throughout the world

N. America	Europe	Asia
□ □ □	□ □ □ □ □ □	□ □ □ □ □
□ □ □	□ □ □ □ □ □	□ □ □ □ □

S. America	Africa	Russia	Australia
□ □	□ □ □ □	□ □	□ □ □ □
□ □	□ □ □ □	□ □	□ □ □ □

Blueprint Inc. Process value

Process cost per transaction

Because process cost has a direct impact on profitability, we aim to reduce this cost per transaction to $1 by introducing more efficient processing methods and eliminating all tasks which do not add value (particularly tasks which occur for internal reasons only).

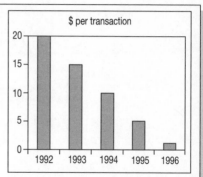

Efficiency rating

We have again participated in the 'PW World Process Benchmarking Study', which has shown that the Company remains in the top quartile of MNCs on process efficiency. While this reflects the investment made in new systems and the interactive database, we believe significant opportunity still remains to enhance our efficiency rating.

Office space

We have successfully reduced the most under-utilized asset in the business – our office space – and have enhanced employee satisfaction by encouraging more staff to telecommute. This has resulted in a reduction of 10,000 sq. metres in our office space require-ments and an increase in capex of $20m for the provision of mobile work stations and technology support services.

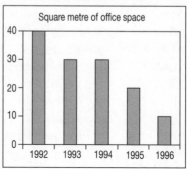

Outsourcing cost

We have continued the strategic push to outsource all non-value-adding activities to major recognized outsourcing providers. As noted earlier, we have outsourced all finance-related functions in the year, saving us $180m over the next 10 years. This follows the outsourcing of information technology, primary manufacturing, and distribution in previous years.

	Annualized cost savings
Financial transactions	$$$$
Primary manufacturing	$$$
Information technology	$$
Distribution	$

279

APPENDIX 2

Glossary of Acronyms

ABC	activity-based costing
ABS	audit and business services
ACBM	activity-based cost management)
ADR	American depositary receipt
ASB	Accounting Standards Board
CAPM	Capital Asset Pricing Model
CCR	cost of capital return
CFROI	cash flow return on investment
DCF	discounted cash flow
DDM	dividend discount mode
EBITDA	earnings before deduction of interest, tax, depreciation and amortization
EPS	earnings per share
EVA™	economic value added
FCF	free cash flow
GAAP	generally accepted accounting principles
IAS	International Accounting Standards
IP	intellectual property
IPO	initial public offering (of stock)
IR	investor relations
IRR	internal rate of return
JSE	Johannesburg Stock Exchange
JV	joint venture
KPI	key performance indicator
MRP	market risk premium
MVA	market value added
NIBL	non-interest-bearing liabilities
NOPAT	net operating profit after tax
NPV	net present value
OCF	operating cash flow
PBIT	profit before interest and tax
P/L, P & L	profit and loss
P/E ratio	price/earnings ratio – share price dividend by earnings per share

PV	present value
ROCE	return on capital employed
ROE	return on equity
ROI	return on investment
RONA	return on net assets
SBU	strategic business unit
SG&A	selling, general and administrative (expenses)
SHV	shareholder value
SVA	shareholder value added
SWOT	strengths, weaknesses, opportunities and threats (as in SWOT analysis)
TQM:	total quality management
TSR	total shareholder return (dividend income plus capital appreciation)
VBM	value-based management
VBR, VR	value-based reporting, value reporting
VROI	value return on investment
WACC	weighted average cost of capital

APPENDIX 3
Some Technicalities

Shareholder value, enterprise value and the value of capital employed (See Chapters 6, 8, and 9.)

Shareholder value ultimately looks at the value attributable to the shareholders in a company. This is often confused with the question of the total enterprise value, or the value of all the assets used in operating the company – which are not the same. At its simplest, shareholder value represents the part of a company's activity owned by the shareholders, and that part only. This is normally defined as the market value of the shares and other hybrid instruments that could become shares. It can also include minority interests in other companies (since these dividends will also flow back to the shareholders of the owning company) and any cash and marketable securities. But it will not include any other claims that debt-holders have on the company.

In our view, neither the EVA™ nor the CFROI approach in fact deal with shareholder value, but rather with the question of *the returns accruing to all capital holders in the company*, which expressly includes debt-holders too.

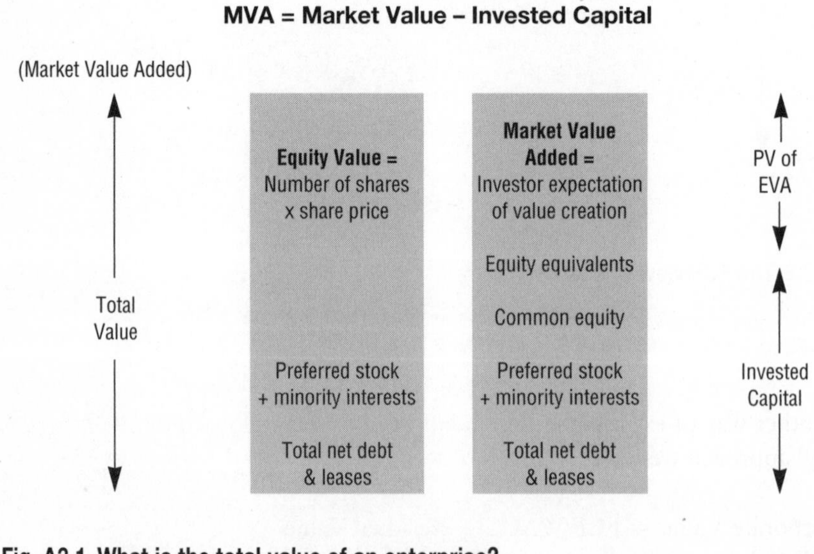

MVA = Market Value – Invested Capital

(Market Value Added)

Total Value

Equity Value = Number of shares x share price	Market Value Added = Investor expectation of value creation	PV of EVA
Preferred stock + minority interests	Equity equivalents / Common equity	Invested Capital
Total net debt & leases	Preferred stock + minority interests	
	Total net debt & leases	

Fig. A3.1 What is the total value of an enterprise?

Fig. A3.1 is the EVA™ view of the world. It shows there are two ways of measuring the total value of the firm (which, it should be noted, is not the same as the market value of the equity in a firm). The left hand column shows the total value of all resources minus cash (since this does not contribute to the creation of shareholder value), with debt and equity added together. This, then, is equivalent to value created – the market value added, plus the sum of the invested capital at par value, shown in the right hand column. In this view of the world, the enterprise value includes the value of debt, and will generally be greater than the sum of the market capitalization of the company and the net debt.

This can be contrasted to the 'entity' or FCF view of the world which is shown in Fig. A3.2 below. Here there is a stricter separation of the cash flows attributable to the shareholders. Debt is seen as a deduction from the resources available to the shareholders, whereas cash is something that will add to the asset value per share.

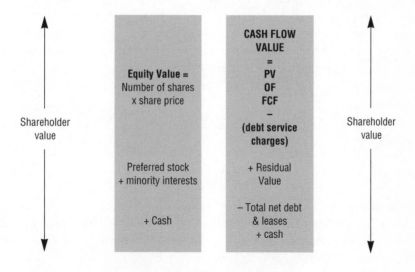

Fig. A3.2 The FCF view of shareholder value

Another way of expressing these relationships is as follows. Following a FCF 'entity' approach we have:

Corporate Value = FCF/WACC + Residual Value
SHV   = Corporate Value – Debt

Under an EVA™ approach we have:

PV ('Spread')   = ROCE – WACC x Capital Employed
Corporate Value = Present Value ('Spread') + Residual Value

where ROCE is the return on capital employed. This is defined as the net operating profit after tax and after depreciation, divided by the total capital
employed. Capital employed includes debt + equity, and the WACC is generated using normal CAPM assumptions. Note, the EVA™/SVA and FCF
approaches are compatible with each other once a suitable adjustment has been
made to the debt figures.

Debt/equity ratios (See Chapter 3.)

Several questions need to be considered on this subject. The first is whether to
use an actual or a prospective debt/equity ratio. Actual figures have the advantage of describing an 'as is' situation, and can be relatively easily compared to
those of other companies in similar lines of business. This helps to provide an
objective measure, and so anchor the WACC calculation in a market-based view
of the world. A prospective view on the debt/equity ratio requires more detailed
calculations about what is a) currently in the pipeline and b) what might be seen
as a desired ratio.

a) refers to the conversion possibilities of various hybrid warrants and convertibles that may be converted back into equity some time during the forecast
period. This needs to be allowed for in any analysis. At its most basic, this will
either add to the equity base of the company, or the debt will have to be repaid
and/or re-issued. Practices vary about whether to use a single WACC for the
whole forecast period, or to adjust it year by year as the debt/equity ratio
changes. This is something that happens using the EVA™/SVA approach. But
there is a further complexity, which is that the analysis permits management to
look carefully at what capital might be best for them. This will refer to a capital
structure that gains the benefits of a lower WACC through higher borrowing,
but will carefully weigh up the implications of higher interest payments against
what is regarded as a sustainable growth in cash flows. Attention has to be paid
here to the costs of changing the capital structure, as well as ensuring that a position adopted today will remain advantageous over time. It also has to relate
changes in the debt/equity ratio to the use to which additional resources might
be put. Gearing up the balance sheet in the pursuit of a lower WACC might not
be helpful in the longer term if there are no useful and profitable ways in which
these resources can be used. A check using the VROI calculation is helpful here
(see Chapter 6, p 60).

INDEX